T0214993

MEMORY AS A PROGRAMMING CONCEPT IN C AND C++

The overwhelming majority of program bugs and computer crashes stem from problems of memory access, allocation, or deallocation. Such memory-related errors are also notoriously difficult to debug. Yet the role that memory plays in C and C++ programming is a subject often overlooked in courses and books because it requires specialized knowledge of operating systems, compilers, and computer architecture in addition to a familiarity with the languages themselves. Most professional programmers learn about memory entirely through experience of the trouble it causes.

This book provides students and professional programmers with a concise yet comprehensive view of the role that memory plays in all aspects of programming and program behavior. Assuming only a basic familiarity with C or C++, the author describes the techniques, methods, and tools available to deal with the problems related to memory and its effective use.

Frantisek Franek is Professor of Computer Science at McMaster University, where he helped found the Algorithms Research Group. Franek's academic career encompasses research in mathematics (from the well-known Balcar–Franek theorem in Boolean algebra to finite combinatorics) as well as in computer science (from algorithms on strings to artificial intelligence). The author earned his Ph.D. at the University of Toronto and has held positions at several universities, including the Wesley Young Researchship at Dartmouth College. Franek has worked as a consultant on many commercial C/C++/Java projects internationally.

MEMORY AS A PROGRAMMING CONCEPT IN C AND C++

FRANTISEK FRANEK

McMaster University

CAMBRIDGE
UNIVERSITY PRESS

CAMBRIDGE UNIVERSITY PRESS
Cambridge, New York, Melbourne, Madrid, Cape Town, Singapore,
São Paulo, Delhi, Dubai, Tokyo, Mexico City

Cambridge University Press
32 Avenue of the Americas, New York, NY 10013-2473, USA

www.cambridge.org
Information on this title: www.cambridge.org/9780521520430

First published 2004
Reprinted 2005, 2006, 2007, 2009, 2010

A catalog record for this publication is available from the British Library.

Library of Congress Cataloging in Publication Data

Franek, F. (Frantisek)
Memory as a programming concept in C and C++ / Frantisek Franek.
   p.   cm.
Includes bibliographical references and index.
ISBN 0-521-81720-X – ISBN 0-521-52043-6 (pb.)
   1. Memory management (Computer science)   2. C (Computer program language)
3. C++ (Computer program language)   I. Title.
QA76.9.M45F73   2003
005.4'35 – dc21   2003051543

ISBN 978-0-521-81720-2 Hardback
ISBN 978-0-521-52043-0 Paperback

CONTENTS

Acknowledgments
page ix

1
Introduction
page 1

2
From Source File to Executable File
page 7

Transformation of a source file to a load (executable) module. Why we can and do discuss source programs and their behavior as if they were executing somewhere in memory in their source form. Concepts of static memory allocation, dynamic memory allocation, program address space, and program system stack.

3
Variables and Objects; Pointers and Addresses
page 21

Variables as "data containers" with names. Values as data – simple (innate or elementary) data, structures, and objects. Referencing variables through pointers. Unnamed "data containers" and their referencing through pointers. The dual role of pointers as address holders and binary code "interpreters". Various interpretations of the contents of a piece of memory. Pointer arithmetic. Why C/C++ cannot be interpreted in a platform-free manner like Java can. Why C/C++ cannot have a garbage collector.

4
Dynamic Allocation and Deallocation of Memory
page 45

Fundamentals of dynamic allocation and deallocation of memory: free store (system heap); per-process memory manager; C memory allocators malloc(), calloc(), *and* realloc(); *and C deallocator* free(). *How to handle memory allocation/deallocation errors.*

5
Functions and Function Calls
page 59

System stack, activation frame, activation frame as the storage for local auto objects and for function arguments. Passing arguments by value as opposed to by reference. Calling sequence. Recursion and its relation to activation frames and the system stack. The price of recursion.

6
One-Dimensional Arrays and Strings
page 81

Static one-dimensional arrays and their representation as pointers. Array indexing as indirection. Why an array index range check cannot be performed in C/C++. The price of run-time array index range checking; the "compile-time checking" versus "run-time checking" philosophies. Passing static one-dimensional arrays as function arguments. Definition versus declaration of one-dimensional arrays. Dynamic one-dimensional arrays. Strings as static or dynamic one-dimensional char *arrays terminated with* NULL. *How to add a custom-made run-time index range checker in C++.*

7
Multi-Dimensional Arrays
page 97

Static multi-dimensional arrays and their representation. Row-major storage format and the access formula. Passing multi-dimensional arrays as function arguments. Dynamic multi-dimensional arrays.

8
Classes and Objects
page 106

Basic ideas of object orientation; the concepts of classes and objects. Operators new, new[], delete, *and* delete[], *and related issues. Constructors and destructors.*

9
Linked Data Structures
page 132

Fundamentals, advantages, and disadvantages of linked data structures. Moving a linked data structure in memory, or to/from a disk, or transmitting it across a communication channel – techniques of compaction and serialization. Memory allocation from a specific arena.

10
Memory Leaks and Their Debugging
page 159

Classification of the causes of memory leaks. Tracing memory leaks in C programs using location reporting and allocation/deallocation information-gathering versions of the C allocators and deallocators. Tracing memory leaks in C++ programs: overloading the operators new *and* delete *and the problems it causes. Techniques for location tracing. Counting objects in C++. Smart pointers as a remedy for memory leaks caused by the undetermined ownership problem.*

11
Programs in Execution: Processes and Threads
page 187

Environment and environment variables, command-line arguments and command-line argument structure. A process and its main attributes – user space and process image. Spawning a new process (UNIX fork() *system call) from the memory point of view. Principles of interprocess communication; System V shared memory segments and "shared memory leaks". Threads and lightweight processes; advantages and disadvantages of threads over processes. The need to protect the "common" data in threads. Memory leaks caused by careless multithreading.*

A
Hanoi Towers Puzzle
page 210

CONTENTS

B
Tracing Objects in C++
page 216

C
Tracing Objects and Memory in C++
page 227

D
Thread-Safe and Process-Safe Reporting and Logging Functions
page 234

Glossary
page 239

Index
page 255

ACKNOWLEDGMENTS

Every book is to a significant degree a team effort; there are always many people essential for the book's publication, from the author(s) all the way to the editors and publisher. This book is no exception, and my sincere gratitude goes to all the people who contributed to its publication. My special thanks go to George Grosman, a musician and man of letters, for his help with the style and the grammar (English is not my mother tongue), and to Dr. Jan Holub, a postdoctoral Fellow in the Department of Computing and Software at McMaster University, for his careful reading of the manuscript and checking of the technical aspects of the text.

Please note that lengthier sections of code – as well as solutions to selected exercises – can be found on my website: www.cas.mcmaster.ca/~franek.

To my parents
　Prof. Dr. Jiří and Zdeňka Franěk for everything;
and my mentors and best friends
　Dr. B. Balcar DrSc., Czech Academy of Sciences,
　Prof. Emeritus Dr. A. Rosa, McMaster University,
　Honorable V. L. Rosicky, Consul of the Czech Republic,
　　formerly president of Terren Corp.
　for everything I know about computers and mathematics;
and my wife Marie and children Jacob and Nicole,
　for their love, support, and understanding

CHAPTER ONE

INTRODUCTION

The motivation for this book came from years of observing computer science students at universities as well as professional programmers working in software development. I had come to the conclusion that there seemed to be a gap in their understanding of programming. They usually understood the syntax of the programming language they were using and had a reasonable grasp of such topics as algorithms and data structures. However, a program is not executed in a vacuum; it is executed in computer memory. This simple fact exerts a powerful influence on the actual behavior of the program – or, expressed more precisely, a subtle yet powerful influence on the semantics of the particular programming language. I had observed that many students and programmers did not fully understand how memory affected the behavior of the C and C++ programs they were designing. This book is an attempt to fill this gap and provide students and programmers alike with a text that is focused on this topic.

In a typical computer science curriculum, it is expected that students take courses in computer architecture, operating systems, compilers, and principles of programming languages – courses that should provide them with a "model" of how memory matters in the behavior of programs.

However, not all students end up taking all these courses, and even if they do, they may not take them in the right order. Often the courses are presented in a disjointed way, making it difficult for students to forge a unified view of how memory affects the execution of programs. Additionally, not all programmers are graduates of university or college programs that feature a typical computer science curriculum. Whatever the reasons, there seems to be a significant number of computer science students and professional programmers who lack a full understanding of the intricate relationship between programs and memory. In this book we will try to pull together the various pieces of knowledge related to the topic from all the fields involved (operating systems, computer architecture, compilers, principles of programming languages, and C and C++ programming) into a coherent picture. This should free the reader from searching various texts for relevant information. However, in no way should this book be viewed as a programming text, for it assumes that the reader has at least an intermediate level of programming skills in C or C++ and hence simple programming concepts are not explained. Nor should this book be viewed as an advanced C/C++ programming text, for it leaves too many topics – the ones not directly related to memory – uncovered (e.g., virtual methods and dynamic binding in C++). Moreover, it should not be seen as an operating system book, for it does not delve into the general issues of the discipline and only refers to facts that are relevant to C and C++ programmers.

Unfortunately, there seems to be no curriculum at any university or college covering this topic on its own. As a result, students usually end up with three or four disjointed views: programming syntax and (an incomplete) C/C++ semantics; algorithms and data structures, with their emphasis on the mathematical treatment of the subject; operating systems; and possibly compilers. Although my ambition is to fill the gaps among these various views – at least from the perspective of C/C++ programming – I hope that the book proves to be a valuable supplement to any of the topics mentioned.

My own experience with software development in the real world shows that an overwhelming number of computer program bugs and problems are related to memory in some way. This is not so surprising, since there are in fact few ways to "crash" a program and most involve memory. For instance, a common problem in C/C++ is accessing an array item with an index that is out of range (see Chapter 6). A program with such a simple bug can exhibit totally erratic behavior during different executions, behavior that ranges from perfect to incorrect, to crashing at the execution of an unrelated instruction with an unrelated message from the operating system, to crashing at the execution of the offending instruction with a message from the operating system that signals an invalid memory access.

With the advent of object oriented programming and the design and development of more complex software systems, a peculiar problem has started to manifest itself more frequently: so-called memory leaks (see Chapter 10). In simple terms, this is a failure to design adequate housecleaning facilities for a program, with the result that unneeded earlier allocated memory is not deallocated. Such undeallocated and ultimately unused memory keeps accumulating to the point of paralyzing the execution of the program or the performance of the whole computer system. It sounds almost mystical when a programmer's explanation of why the system performs so badly is "we are dealing with memory leaks", as if it were some kind of deficiency of the memory. A more concrete (and accurate) explanation would be "we did not design the system properly, so the unneeded but undeallocated memory accumulates to the point of severely degrading the performance of the system". The troubles that I have witnessed in detecting and rectifying memory leaks strongly indicate that many students and programmers lack a fundamental appreciation of the role and function of memory in programming and program behavior.

We are not really interested in technical, physical, or engineering characteristics of memory as such (how it is organized, what the machine word is, how the access is organized, how it is implemented on the physical level, etc.); rather, we are interested in memory as a concept and the role it plays in programming and behavior of C/C++ programs. After finishing this book, the reader should – in addition to recognizing superficial differences in syntax and use – be able to understand (for example) the deeper differences between the "compile-time index range checking" philosophy used in C/C++ and the "run-time index range checking" philosophy used in Pascal (Chapter 6) or between the "recursive procedure calls" philosophy used in C/C++ and the "nonrecursive procedure calls" philosophy used in FORTRAN (Chapter 5). As another example, the reader of this book should come to appreciate why Java requires garbage collection whereas C/C++ does not (and in general cannot); why C/C++ cannot be interpreted in a manner similar to Java; and why Java does not (and cannot) have pointers whereas C/C++ does (Chapter 3) – because all these aspects are related in some way to memory and its use. The reader should understand the issues concerning memory during object construction and destruction (Chapter 8); learn how to compact or serialize linked data structures so they can be recorded to a disk or transmitted across a network (Chapter 9); and learn how to design programs that allow monitoring of memory allocation/deallocation to detect memory leaks (Chapter 10). The reader will also be exposed to important concepts not exclusively related to C/C++, concepts that are usually covered in courses on operating systems but included here by virtue of being related to memory: for example, concepts of process and thread and interprocess communication (Chapter 11) facilitated by memory (shared memory segments, pipes, messages). Of course, as always, our interest will be on the memory issues concerning both the processes and the threads.

The book is divided into eleven chapters. Chapter 2 deals with the process of compilation, linking, and loading in order to explain how the behavior of programs can be discussed and examined as if they were executing in the source form, how the static and the dynamic parts of memory are assigned to a program, and how the abstract address space of the program is mapped to the physical memory. Most of the topics in Chapter 2 are drawn from the field of the principles of operating systems. We cover the topics without referring to any particular operating system or any low-level technical details. Otherwise, the text would become cumbersome and difficult to read and would distract the reader from focusing on memory and its role in C/C++ programming. However, knowledge of the topics covered in Chapter 2 is essential to almost all discussions of the role of memory in the subsequent chapters.

Chapter 3 deals with variables as memory segments (data containers) and the related notions of addresses and pointers, with a particular emphasis on various interpretations of the contents of memory segments and possible memory access errors. In Chapter 4, dynamic memory allocation and deallocation are discussed and illustrated using the C allocators `malloc()`, `calloc()`, and `realloc()` and the C deallocator `free()`. In Chapter 5, function calls are explained with a detailed look at activation frames, the system stack, and the related notion of recursion. In Chapter 6, one-dimensional arrays and strings, both static and dynamic, are discussed. Chapter 7 extends that discussion to multi-dimensional arrays.

Chapter 8 examines in detail the construction and destruction of C++ objects together with the C++ allocators (the operators `new` and `new[]`) and the C++ deallocators (the operators `delete` and `delete[]`) in their global and class-specific forms. The focus of the chapter is not the object orientation of C++ classes but rather the aspects of object creation and destruction related to memory. Similarly, in Chapter 9 we discuss linked data structures but not from the usual point of view (i.e., their definition, behavior, implementation, and applications); instead, our point of view is related to memory (i.e., how to move linked data structures in memory, to or from a disk, or across a communication channel). Chapter 10 is devoted to a classification of the most frequent problems leading to memory leaks and their detection and remedy for both C and C++ programs.

We started our discussion with operating system topics related to programs – compilation, linking, and loading – in Chapter 2, and in Chapter 11 we finish our book by again discussing operating system topics related to programs in execution: processes and threads, and how they relate to memory. Of course, this chapter must be more operating system–specific, so some notions (e.g., the system call fork() and the sample code) are specific to UNIX.

Finally, in the appendices we present some complete code and discuss it briefly. In Appendix A we describe the Hanoi towers puzzle and provide a simple C program solving it (for completeness, as the puzzle is mentioned in Chapter 5 in relation to recursion). In Appendix B we present a simple C++ program on which we illustrate object tracing: how to keep track of objects and of when and where they were allocated (this includes localization tracing as well). We go through various combinations of turning the features on and off. In Appendix C, a similar C++ program is used and object tracing, localization tracing, and memory allocation tracing are all demonstrated. Appendix B and Appendix C both illustrate debugging of memory leaks as discussed in Chapter 10. Finally, Appendix D contains process-safe and thread-safe UNIX logging functions (used in examples throughout the book) that serve to illustrate some of the topics related to processes and threads discussed in Chapter 11.

Every chapter includes a Review section that contains a brief and condensed description of the topics covered, followed by an Exercises section that tests whether the reader has fully grasped the issues discussed. This is followed by a References section, pointing the reader to sources for examining the issues in more depth. All special terms used in the book are defined and/or explained in the Glossary, which follows Appendix D.

I have tried to limit the sample computer code to the minimum needed to comprehend the issues being illustrated, leaving out any code not relevant to the topic under discussion. Hence some of the fragments of code within a given chapter are not complete, though all were tested within larger programs for their correctness.

I wish you, dear reader, happy reading, and I hope that if somebody asks you about it later you can reply: "if my *memory* serves, it was a rather useful book".

CHAPTER TWO

FROM SOURCE FILE TO EXECUTABLE FILE

Transformation of a source file to a load (executable) module. Why we can and do discuss source programs and their behavior as if they were executing somewhere in memory in their source form. Concepts of static memory allocation, dynamic memory allocation, program address space, and program system stack.

It is useful and practical to discuss the behavior (often referred to as the semantics) of a computer program written in a high-level language like C or C++ as if it were executing in computer memory in its source form. For instance, the semantics of the statement x = x+1 might be described as "the value of the variable x is incremented by 1", yet nothing could be farther from the truth because the program in its source form is a simple ASCII text file sitting quietly somewhere on a disk doing nothing. On the other hand, speaking conceptually, this is exactly what happens to the variable x when the program executes – although, to confuse matters even more, there is no variable x to speak of when the program is running. In order to understand all of this, we must discuss the process of compilation, linking, loading, and execution of programs. Most of the facts discussed in this chapter can be found in various books and texts dealing with compilation and compilers, operating systems, and computer architecture.

Both C and C++ belong to a family of high-level symbolic languages, meaning that certain entities in such programs can be referenced by their names (symbols). In C these entities can be data items called variables (innate data like char or int, or user-defined structures using the struct construct or the array construct) and functions, whereas in C++ the data items also include objects (defined by the user via classes) and functions include class methods. In order to discuss C and C++ as if they were the same language, we will thus use the term *objects* to denote innate data, data structures, or arrays in C and innate data, data structures, arrays, or true objects in C++. The term *function* will refer to functions in C and to functions and class methods in C++.

High-level symbolic languages were invented for one and only one purpose: to make it simpler and more convenient for the programmer to write a program. Toward this end, such languages exhibit (in highly simplified and reduced form) the syntax and symbolic character of natural languages. As such they are not suitable for computers that understand only one language, the machine code in its binary form. The instructions of machine code can (oversimply) be described as instructions of the type "copy data from memory to register", "copy data from register to memory", "copy data within memory", or "do some calculation with data in one or two registers". It is the role of a computer program known as the *compiler* to translate the program written in a high-level symbolic language to the machine code. It is quite standard to call the simple ASCII text file in which the "sentences" of the high-level symbolic language are stored the *source file* or *source module*. The high-level symbolic language in which the program is written is customarily referred to as *source language*, while the program written in the source language is referred to as *source code*. The main purposes of the compiler are translating each complex instruction of the source language into a set of machine instructions and, of most interest to us, *replacing each symbolic reference by an address reference*.

Usually, the result of compilation is a binary file referred to as *object file* or *object module*, in which is stored the *object code*. Very often the program we are interested in is divided (for convenience) into a set of many source files, and thus the compiler will produce a set of object files. Almost any program written in C/C++ uses so-called standard functions (i.e., subprograms written by others and included with the compiler for the convenience of its users) that are prepared in object form. Therefore, after compilation, we are presented with a group of object files. These must be somehow forged together – in a process known as *linking* – into a single binary file called the *load file* (or *load module*) or the *executable file* (*module*). The careful reader should note that the term "linking" is commonly but misleadingly used for the whole process, which actually consists of two distinct phases and activities, relocation and linking; similarly, the

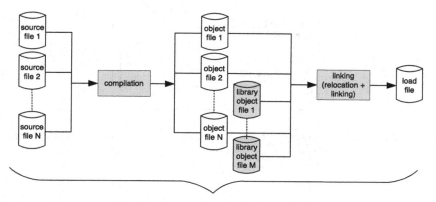

usually performed by a compiler, usually in one uninterrupted sequence

Figure 2.1   Compilation and linking

term "compilation" is often used for the whole two-step process of compilation and linking. See Figure 2.1.

The load module is ready to be executed. The term "load" indicates the main purpose of the file: it can be loaded into memory (i.e., a complete copy of the file is stored in the memory with some additional changes to address references in the load module) and executed. The process of loading is rather complex and so we do not explain it in any fine detail; instead, we simply paint a broad picture that is relevant to how a program executes in memory.

Before we can embark on describing the main features of an object module, we must clarify some important terminology concerning programs written in C and C++ languages. The structure of a C program is rather simple. It is often called a *flat-table* approach, when a program consists of at least one function (and possibly more) and some definitions of objects. In C++ the picture becomes a bit more complicated because functions, data definitions, and objects can be lumped together into classes, but for the time being we may ignore this added complexity. Objects defined outside of functions have storage class *static*, meaning that they exist for the duration of the execution of the program. They are often referred to as *global* objects, for they can be referenced by their name in any function of the program (with some restrictions) regardless of the particular source file in which they reside. Confusingly enough, defining a global object with the keyword "static" does not change its storage class but does make it impossible for the object to be referenced in a different

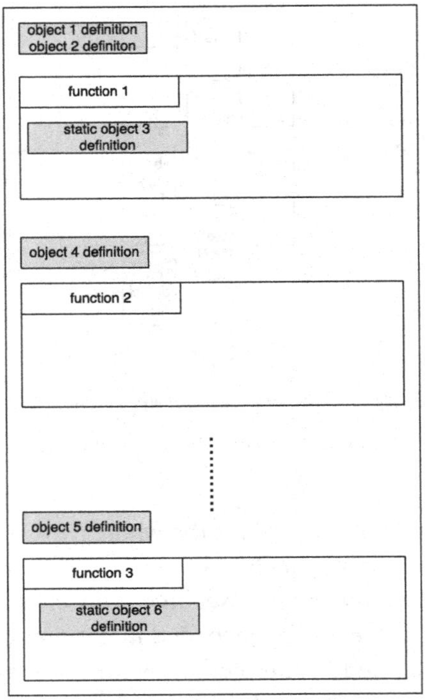

Figure 2.2   Layout of a C/C++ source program and static objects

source file. Objects defined within functions (or within blocks) are referred to as *local* objects (i.e., local to the function or to the block). Their
storage class is by default *auto*, for they are "created" automatically upon
activation of their function and are automatically destroyed upon deac-
tivation of that function. However, if a local object is defined with the
keyword "static" then its storage class is changed, and it becomes a static
object that exists throughout the duration of the program's execution (yet
this does not make it a global object for the purpose of symbolic reference).
Thus, when we speak of *static data*, we mean all global objects and all local
objects that are defined as static. In Figure 2.2, objects 1–6 are static.

In order to discuss how an object module is created, we use the following simple C program. The array a[] represents the initialized (global)
static data, the local variable k in main() represents the initialized (local)
static data, and the array b[] represents the uninitialized (global) static
data. The local variable i in main() does not enter our discussion until the
end of this chapter.

```
#include <stdio.h>

int a[10]={0,1,2,3,4,5,6,7,8,9};
int b[10];

/* function main ---------------------------------- */
void main()
{
    int i;
    static int k = 3;

    for(i = 0;  i < 10;  i++) {
      printf("%d\n",a[i]);
      b[i] = k*a[i];
      }/*endfor*/

}/*end main*/
```

An object module contains all source code statements translated to machine instructions (this is one of the reasons why an object file must be binary). The header section (see Figure 2.3) contains the sizes of all the other sections involved – including the size of the uninitialized data section, which is not created until load time – in order to parse the object module (because it is a binary file, no binary value can be used to indicate the end or beginning of a section). We are mostly interested in the initialized data and symbol table sections.

Figure 2.4 shows a simplified version of the object module for the sample program. The X indicates some binary data whose precise nature is

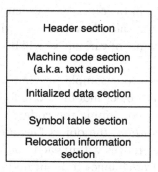

| Header section |
| Machine code section (a.k.a. text section) |
| Initialized data section |
| Symbol table section |
| Relocation information section |

Figure 2.3   Object module structure

Offset	Contents	Comment
Header section		
0	124	number of bytes of Machine code section
4	44	number of bytes of initialized data section
8	40	number of bytes of Uninitialized data section (array b[])
		(*not part of this object module*)
12	60	number of bytes of Symbol table section
16	44	number of bytes of Relocation information section
Machine code section (124 bytes)		
20	X	code for the top of the **for** loop (36 bytes)
56	X	code for call to **printf()** (20 bytes)
76	X	code for the assignment statement (12 bytes)
88	X	code for the bottom of the **for** loop (4 bytes)
92	X	code for exiting **main()** (52 bytes)
Initialized data section (44 bytes)		
144	0	beginning of array a[]
148	1	
:		
176	8	
180	9	end of array a[] (40 bytes)
184	3	variable k (4 bytes)
Symbol table section (60 bytes)		
188	X	array a[] : offset 0 in Initialized data section (12 bytes)
200	X	variable k : offset 40 in Initialized data section (12 bytes)
210	X	array b[] : offset 0 in Uninitialized data section (12 bytes)
222	X	**main** : offset 0 in Machine code section (12 bytes)
234	X	**printf** : external, used at offset 56 of Machine code section (14 bytes)
Relocation information section (44 bytes)		
248	X	relocation information

Figure 2.4 Object module (simplified) of the sample program

not important and would be overly technical for understanding the principles behind creation of an object module. An important aspect for our discussion is the transformation of symbolic references (of the arrays a[] and b[], the variable k, the function main(), and the standard function printf()) into address references in terms of offset (distance in bytes) from the beginning of the object module (or a section). Thus "start executing function x()" will become "start executing instructions at address y". Likewise, "store value in variable x" will become "store value at address y" and "get value of variable x" will become "fetch value from address y".

The object module of our sample program is then linked together with at least two library object modules, one for the standard function printf() and the other containing the code for program termination. In the first phase, *relocation,* the object files are merged together and the internal address references within each object module must be updated to reflect the offset changes brought on by merging all three object modules into one. In the following phase, *linking,* external address

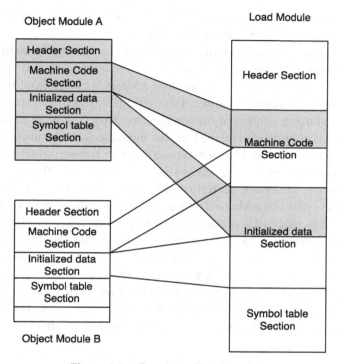

Figure 2.5 Creation of load module

references in each object module must be resolved. In our example, the linker must resolve the explicit reference from the object module of our sample program to the standard function printf() (i.e., replace it by the appropriate address reference through the offset with respect to the beginning of the load module being created) in the library object module and also resolve the implicit reference from the object module of our sample program to program termination code in another library object module. See Figure 2.5 for a schematic diagram of the whole process.

The load module (still without the uninitialized data section) represents the abstract notion of the program address space. The loader finds all the required information about the program address space in the load module. As mentioned previously, all address references in the load module are in the form of the offset from the beginning of the load module. Such addresses are often called *relative* (or *logical*) *addresses*. The loader and/or operating system must map the logical addresses to *physical addresses* in the main memory and then copy the binary information or data to these memory locations.

The process of memory mapping is quite complicated and depends in its technical details on the particular operating system and hardware platform. In the simplest case, a logical address is mapped onto a physical address by a simple addition of the logical address (offset) to the base register (starting address of the loaded program). The issue of memory mapping is complicated by the fact that most modern operating systems (like UNIX or Windows) employ *virtual memory systems*, which allow execution of programs with address spaces that are larger than the physical memory. Moreover, such memory systems allow for noncontiguous mapping – that is, two logical addresses that are consecutive in the logical address space of a program are mapped onto two nonconsecutive physical addresses. *Caching*, which is offered by most modern hardware platforms to speed up the execution of software, further complicates the issue of memory mapping. As we discuss in Chapter 11 (which covers the fundamentals of interprocess communication related to memory), shared memory segments are treated as memory-mapped files, and this makes memory mapping even more complicated. Figure 2.6 – rather schematic,

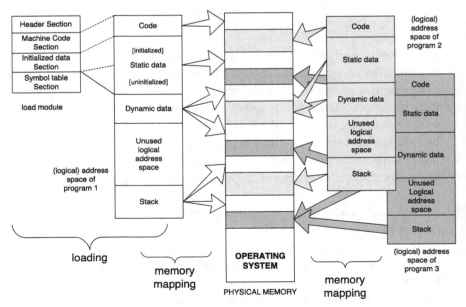

Figure 2.6   Loading and memory mapping

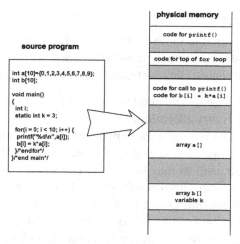

Figure 2.7 From source program to its "placement" in memory during execution

but sufficient for our purpose – illustrates a program being loaded into memory.

Notice that the loader "created" the uninitialized data as a part of static data of the program address space; to do so, the loader only needs to know the section's size, which is stored in the header section of the load module. We have seen that there is a well-defined unequivocal process that leads from the source file (or files) to the program address space. The program address space is mapped also in a well-defined unequivocal process to various segments in the physical memory. It is thus possible for us to make a mental quantum leap and discuss the behavior of a program based on its address space as it is mapped into the memory; this is illustrated in Figure 2.7.

The code and the static data parts of the program address space were in essence prepared by the compiler and thus we speak of *static memory allocation* (or *memory allocation at compile time* or *memory allocated by the compiler*) even though, strictly speaking, the compiler does not allocate any memory when the program is run. It may even be the case that, when a program is run, the compiler used to compile the program no longer exists. The size and structure of code and static data sections will not change during the execution of the program, though at various times they may be mapped into various segments of physical memory.

The curious reader may at this point have three questions.

1. Where is the variable i located in the physical memory?
2. What is the stack section pictured in Figure 2.6?
3. What is the dynamic data section pictured in Figure 2.6?

The rest of this chapter is devoted to answering these questions that deal with dynamic memory allocation.

Both C and C++ are recursive languages. We will discuss this in detail in Chapter 5, but for now suffice it to say that this allows a function to eventually call itself (it may be a direct call when a function A() calls the function A(), or an indirect call when a function A() calls a function B() that calls a function C() ... that calls the function A()). There is a certain penalty to be paid in speed of execution and memory requirements for facilitating recursion, but it is more than balanced out by the problem-solving power gained. The memory role in recursion is what interests us, bringing us to the *program system stack* and *dynamic memory allocation*.

Very often a running program requires more memory than anticipated during its design or even when its execution begins. Take, for example, a simple program that repeatedly prompts the user for a word and then stores the word in the memory until the user enters quit. Nobody can anticipate how much memory will be required. Thus, programs in general need the ability to request and obtain more memory dynamically – that is, during the program's execution. We will discuss the details of dynamic allocation and deallocation in Chapter 4, but for now we simply state that the section marked as "dynamic data" in the address space of a program (see e.g. Figure 2.6) can be increased to accommodate the requested increase in memory (using high logical addresses from the unused logical address space) and properly mapped to the physical memory, as illustrated in Figure 2.8. This memory allocation is managed by the *program memory manager* (which basically is the C allocator malloc() or the C++ allocator new).

When a function is called, an *activation frame* (or *activation record*) is dynamically created (i.e., the required memory is dynamically allocated using low addresses of the unused logical address space and the required data are stored in it) and pushed on the stack. (Simply stated, a *stack* is a data structure resembling a deck of cards: you can only put a new card on the top of the deck, which is called operation *push*, or remove the top card from the deck, which is called operation *pop*.) The activation frame

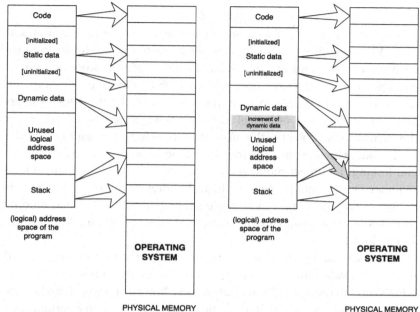

Figure 2.8 Dynamic memory allocation

of the function is its "address space", and all local automatic variables are "located" there. That is why the variable i in our sample program has not figured in our discussion so far. It is located in – and is part of the activation frame for – the function main(). The compiler translates the symbolic references of the variable i to address references relative to the beginning of the activation frame. Thus, when a function is called many times, there will be many unrelated activation frames on the stack for that function and hence many unrelated copies of the local variables of that function.

We conclude with a short note: For the purist, a program in execution is usually called a *process*. Therefore, it would be more precise to talk of "process address space", "process memory management", and a "process system stack". We will use such proper terminology in later chapters, but in this introductory chapter we really wanted to focus on what happens to a program and did not wish to sidetrack a reader not well versed in operating system terminology. For the sake of simplicity, we will often refer to the "system stack" instead of the "process system stack".

Review

A program written in C/C++ is stored in one or more source modules as plain ASCII text files. These are compiled into object modules. Because we are focused on all memory-related aspects of this process, we emphasize the fact that all symbolic references from the source program are replaced by address references in the object module; the address references are in the form of logical (or relative) addresses, which represent the location of an object as the offset (distance) from the beginning of the load module (or an activation frame for a local object). During relocation and linking, all object modules are "forged" together into a single load module. During that process, all logical addresses are updated vis-à-vis the beginning of the new load module being created. This load module contains all information about what the abstract program address space should look like.

When we request the operating system to execute a program, its load module is loaded into memory – that is, the program address space is created and mapped to physical addresses. Now the program can be executed one instruction at a time, in the usual way. Thus, on a certain level of abstraction, we can pretend that the C/C++ instructions of the source program are mapped onto sets of machine instructions stored in the memory and that data (variables, objects, etc.) of the program are mapped to appropriate segments of the memory. (Static data – i.e., global objects and local objects defined with the storage class "static" – are mapped into the static data region of the program's memory, while dynamic data are mapped into the dynamic data region of the program's memory.) This level of abstraction is useful for discussions of programs and their semantics. Each object in a program thus corresponds to a well-defined segment of memory, and the program's instructions merely modify these objects; that is, the instructions either read the data from or store new data in these memory segments.

Exercises

2.1　In a C/C++ program, can you define a global variable that is not accessible by a certain function?

2.2　Can a global variable in a C/C++ program be located in the static data section of the object module of the program? Can it be located in the dynamic section of the load module?

2.3　What is the difference between logical address and physical address?

2.4 What is the difference between object module and load module?

2.5 What does "address space" refer to?

2.6 What is the system stack for?

2.7 Why does the load module have no dynamic data section even though the address space does?

2.8 The statements of a C/C++ program are translated by the compiler to machine instructions. Where are these instructions stored?

2.9 Is there any difference between linking and relocation? If so, describe it.

References

Some very good contemporary textbooks on principles of operating systems:

Crowley, Ch., *Operating Systems, A Design-Oriented Approach,* Irwin / McGraw-Hill, New York, 1997.

Silberschatz, A., Galvin, P. B., and Gagne, G., *Operating System Concepts,* Wiley, New York, 2002.

Stallings, W., *Operating Systems – Internals and Design Principles,* Prentice-Hall, Englewood Cliffs, NJ, 2001.

Tanenbaum, A. S., *Modern Operating Systems,* Prentice-Hall, Englewood Cliffs, NJ, 2001.

An excellent text (recommended in several chapters of this book) that is focused on C++ and includes topics on effective memory management:

Sutter, H., *Exceptional C++,* Addison-Wesley, Reading, MA, 2000.

Fundamentals of compilers principles and techniques; an oldie, but still the best text around:

Aho, A. V., Sethi, R., and Ullman, J. D., *Compilers – Principles, Techniques, and Tools,* Addison-Wesley, Reading, MA, 1988.

Other texts on the fundamentals of compiler principles and techniques:

Pittman, T., and Peters, J., *The Art of Compiler Design, Theory and Practice,* Prentice-Hall, Englewood Cliffs, NJ, 1992.

Waite, W. M., and Carter, L. R., *An Introduction to Compiler Construction,* HarperCollins, New York, 1993.

Fundamentals of computer architecture:

Hamacher, C., Vranesic, Z., and Zaky, S., *Computer Organization,* McGraw-Hill, New York, 2002.

Hennessy, J., and Patterson, D., *Computer Architecture: A Quantitative Approach,* Elsevier, New York, 2002.

Murdocca, M., and Heuring, V. P., *Principles of Computer Architecture,* Prentice-Hall, Englewood Cliffs, NJ, 1999.

Stallings, William, *Computer Organization and Architecture – Principles of Structure and Function*, Prentice-Hall, Englewood Cliffs, NJ, 1996.

Fundamentals of programming languages:

Clark, R. G., *Comparative Programming Languages*, Addison-Wesley, Reading, MA, 2001.

Mitchell, J. C., *Concepts in Programming Languages*, Cambridge University Press, 2002.

Pratt, T. W., and Zelkowitz, M. V., *Programming Languages – Design and Implementation*, Prentice-Hall, Englewood Cliffs, NJ, 2001.

The Internet is an excellent source for technical details about memory and memory management in various operating systems, but there is no guarantee of how the links will be maintained in the future:

Gorman, M., "Code Commentary on the Linux Virtual Memory Manager", http://www.csn.ul.ie/~mel/projects/vm/guide/pdf/code.pdf.

Gorman, M., "Understanding the Linux Virtual Memory Manager", http://www.csn.ul.ie/~mel/projects/vm/guide/pdf/understand.pdf.

Myers, N. C., "Memory Management in C++", *C++ Report*, July/August 1993 (part 1) and December 1993 (part 2); also at http://www.cantrip.org/wave12.html.

Russinovich, M., "Inside Memory Management", part 1, *Windows & .NET Magazine*, http://www.winntmag.com/Articles/Index.cfm?IssueID=56&ArticleID=3686.

Russinovich, M., "Inside Memory Management", part 2, *Windows & .NET Magazine*, http://www.winntmag.com/Articles/Index.cfm?IssueID=58&ArticleID=3774.

An excellent site for links concerning technical knowledge of memory management for various operating systems:

http://www.memorymanagement.org.

CHAPTER THREE

VARIABLES AND OBJECTS;
POINTERS AND ADDRESSES

Variables as "data containers" with names. Values as data – simple (innate or elementary) data, structures, and objects. Referencing variables through pointers. Unnamed "data containers" and their referencing through pointers. The dual role of pointers as address holders and binary code "interpreters". Various interpretations of the contents of a piece of memory. Pointer arithmetic. Why C/C++ cannot be interpreted in a platform-free manner like Java can. Why C/C++ cannot have a garbage collector.

During the execution of a program, a variable of the program corresponds to a location in memory, and the address of that location replaces all symbolic references to the variable in the load module. This is one of the important facts touched upon in Chapter 2 when we discussed why we can behave as if the program in its source form executes in the memory. In this chapter we will refine this notion and discuss its consequences.

The idea of variable as "data container" is very natural. In its crudest form we can imagine a variable to be a box, and whatever is in the box is the value of that variable. If we want to evaluate the variable (i.e., find its value), all we need do is look in the box and see what is in there; when we want to store something in the variable, we simply put it into the box. In fact, this crude notion is not that far from reality.

Instead of a box, a variable corresponds to a segment in memory. The contents of that segment – or, more precisely, the binary code stored in that segment – is the value of the variable. If a program needs to *evaluate* the variable, it must *fetch* or *read* the binary code stored in that memory segment and then *interpret* it as the appropriate value. If a program needs to *store* a value in a variable, is must first *convert* the value to the appropriate binary code and then store the binary code in the memory segment that corresponds to the variable.

There are several important issues to ponder in the previous paragraph alone.

The first important issue concerns binary codes. Memory can store only binary codes. Yet even the C language requires several different data types: characters, integers, floats, and so forth. Thus, different kinds of data must be converted to binary code in different ways. This is why a compiler, when dealing with a particular data type, must first include instructions to perform the conversion (or do the conversion itself if possible) to the appropriate binary code before it can include instructions for storing it in memory or using it in any way.

The second important issue concerns the size of the memory segment that corresponds to a variable, and hence the length of the binary code stored there. As stated previously, each symbolic reference in the source code is replaced by an address reference of the the beginning of the segment that corresponds to it (we will refer to this as the "address of the variable"). But there is no record of where the segment ends, so how does the computer know if it is to fetch 1 bit, 10 bits, or 100,000 bits? The solution is rather simple, though with poignant consequences. *Each particular data type has a definite size.* That size may differ from platform to platform, but for a particular platform it is fixed and unchangeable. For example, char has the size of 1 byte on any machine, while int may have the size of 2 bytes on the old 16-bit machines or the size of 4 bytes on today's most common 32-bit machines (and will be the size of 8 bytes on the coming 64-bit machines). We will use the term "size of variable" for the size of the memory segment that corresponds to it, which in turn is determined by the data type of the variable.

One of the major consequences of a definite size for each data type is a kind of "physical" aspect of the behavior of variables. Just like a physical box, a memory segment of a definite size cannot be used to store something that is "bigger". With a box it is physically impossible (without either breaking the box or the item being stored therein), but with a segment of memory the situation is different. We could choose different strategies for attempting to store a binary code longer than the size of the variable, a problem commonly referred to as *overflow*. One strategy for dealing with overflow is to prevent it by truncating the code to fit the space; another is to treat it as an error or exception; and yet another is simply to let it happen and try to store the longer binary code at that address anyway.

The C and C++ languages employ a mixed strategy: should overflow occur as a result of a numeric operation (sort of left-end overflow), it is prevented by truncation; otherwise (sort of right-end overflow), it is allowed to happen and the binary code is stored "as is", regardless of the consequences (for which the programmer is held ultimately responsible).

Thus, the result of incrementing a value of a variable may be larger than the variable and hence truncated. Let us discuss the following simple for-loop.

```
char i;
...
for(i = 0; i < 256; i++)
  printf("%d\n",i);
```

Though seemingly correct, it is an infinite (i.e., never-ending) loop. The problem is caused not by the logic of the loop nor by the mathematical abstraction of the loop but rather by the "physicality" of the variable i as represented by a memory segment. Since i is of data type char, it follows that i has the size of 1 byte. Hence i attains the value of 255 when the binary code stored in it is 11111111. When i is incremented by 1, the code 11111111 should be replaced by 100000000, but the leftmost bit is truncated and so 00000000 is stored in i. The value of i ranges from 0 to 255, and after reaching 255 the next value is zero again (like odometers in cars). Thus, i will never reach the terminating value of 256 and so the loop goes on for ever and ever, or until the program is terminated from the outside (a more likely scenario). A good compiler should alert us to the possible danger and give a warning message that we are comparing distinct data types (char on the left-hand side is being compared to int on the right-hand side in the expression i < 256) and that it could be risky (or better yet, that the expression is always true). But not all compilers are good, and many programmers completely ignore warning messages or leave too many seemingly harmless warning messages unattended, so that an occasional important warning message is overlooked. Furthermore, the operator < may be overloaded for this particular combination of data types and hence no warning message will be produced by any compiler (of course the overloading of < could not be done in C++ for this trivial example, since classes or enumerated types would have to be involved instead of elementary data types, but the principle is the same).

The same problem can manifest itself in an even more innocuous form that would not be detected by a compiler unless it is set to report all potential overflow errors. The code

```
char i;
int j;
...
i = 255;
...
i++;
...
j = 510/i;
```

will crash the program (i.e., the operating system will terminate its execution) because the value of the variable i is 0 when the division is performed. Syntactically, everything is absolutely correct; there is nothing obvious a compiler could flag as potentially dangerous. Logically and mathematically it is correct. The only trouble is the definite size of i as a piece of memory, which results in i inadvertently having a zero value owing to overflow.

We have just illustrated that n incremented by 1 does not necessarily have the value of n+1. This is something that we all take for granted. Thus, numbers as they are represented in memory are not a very faithful model of the abstract numbers we are used to. They are sufficient for a wide variety of applications, but they must be treated with respect and understanding to prevent programs from being unreliable in their performance and in the results they produce. The notion of variables as "data containers" or "memory segments" of definite sizes is helpful for avoiding errors like the ones just shown.

The other C/C++ strategy – of right-end overflows being ignored – is even more significant. Consider the following fragment of a simple program:

```
char i;
int* p = (int*) &i;
...
*p = 1234567892;
...
```

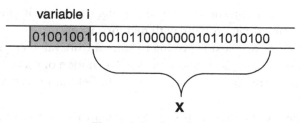

Figure 3.1   Overflow

No compiler will complain; everything seems fine. Yet clearly we are storing a binary code for the integer value 1234567892 that takes 32 bits (01001001001011000000001011010100) at the address of the variable i that has the size of 8 bits (see Figure 3.1).

There are several possible outcomes.

1. If the whole part **X** of the memory in Figure 3.1 belongs to the running program (process), then:
    (a) if **X** does not contain any data important for the rest of the execution of the program, then the program runs fine and there is no apparent problem;
    (b) if **X** does contain important data that are overridden by the 10010110000001011010100 tail of the binary code *but* by pure chance this does not change anything (as the data stored therein just happened to be the same), then the program runs fine and there is no apparent problem;
    (c) if **X** does contain important data that are overridden and thus changed, then
        (i) incorrect results may be produced or
        (ii) the program may crash with all kinds of possible error messages.
2. If all or part of **X** belongs to some other process, then the program is terminated by the operating system for a memory access violation (the infamous UNIX segmentation fault error).

Any of these situations could occur at any time during execution, and the program's user has no control over the circumstances. Such a program exhibits erratic behavior: sometimes runs fine, sometimes runs wrong, sometimes crashes for one reason, another time crashes for a different reason. In fact, an erratically behaving program should immediately be suspected of a hidden problem with memory access.

All these troubles just for trying to store an int value at the location of a char variable? A most emphatic *Yes!* The notion of variables as "data containers" or "memory segments" is again helpful in preventing such problems.

The sizeof operator can be used to calculate the size in bytes either of the result of an evaluation of an expression (sizeof *expr*) or a data type (sizeof(*type*)). The size calculation is performed during compilation and hence according to whatever platform the program is being compiled on, and this becomes an important aspect of portability. In particular, the size of a variable x can be calculated by sizeof x or sizeof(x) expressions. On a typical 32-bit machine, the C/C++ *innate* (or *built-in* or *elementary* or *fundamental*) data types have the following sizes:

- char and unsigned char values and variables have the size of 1 byte;
- short and unsigned short values and variables have the size of 2 bytes;
- int and unsigned int values and variables have the size of 4 bytes;
- long and unsigned long values and variables have the size of 4 bytes;
- float values and variables have the size of 4 bytes;
- double values and variables have the size of 8 bytes;
- any pointer value or variable has the size of 4 bytes.

In C/C++ programs one can define more complex data values and "data containers" (commonly called *structures* or *records*, though the latter term has lately become obsolete) using the struct construct. This construct can be used recursively (hierarchically), allowing us to explicitly describe how a structure consists of simpler or elementary components.

```
struct {
  char a;
  int b;
} x;
```

The structure variable x consists of two components: the first, named x.a, has data type char and so has a size of 1 byte; the second, named x.b, has data type int and so has the size of 4 bytes. *The memory of a structure is contiguous.* This simple example brings us to the topic of padding.

The memory usually cannot be accessed one bit or byte at a time. Its physical realization most commonly allows an access by one "machine

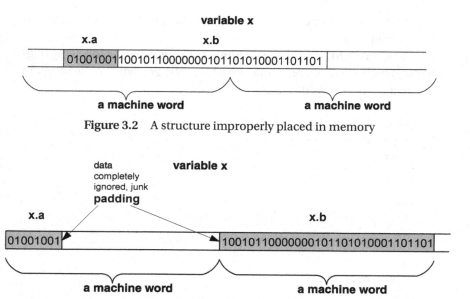

Figure 3.2 A structure improperly placed in memory

Figure 3.3 A structure properly placed in memory with the use of padding

word" at a time. Thus, when the computer is fetching the value of x.a from memory, it must in fact fetch the whole machine word of which x.a is a part. The same is true for storing; when the computer is storing a new value in x.a, the whole machine word must be stored anew in memory.

If the structure x were placed in the memory improperly (see Figure 3.2) then access to x.b would be rather inefficient, for fetching the value from or storing a value in x.b would require fetching or storing two machine words, even though x.b on its own would fit into a single machine word. It is much more efficient to waste some memory and *align* the components with machine-word boundaries in the physical memory, as indicated in Figure 3.3.

Now, access to x.a or x.b requires a single memory access. The inclusion of this extra (otherwise unused) memory by the compiler is called *padding*, and the data stored in it are never accessed by the program and thus are complete junk, so in that respect the memory is wasted. The only purpose of padding is to align items of the structure with machine-word boundaries for efficient memory access. From a logical point of view the padding does not matter. But it does affect the size of a structure, and since it depends on the platform and the compiler, the same structure may have different sizes on different machines or when compiled by different compilers.

A frequent error of ignoring padding is illustrated by the following fragment of code. Such an error may lead to erratic behavior of the program due to an overflow, as discussed previously.

```
struct mystruct {
  char a;
  int b;
};
...
...
void copy(void*,void*); /* prototype */
...
...
char* p;
struct mystruct x;
...
p = malloc(5);
...
copy(p,&x);
...
```

The programmer has calculated the size of mystruct to be 5 bytes, yet with padding the size of mystruct is 8 bytes. In the program, 5 bytes are allocated for a copy of the variable x, but when the contents of x are copied to the location that p points to, this causes an overflow because the function copy() correctly copies 8 bytes.

It should be noted that the previous code fragment also illustrates the common programming problem of using inconsistent conceptual levels. The programmer of the code fragment is dealing inconsistently with mystruct on two distinct conceptual levels: as a structure consisting of various components, and as a contiguous segment of memory or *buffer*. The function copy() is dealing with mystruct in a consistent manner, as a buffer with size 8 bytes.

Using the sizeof operator would remedy the overflow problem,

```
struct mystruct {
  char a;
  int b;
};
```

```
...
...
void copy(void*,void*); /* prototype */
...
...
char* p;
struct mystruct x;
...
p = malloc(sizeof(struct mystruct));
...
copy(p,&x);
...
```

though it does not address the problem of using inconsistent conceptual levels. The most consistent and hence the safest approach is to deal with mystruct as a structure only and leave the compiler to deal with it entirely:

```
struct mystruct {
  char a;
  int b;
};
...
...
struct mystruct* p;
struct mystruct x;
...
p = malloc(sizeof(struct mystruct));
...
*p = x;
...
```

The following code shows another error of ignoring padding (and using inconsistent conceptual levels) that may lead to incorrect results:

```
struct mystruct {
  char a;
  int b;
};
...
...
...
void bytecopy(void*,void*,int);
```

```
...
...
char* p;
struct mystruct* p1;
struct mystruct x;
...
p = malloc(sizeof(struct mystruct));
...
bytecopy(p,(char*)&x.a,1);
bytecopy(p+1,(char*)&x.b,4);
p1 = (struct mystruct*) p;
...
```

Here the value of item p1->a is correct (the same as x.a), but the value of p1->b is incorrect because bytecopy(s1,s2,n) copies n bytes from s2 to s1.

We have illustrated that improper programming and ignoring padding can lead to errors. However, ignoring padding can itself lead to inefficient use of memory:

```
struct mystruct1 {
  char a;
  int b;
  char c;
}
```

requires 12 bytes on a typical 32-bit machine, while

```
struct mystruct2 {
  char a;
  char c;
  int b;
}
```

requires only 8 bytes.

In Chapter 8 we will discuss classes and objects of C++ and their relation to memory in detail. At this point let us state that objects without methods are in fact very much like structures created by the struct construct. In fact, struct in C++ is treated as a class with no explicit methods and with all members being public. Nevertheless, for the purpose of our discussion of the memory aspects of variables, this has no relevance and thus all we have said about structures almost fully applies to objects as well.

Memory can never be empty. Therefore, when a variable is created as a "data container", it cannot be empty. The value of the variable is then arbitrary because the contents of the container are arbitrary, depending on circumstances that are totally beyond the programmer's control or prediction. It is a common error to leave a variable uninitialized or unset and then use it in an expression, which leads to incorrect results or crashing programs. A good compiler, though, can detect the first use of an uninitialized or unset variable in an expression and issue a warning message.

It may be important to know the logical address of a variable (e.g., in C it is used to emulate passing of arguments by reference; see Chapter 5). Of course, the address can only be known at the time of compilation. A C/C++ *address operator* & allows us to obtain that address in the form of an appropriate pointer (more about pointers later). We used it to pass the address of x.a or the address of x.b in the call to bytecopy() and to pass the address of x in the call to copy() in the previous code samples.

In order for a program to work with a "data container" it must know three attributes of that container: its address, its size, and its coding. The last two are determined by the data type of the container, so in a sense we need only two attributes: address and data type. During compilation, the compiler keeps tabs on variables in its symbol section and consequently knows all the attributes. Since each symbolic reference is ultimately replaced by an address reference, it is natural to consider whether we could reference the data containers directly by address and so avoid giving them explicit names. Having data containers without explicit names is crucial if we want to create them dynamically during program execution. For that we must somehow supply both attributes. This is the main purpose and role of the special values and variables in C and C++ called *pointers*. A pointer as a value is a simple address, and a pointer as a variable is a simple data container to hold an address. Moreover, the data type of the pointer determines the type of the data container being referenced via that pointer. The exception is void*, which represents just a plain address with no data type reference. We say that a pointer *points to address* x if the value of the pointer is x (see Figure 3.4).

Notice the subtle distinction: a pointer points to an address (a single byte), not to a data container of any kind. To determine what "lies at the

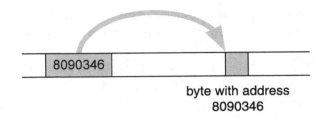

byte with address
8090346

Figure 3.4   A pointer points to a memory location

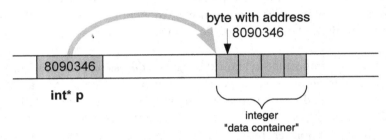

Figure 3.5   A pointer points to a "virtual data container"

end of the arrow" we must know the data type of the pointer, and (as indicated in Figure 3.5) a "virtual data container" of the same type is expected
at the end of the arrow.

Referencing of a data container through its pointer is done by the *indirection* operator *, and this operation is often called *dereferencing* of the
pointer. If used as a so-called l-value (roughly speaking, a value that can
occur on the left-hand side of the assignment expression, indicating storage), then dereferencing translates as "store the appropriate binary code
for the data type at the address the pointer is pointing to":

```
char* p;
...
*p = 'A';
```

More precisely, this example translates as "store the 8-bit ASCII binary
code for character 'A' at the address stored in p". In any other context,
dereferencing translates as "fetch the binary code of the appropriate
length from the address the pointer is pointing to":

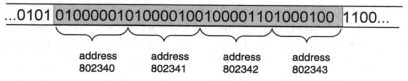

Figure 3.6 What is the value stored in the four bytes starting at address 802340?

```
char* p;
char x;
...
x = *p;
```

More precisely, this code translates as "fetch the binary code of length 1 byte from the address stored in p and store it in the variable x".

Pointers and their dereferencing are powerful programming features. Not only do they make it possible to access any memory location, they also make it possible to interpret the binary code stored in a certain memory location in different ways. My favorite "tricky" question for beginning computer science students is depicted in Figure 3.6.

If you, dear reader, did not answer "I cannot tell", then you should brush up on the fundamentals of C programming. The truth is that the binary code stored in the four bytes starting at location 802340 can be interpreted in various ways; that is, the value is "in the eye of beholder". The value could be interpreted as two short integer values 16916 and 17475 in a row, or as an integer value of 1145258561, or as a float value of 781.035217, or as four consecutive characters 'A', 'B', 'C', and 'D' in a row, and so on. Somebody may run the program code given next and come up with different values than given here.

This discrepancy is related to *byte order* – the order of significance of bytes. Imagine a 2-byte short integer with value 1. One byte contains all 0s, while the other byte contains all 0s and a single 1. In the *big endian* byte order, the byte with all 0s (the more significant byte) is on the left, while the byte with 1 (the less significant byte) is on the right. The *little endian* byte order is reversed: the less significant byte is on the left, while the more significant byte is on the right. The same applies to data of more than 2 bytes such as long integers.

For networking purposes (to establish in what order to transfer data across a network), the standard *network byte order* is defined as the big endian order. For the reasons just discussed, we have included a run-time check for "endianess" in the following sample program, which illustrates the technique of interpreting the contents of memory in different ways.

```c
#include <stdio.h>

char* Bits(char c);
int AmBigEndian();

    /* create a segment of static memory with the right data */
    char a[4] = {'A','B','C','D'};

/* function main ------------------------------------------- */
int main()
{
    char* b = a;           /* b points to the beginning of a */
    short* s = (short*) s;  /* s points to the beginning of a */
    int* p = (int*) a;      /* p points to the beginning of a */
    float* f = (float*) a;  /* f points to the beginning of a */

    if (AmBigEndian())
      printf("I am big endian\n");
    else
      printf("I am little endian\n");

    /* show the data as a sequence of bits */
    printf("%s",Bits(a[0]));
    printf("%s",Bits(a[1]));
    printf("%s",Bits(a[2]));
    printf("%s",Bits(a[3]));
    putchar('\n');

    /* show the data as 4 characters */
    printf("'%c','%c','%c','%c'\n",*b,*(b+1),*(b+2),*(b+3));

    /* show the data as 2 short integers */
    printf("%d,%d\n",*s,*(s+1));

    /* show the data as 1 integer */
    printf("%d\n",*p);

    /* show the data as 1 float */
    printf("%f\n",*f);
```

```c
    return 0;

}/*end main*/

/* function Bits ------------------------------------------ */
char* Bits(char c)
{
    static char ret[9];
    int i;

    i = (int) c;
    if (!AmBigEndian()) i = i >> 24;

    ret[0] = ((c&128) == 128)+'0'
    ret[1] = ((c&64) == 64)+'0'
    ret[2] = ((c&32) == 32)+'0'
    ret[3] = ((c&16) == 16)+'0'
    ret[4] = ((c&8) == 8)+'0'
    ret[5] = ((c&4) == 4)+'0'
    ret[6] = ((c&2) == 2)+'0'
    ret[7] = ((c&1) == 1)+'0'
    ret[8] = '\0';

    return ret;
}/* end Bits */

/* function AmBigEndian ------------------------------------ */
int AmBigEndian()
{
  long x = 1;
  return !(*((char *)(&x)));
}/* end AmBigEndian */
```

When executed on a big endian machine (most UNIX boxes), this program will give the following output:

```
I am big endian
'A','B','C','D'
01000001010000100100001101000100
16706,17220
1094861636
12.141422
```

while on a little endian machine (Intel processors) the output is

```
I am little endian
'A','B','C','D'
01000001010000100100001101000100
16961,17475
1145258561
781.035217
```

A crude yet useful analogy can be made: a pointer has two attributes. First, it points to a memory location, and second, it wears "data type glasses" – wherever it points, there it sees (through these "glasses") a virtual data container of the data type of the "glasses". The pointer "sees" the data container there no matter what, which is why we call it a "virtual" data container. This segment of memory might have been defined as that kind of data container or it might not; it makes no difference, as the sample program shows. The pointer b looks at the address 802340 and through its char "glasses" sees a char data container of 1 byte there (see Figure 3.7). The pointer s looks at the address 802340 and through its short "glasses" sees a short data container of 2 bytes (Figure 3.8). The pointer p looks at the address 802340 and through its int "glasses" sees a int data container of 4 bytes (Figure 3.9). The pointer f looks at the address 802340 and through its float "glasses" sees a float data container of 4 bytes (Figure 3.10).

The analogy of virtual data containers makes the pointer arithmetic relatively simple and clear. Pointer arithmetic expressions should always have the form of "pointer ± nonnegative integer". The semantics of p+n is: "the address of the beginning of nth data container to the right of where p is pointing now"; more formally, the address is calculated as p+n*sizeof(X),

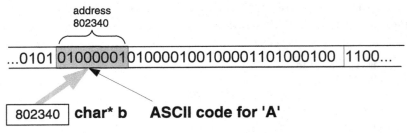

Figure 3.7 Looking through char* "glasses" at a char virtual data container

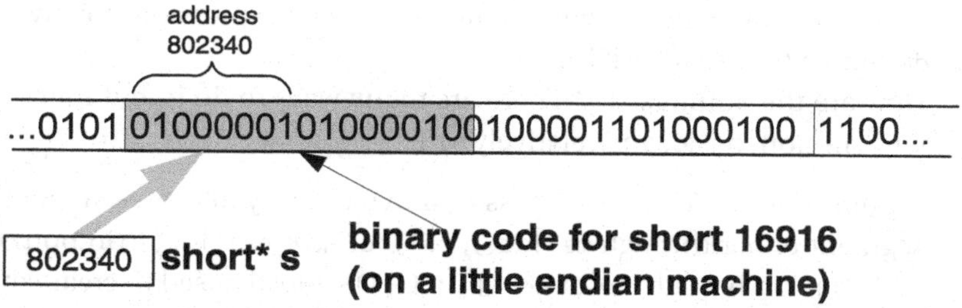

address
802340

...0101 `01000001010000100`100001101000100 1100...

802340 | **short* s**

**binary code for short 16916
(on a little endian machine)**

Figure 3.8 Looking through short* "glasses" at a short virtual data container

address
802340

...0101 `01000001010000100010000 1101000100` 1100...

802340 | **int* p**

**binary code for int 1145258561
(on a little endian machine)**

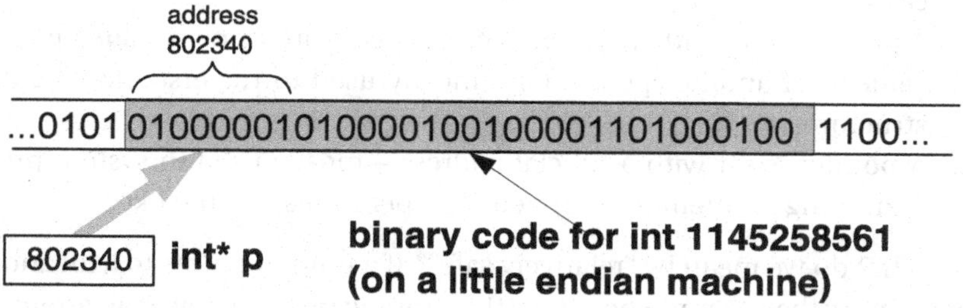

Figure 3.9 Looking through int* "glasses" at an int virtual data container

address
802340

...0101 `0100000101000010001000011101000100` 1100...

802340 | **float* f**

**binary code for float 781.035217
(on a little endian machine)**

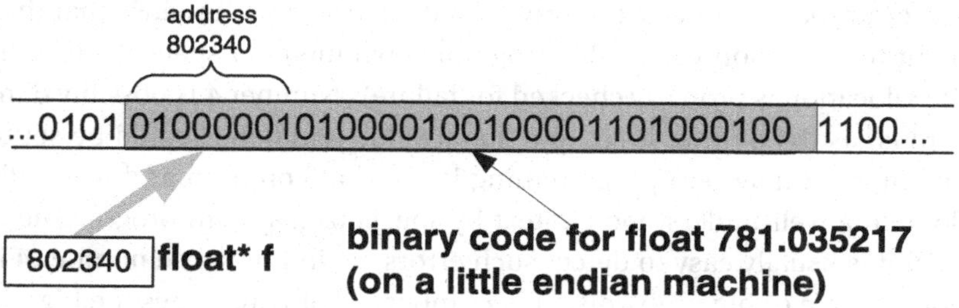

Figure 3.10 Looking through float* "glasses" at a float virtual data container

where X is the data type of the pointer p. Likewise, the semantics of p-n is: "the address of the beginning of nth data container to the left of where p is pointing now"; more formally, the address is calculated as p-n*sizeof(X). Thus, the arrow where a pointer points can only move in discrete steps, from the beginning of one virtual data container to the beginning of another. It should come as no surprise that void* pointers cannot be involved in pointer arithmetic (of course, there are some compilers that may complain but still evaluate pointer arithmetic expressions involving void*, which they treat as if it were char*).

How are the pointers set? There are many ways to do it, but four are rather common, basic, and relatively safe.

1. A pointer is set with an address of a dynamically allocated memory segment either through malloc(), calloc(), or realloc() (in both C and C++) or through new or new[] (in C++) – mostly used to create dynamic objects and linked data structures.
2. A pointer is set with an address of a named object through the address operator & – mostly used to emulate passing by reference in C function calls.
3. A pointer is set with an address calculated from its own value and/or value(s) of another pointer(s) – mostly used to traverse linked data structures.
4. A pointer is set with a special address – mostly used in system programming for memory-mapped I/O operations and the like.

What do we mean by "relatively safe"? If a pointer points to a location in memory that does not belong to the running program and if an attempt is made to store any value there, then most modern operating systems will terminate the program immediately for a memory access violation. It is clear that pointers set in ways 1 and 2 are safe in the sense that they point to a location within the program's own memory space (as long as the allocation is properly checked for failure). Number 4 is possibly dangerous, as the pointer is set to a literal value and hence could be set to anything. But system programming is not that common and is usually done in a well-understood context by specialized system programmers; also, it is usually easy to detect such errors, so in this sense number 4 is not a source of big problems. It is number 3 that constitutes the biggest source of possible memory access violations: the calculations may be incorrect, leading to incorrect locations being pointed to. Since the actual value of the pointer that caused the violation may only be known at the moment of executing the expression of which it is a part, these errors can only be detected and debugged at run time.

There are two common situations associated with pointers that lead to memory access violations. In the first, the *uninitialized pointer*, a pointer is not initialized or set and so it can point to any random location (as discussed previously for uninitialized or unset variables). An attempt to store something at the location the pointer is pointing to may result in a memory access violation. The other situation is the *dangling pointer* (or *dangling reference*). If a pointer is pointed to an object that is later deallocated, the pointer is left dangling (i.e., pointing to a previously meaningful address that is no longer meaningful). There are two ways for dangling to happen, explicit and implicit. In the explicit way, the pointer is first pointed to a dynamically allocated segment that is later explicitly deallocated without resetting the pointer appropriately. In the implicit way, the pointer is first pointed to a local object that is then later deallocated (as a part of the activation frame) when its function terminates, again without appropriate resetting of the pointer.

It has already been mentioned that a memory segment cannot ever be empty. This brings us to the notion of a null pointer, a pointer that points nowhere. An "empty" pointer would be ideal but is not possible, so we must find a possible address to mean *null*. Since it is standard to reserve the lowest memory addresses for the operating system, no application program ever stores anything at the very first byte – the byte with address zero. Thus we can (and do) use the value of 0 as meaning "no address whatsoever". The C language makes a conceptual distinction: in the stdio.h header file, a value NULL is defined (to be actually '\0'). We can thus compare the value of pointer p with NULL or set p to NULL, because the compiler expands '\0' to the appropriate value. However, the stricter C++ compilers treat such expressions as a type mismatch, and thus it is usually the best to simply use 0 for null pointers; it does not stand out as nicely as NULL, but at least it does not irritate the compiler. Lately the definitions of NULL have started to vary, using 0 or (void*)0. In such cases, strict ANSI or C++ compilers have no problems dealing with NULL.

A program written in a programming language does not necessarily have to be compiled before it can be executed; instead, it may be *interpreted*. The interpretation is done by a special program (interpreter) that reads the source statements, parses them, understands them, and executes the necessary instructions to achieve the same goals as the original source statements. It is clear that interpretation imposes certain restrictions on the expressiveness of the language (the language constructs can only allow actions that the interpreter is capable of) and that it is slower in execution when compared with compiled programs (the parsing and understanding of the source statements is done at run time rather than compile time). On the other hand, as long as you have the right interpreter on a machine, any program can be run there. The Java designers opted for this platform-free portability. To alleviate the problem with the speed of execution, Java programs are first compiled to *byte code* and then interpreted by the *Java virtual machine* interpreter, which greatly improves the speed of execution. Nevertheless, our comment about restrictions imposed on a language designed for interpretation still applies.

There is a price to pay for the power of pointers and dereferencing: it allows so much flexibility that it would be virtually impossible to design an interpreter capable of dealing with them. Their use makes C/C++ programs possibly too platform-oriented. For instance, special address locations for memory-mapped I/O operations are highly dependent on the particular platform and could be totally meaningless on any other platform. Such a program cannot and should not be made portable. Thus, any possible C/C++ interpreter would have to be platform-specific in its capabilities, voiding the main advantage of interpretation while leaving the disadvantages in place.

In Chapter 4 we will discuss dynamic memory allocation in more detail. From our discussion of pointers it should be clear that explicit dynamic memory allocation is fraught with a number of perils. In Chapter 10 we will discuss memory leaks resulting from improper memory deallocation. Simply put, having explicit memory allocation and deallocation gives C/C++ programs immense flexibility while keeping overhead to a minimum, but it opens the door to many possible problems.

The Java designers opted for a different strategy. Java does not allow any explicit memory allocation and deallocation, all allocations are done implicitly through reference variables, and the deallocation takes place automatically through *garbage collection*. The principles of garbage collection are simple: every portion of dynamically allocated memory has been allocated through a symbolic reference and so, as long as it is being referenced by an object, the garbage collector leaves it intact. But when memory is no longer referenced by any "live" object, the garbage collector can deallocate it. This strategy removes quite a few problems with memory access, but it requires explicit symbolic referencing (and hence no pointers). Besides that, the garbage collector can kick in any time more memory is needed, degrading the performance of a program at unpredictable moments.

Thus pointers prevent C/C++ from having a built-in garbage collector. This does not mean that you cannot write your own garbage collector (or download somebody else's) and then have all your programs written in compliance with the requirements of the garbage collector. Rather, this means that garbage collection cannot be a generic feature of C/C++ compilers that is transparent to programmers as it is, for example, in Java.

Review

A variable in a C/C++ program can be conveniently viewed as an appropriate "data container" of a definite size. In this (and the previous) chapter we have discussed this container as a segment of memory. The address of the segment (i.e., the address of its first byte) is referred to as the address of the variable and the length of the segment as the size of the variable. The symbolic references to the variable in the source program are replaced by the compiler with the address references to that segment. The data type of the "container" determines which binary code is used to store the value or to interpret the value stored there.

Pointers are special values and variables with two attributes – the first is an address, the other is a data type. Thus a pointer determines which location in the memory we are referencing as well as how to interpret the binary code at that location. In essence, looking through the pointer's eyes, we can see where it points to a "virtual object" of the appropriate data type. Thus, pointers allow us to interpret the contents of a memory segment in various ways and to reference such virtual objects without using their names or even giving them names. This gives C/C++ programs a lot of flexibility and problem-solving power, but on the other hand it can be dangerous (since dangling or incorrectly set pointers cause memory access faults) and in general prevents C/C++ programs from being portable or interpretable in a Java-like platform-free manner.

Explicit dynamic memory allocation and deallocation goes hand in hand with pointers, putting the onus for memory handling on the programmer. This has both positive and negative consequences: memory handling can thus be made predictable and highly efficient, but it can also end up being unpredictable, inefficient, or (even worse) outright incorrect. The infamous "memory leaks" are result of such improper handling of memory allocation and deallocation: not all the allocated (but no longer needed) memory is deallocated and hence, as the program executes, the unused yet allocated memory keeps accumulating to the point of becoming detrimental to the running program, other running programs, or even the operating system. Thus, in a general setting, C/C++ cannot have a garbage collector – unless you are willing to refrain from a

MEMORY AS A PROGRAMMING CONCEPT

free-format explicit memory allocation in favor of a restricted allocation handled through mechanisms with which your custom-made garbage collector can work.

Exercises

3.1 While compiling a C program, the GNU C compiler gave us the error message "warning: comparison is always true due to limited range of data type". Does this message warrant a closer inspection of the statement it refers to, or can it be safely ignored? If you think that it cannot be safely ignored, give an example of where it may be essential.

3.2 Assume that the value of an int variable i is not zero. Is it possible that i += 3*i will set the value of i to zero? If so, under what circumstances?

3.3 Consider an int variable x and consider a pointer float* p = (float*)&x pointing to x. If we store a float value 2.35 in x directly using x = 2.35 or indirectly using *p = 2.35, will we get the same bit pattern stored in x in both cases or instead different patterns?

3.4 Storing an int value in memory using a char* pointer can cause all kinds of errors. Can storing an int value in a char variable cause the same errors?

3.5 Calculate the size in bytes of the following structure:

```
struct{
   int b;
   char a;
   int c;
}
```

3.6 In a C program, we store two short integers in an int variable; we then retrieve and display them later in the program:

```
short* p;
int x;
...
p = (short*) &x;
*p++ = 1;
*p = 2;
...
printf("first short=%d,second short=%d\n",*p, *(p+1));
```

During execution, the screen displays `first short=1, second short=2`. What will the screen display if we compile and execute our program on a machine that has the opposite "endianess"?

3.7 Interpret the binary code `10010101010001010101010101000001` that is stored at the address 8023456. Assume that the machine is a "little endian" one; if you still have a problem with the interpretation, assume that the address is located in the static section of the address space rather than the dynamic data section.

3.8 In our C program we have

```
char* p;
...
p = "ab";
```

The compiler does not complain and the program works fine. If we change this to

```
int* p;
...
*p = 23;
```

then will everything continue to work fine?

3.9 We are using a garbage collector with our C program. We know that, whenever a memory segment previously allocated is no longer referenced in our program, the garbage collector may deallocate it. In order to prevent an unwanted deallocation, we keep (in a special file) addresses of segments that we do not want to lose. Will this help us?

3.10 Since we did not want to make an error in counting of bytes, we used the code

```
char *p;
...
p = malloc(strlen("hello")+1);
strcpy(p,"hello");
```

instead of the intended

```
char *p;
...
p = malloc(6);
strcpy(p,"hello");
```

Compare the memory requirements of each version: which one requires less memory?

References

The following are very good texts on C or C++ programming and cover most of the topics from this chapter:

Carrano, F. M., and Prichard, J. J., *Data Abstraction and Problem Solving with C++: Walls and Mirrors*, Pearson, Harlow, U.K., 2002.

Harbison, S. P. III, and Steele, G. L., Jr., *C: A Reference Manual*, Prentice-Hall, Englewood Cliffs, NJ, 2002.

Keogh, J., *Introduction to Programming with C*, Prentice-Hall, Englewood Cliffs, NJ, 1996.

Kernighan, B. W., and Ritchie, D. M., *The C Programming Language*, Prentice-Hall, Englewood Cliffs, NJ, 1988.

Kirch-Prinz, U., and Prinz, P., *A Complete Guide to Programming in C++*, Jones & Bartlett, Sudbury, MA, 2002.

Perry, J., *Advanced C Programming by Example*, Thomson Learning, Boston, 1998.

Schildt, H., *Advanced C*, McGraw-Hill, New York, 1988.

Stroustrup, B., *The C++ Programming Language*, Addison-Wesley, Reading, MA, 1997.

Tondo, C. L., Gimpel, S. E., and Kernighan, B. W., *The C Answer Book*, Prentice-Hall, Englewood Cliffs, NJ, 1988.

An excellent C/C++ based web portal:

"C and C++ Programming Language Resources around the World",
http://www.eeng.brad.ac.uk/help/.packlangtool/.langs/.c/.resource.html.

The following Internet links are a great source of information on garbage collection in general and on C/C++ based programs in particular:

http://www.cs.ukc.ac.uk/people/staff/rej/gc.html;
http://www.hpl.hp.com/personal/Hans_Boehm/gc/;
http://www.cs.princeton.edu/~appel/modern/c/software/boehm/;
http://www.memorymanagement.org.

A good overview of Java:

Bolker, E. D., and Campbell, W., *Java Outside In*, Cambridge University Press, 2003.

Texts on the Java virtual machine:

Meyer, J., and Downing, T., *Virtual Machine*, O'Reilly, Sebastopol, CA, 1997.

Venners, B., *Inside the Java Virtual Machine*, McGraw-Hill, New York, 2000.

CHAPTER FOUR

DYNAMIC ALLOCATION AND DEALLOCATION OF MEMORY

Fundamentals of dynamic allocation and deallocation of memory: free store (system heap); per-process memory manager; C memory allocators malloc(), calloc(), *and* realloc(); *and C deallocator* free(). *How to handle memory allocation/deallocation errors.*

In previous chapters we have mentioned dynamic allocation of memory several times. In Chapter 2 we had quite a detailed look at the static allocation when we discussed the process of compilation, linking, loading, and execution of a program. We mentioned dynamic allocation from a general point of view or, to be more precise, from the operating system point of view.

The reader should be comfortable with the idea that a running program is allocated several segments – not necessarily contiguous – of memory to which its address space is mapped during program execution. These segments together constitute "the program's memory space", or the "memory it owns", where all the program's instructions and data needed for the execution are stored and accessible. It is obvious that many programs need to increase their memory during their execution; for instance, they might need to store more data or even more instructions.

As mentioned at the end of Chapter 2, it would be more precise to talk about a process rather than a running program. Modern operating systems like UNIX thus have a *process memory manager,* software that is responsible for providing additional allocation of memory to its process and for deallocation when the memory is no longer needed. Since it is

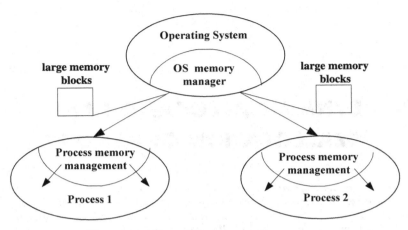

Figure 4.1   Two-tier memory management

not our aim to discuss operating system issues (unless they are directly related to programming in C/C++), suffice it to say that memory management on the operating system level is usually a two-tier affair (see Figure 4.1): first an operating system memory manager allocates rather large "chunks" of memory to individual process memory managers and also keeps track of them. Then each process memory manager allocates smaller "chunks" of the memory to its process and keeps track of allocated and free segments: when its process requests deallocation of a segment, it puts that segment on the list of free segments; if running out of memory, it requests another big chunk from the operating system memory manager.

But what does it really mean to "allocate a segment of memory"? In essence, memory management is a very simple "accounting" of what process owns what part(s) of the memory. (The reader must forgive us this oversimplification, but as stated previously we do not want to be sidetracked by operating system issues not pertinent to C/C++ programming concepts.) Thus, memory allocation is nothing more or less than making an entry in the "accounting book" that this segment is given to this process for keeps, and memory deallocation is an entry that this segment is not needed by this process and hence is "free". Obviously, decisions concerning which segment to allocate, how to make sure that the fragmentation (subdividing bigger segments into smaller ones) does not degrade performance, and many other issues are rather important and complex to solve. However, the programmer must seek to understand the concepts of allocation and deallocation of memory and so need not bother with such technical issues.

It is clear that we are interested in the process memory manager: what is happening (and how) when our program requests more memory or returns some memory no longer needed. It is actually more efficient *not* to have the process manager "return" freed memory segments to the operating system memory manager; thus both allocated and freed memory segments remained assigned to the process. The freed segments are kept by the process memory manager for serving future requests and possibly for unifying adjacent segments into bigger ones (to partially alleviate the fragmentation caused by previous allocations). This may be surprising to some programmers because, with most operating systems, frequent checks of memory usage while a program is running will show that it never decreases (in LINUX it seems to decrease, but this is caused by the way memory use is reported rather than by segments being returned to the operating system). This does not necessarily mean that the program is suffering memory leaks. Normally, memory usage should reach a certain steady state as either no new memory is requested or the requests can be served by using the freed segments. Only if memory usage keeps growing and growing do we face the ignominious memory leakage.

The operating system process manager usually keeps track of allocated blocks in a data structure called the *binary heap* (a binary tree in which each node is labeled by a label that is smaller than labels of all its descendants), whose purpose is to facilitate fast and efficient searching for a suitable free block. This heap is sometimes referred to as the *system heap* or *free store*. The process memory manager usually keeps a dynamic list of free segments. One implication is that, every time your program requests more memory, the process memory manager must search through the list to find a suitable segment; if none is found, more memory must be requested from the operating system memory manager, which must search the system heap for a suitable block. After delivery to the process memory manager, a suitable segment must be carved out from the freshly allocated block. It is therefore impossible to estimate how long it will take to execute a memory allocation request. Even though modern computers and operating systems are very fast, if our program performs a significant number of allocations and deallocations then the attendant yet unpredictable delays may affect the program's performance. These issues must be considered for real-time software systems and for all programs where performance is essential. We will look at these issues when we discuss the concept of "allocation from arena" in Chapter 9.

In modern operating systems, the operating system manager is not a part of the process code but instead is engaged by a system call from the process. The appropriate system call is thus particular to each operating system and each hardware platform. It is desirable and practical to shield an applications programmer from such idiosyncrasies, so C/C++ compilers come equipped with standard functions that provide OS- and platform-independent interfaces to the appropriate system calls. These C standard functions are malloc(), calloc(), realloc(), and free() (the appropriate prototypes and other relevant definitions can be found in the slightly obsolete header file malloc.h or in the more up-to-date header file stdlib.h); even though these C functions can be used without penalty in C++ programs, more sophisticated versions of these are the C++ operators new, new[], delete, and delete[], and programmers are strongly encouraged to use them. In this chapter we focus on the "plain" C functions; we will discuss specific issues pertinent to the C++ operators in Chapter 8. From now on we may consider (albeit somewhat imprecisely) these functions as programming interfaces to the process memory manager.

The synopsis (function prototype together with the necessary header files) of malloc() is rather simple:

```
#include <stdlib.h>

void *malloc(size_t size);
```

The argument size is the size of memory requested in bytes; malloc() either returns NULL if unsuccessful or returns the address (void* is just a plain address) of the beginning of the allocated segment. The segment allocated is properly aligned. Note that malloc() can fail for any of three reasons: if there is not enough memory left for allocation (the free store is depleted); if the size requested exceeds the limit allowed for allocation; or if the process memory manager has somehow been corrupted.

Let us state that we do not really need this previously unmentioned data type size_t, since it is just the good old unsigned long in disguise. However, it is defined according to ANSI-C standard to provide for more careful type checking.

It might come as a surprise to some, but malloc() may in fact allocate a bigger segment than requested. You are guaranteed to receive at least as many bytes you have requested, but you may also get more. The reasons concern both the way malloc() works and the way memory and access to it are organized. From the programmer's point of view it should not matter, for we can never be certain how many bytes were in fact allocated to us; thus, we can only count on the number of bytes we requested. This note's sole purpose is to put some programmers at ease when they check their running program and notice that the memory allocated is more than what the program is asking for (i.e., this is not necessarily symptomatic of a memory leak).

Let us repeat once again that memory can never be "empty". What, then, are the contents of a malloc() allocated segment? A common error is to assume that it is *blanked* (or *cleared*) when all its bits are set to 0. Even though it often happens this way (depending on where the segment is drawn from), in fact the contents of the segment are arbitrary and hence meaningless. Thus, the contents of a segment allocated by malloc() should not be used until it is set by the program to hold some meaningful value or values.

Besides assuming that the contents of a malloc() allocated segment are somehow set, another common error is allocating an insufficient number of bytes, which results in overflow when storing value(s) requiring more bytes. The reader is encouraged to refer to Chapter 3 for more detailed discussion of this topic.

The synopsis of calloc() is as simple as that of malloc():

```
#include <stdlib.h>

void *calloc(size_t nelem, size_t elsize);
```

Whatever has been said for malloc() applies also to calloc(), except that calloc() blanks (clears) the allocated segment and that the number of bytes allocated is nelem*elsize (in simple words, we are asking calloc() to allocate enough bytes for nelem elements of size elsize).

The synopsis of realloc() is also simple:

```
#include <stdlib.h>

void *realloc(void *ptr, size_t size);
```

though its semantics is more complex and its use is rather controversial.

Let us first address the semantics of realloc(). It is designed to expand or reduce an already allocated segment. The role of the argument ptr is exactly that – it is a pointer to the segment that we want to expand or reduce, while size stipulates the size in bytes of the expanded or reduced segment (which we will refer to as *new size*; we use *old size* when referring to the size of the segment prior to the call to realloc()). A null value of ptr is interpreted as there being no segment yet to expand or reduce, and then realloc() behaves like malloc(). If size is 0, then realloc() works like free() and the segment is deallocated. Note that realloc() guarantees the contents of the segment to be unchanged (up to the smaller of the old size and the new size).

All that has been said so far about realloc() is rather straightforward and plausible, so where is the controversy mentioned earlier? First, unless ptr points to a segment previously allocated via malloc(), calloc(), or realloc(), unpredictable problems may occur – including corruption of the process memory manager. Second, though it is not a problem to reduce a segment, it may be a problem to expand it. If there is not enough memory available to the right of the segment's end, then realloc() creates a new segment of the extended size somewhere else in the memory, copies the contents of the old segment up to the old size to the new segment, frees the old segment (see our discussion of free() that follows), and returns the pointer to the new segment. In essence, while the old segment is being extended, it may or may not move in the memory. For many purposes it does not matter that the extended segment has moved, but any meaningful links to the old segment in the program become dangling pointers, with all the consequences discussed in Chapter 3.

Let us illustrate this problem on a small example that is actually quite common. Assume that a program works with a binary tree, a fragment of which is depicted in Figure 4.2. Let us further assume that the program

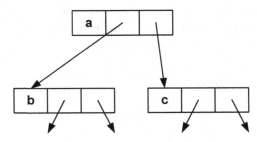

Figure 4.2   Fragment of a binary tree

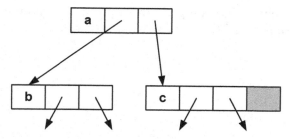

Figure 4.3   Node **c** was extended but has not moved

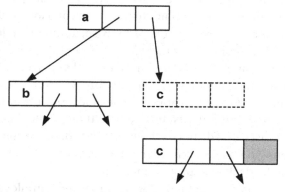

Figure 4.4   Node **c** was extended and has moved

needs to extend the node **c** and does so using `realloc()`. Consider the situation when the expanded node (segment) did not move, depicted in Figure 4.3. The fragment of the tree (and hence the whole tree) is sound.

Now consider the situation depicted in Figure 4.4, where the node (segment) moves while it is extended. The fragment of the tree is no longer sound; in fact, it is no longer a tree because the right child link of the node **a** is dangling.

It is no accident that the modern and better-designed memory allocators of C++ (`new` and `new[]`) have no counterpart to `realloc()`. It is always safer to manage such situations through an explicit allocation of a new segment, an explicit update of all links pointing to the old segment so that they point to the new segment, an explicit copying of all data from the old to the new segment, and finally an explicit deallocation of the old segment.

The previous paragraphs have covered the fundamentals of dynamic memory allocation in C. We are left with the task of returning the

MEMORY AS A PROGRAMMING CONCEPT

unneeded memory by a program to its process memory manager, or memory *deallocation*. This is the role of the C deallocator `free()`, whose synopsis is:

```
#include <stdlib.h>

void free(void *ptr);
```

The function `free()` inserts the segment pointed to by `ptr` back into the list of free segments kept by the process memory manager. As with the `realloc()` function, `ptr` must point to a segment previously allocated via `malloc()`, `calloc()`, or `realloc()`. Otherwise, unpredictable problems may result, which could even include corrupting the process memory manager. If the value of `ptr` is `NULL`, no action takes place.

Throughout this chapter, we have mentioned the errors that can arise during dynamic memory allocation and deallocation. Let us briefly summarize these errors and suggest how to treat them. Note that the C functions we have discussed do not have any error handling mechanisms (such as "exceptions" in C++), so it is up to the programmer to decide how the errors should be dealt with programmatically.

Allocation (using `malloc()`, `calloc()`, or `realloc()` in allocation mode) can fail for three reasons only: (i) not enough memory; (ii) asking for a bigger segment than the limit allows; or (iii) some kind of corruption of the data kept by the process memory manager. We therefore suggest immediate program termination in the event of a memory allocation failure. Of course, the termination should provide the user with a report that is as detailed and localized as possible (the most appropriate form is through logging, discussed in Chapter 10) so that the nature of the error can easily be determined if necessary.

Of course, such an approach cannot be used for safety-critical and/or fault-tolerant software. Such software should be designed differently – for instance:

- the dynamic memory allocation should be done *prior* to the execution of the critical section of the program, so a crash would not cause severe problems;
- the program should obtain as much dynamic memory as possible at the beginning and then use its own memory manager to manage it (we will discuss this together with "allocation from arena" in Chapter 9); or

▪ the program should have the ability to build the most important dynamic data structures it needs and work with them on disk in a special "error mode" – although this degrades performance, it nevertheless allows execution of the critical section to continue (even though in most cases the virtual memory system of the operating system does exactly that).

Reallocation (using `realloc()` in reallocation mode) may fail for the additional reason that the pointer of the segment to be reallocated is incorrect. Unlike allocation errors, which do not usually indicate a badly designed program, a reallocation failure is usually a programming error and as such should be discovered and treated during testing and debugging. A debugging version of `realloc()` should be able to check if the pointer value is correct (i.e., previously allocated) and, if not, allow for detailed debugging (see Chapter 10).

Similarly, `free()` should only be checked in the testing and debugging phase, and only for the purpose of preventing memory leaks (see Chapter 10). A debugging version of `free()` should work along the same lines as indicated for `realloc()`.

Errors caused by improper use of allocated and/or deallocated memory were covered in Chapter 3.

It is clear that different versions of these functions, including custom-made ones, can be used instead of the standard versions. There are many such replacements available, providing either faster and more efficient allocation/deallocation or additional features (such as debugging or reporting). We will discuss this further in Chapter 10.

Review

On the operating system level, memory management consists of keeping an account of what process owns what memory block and allocating more memory to a process when requested (thus the operating system can determine when a process is trying to access a memory location that is not its own – and terminate the process for faulty memory access). On the process level, memory management consists of keeping account of free segments or reclaiming those segments that the process no longer needs.

Statically allocated memory for a process is the memory into which the program is loaded prior to its execution. It does not change throughout the program's execution, and its layout is completely determined by the compiler. Both the data and the instructions of the program are stored in the statically allocated memory.

It is clear that many programs require more memory to store data or possibly additional instructions. These requests for additional memory allocation during the execution of a program – and the manner in which they are served – are generally referred to as "dynamic memory allocation".

In modern operating systems, memory management is a two-tier affair with a single operating system memory manager and different process memory managers specific for each running process. The operating system manager allocates rather big "chunks" (blocks) of memory to the process memory managers. A process memory manager divides these blocks into suitable memory segments, which it allocates to its process. For the process memory manager, dynamic memory allocation includes deciding which segment to allocate (if need be, divide a bigger segment into two smaller ones) and removing it from the list of free segments. The fragmentation caused by this division is inevitable and may degrade program performance. Therefore, deallocation includes (besides adding the freed segment to the list of free segments) possibly joining the freed segment with adjacent free segments to counter somewhat the fragmentation.

When a request for more memory is issued by a program (through a malloc(), calloc(), or realloc() call), its process memory manager allocates it a segment of a size equal to or bigger than the size requested (if such a segment is not ready, the process manager creates it from a bigger one; if this is not possible, the process memory manager requests a new block from the operating system manager). If there is not enough memory, the allocators return NULL; otherwise, they return the address of the allocated segment. The contents of the allocated segment are arbitrary for malloc(). All bits are cleared for calloc() and are preserved up to the minimum of the old size and the new size for realloc() (in the extended/reduced part, the contents are arbitrary). Allocation fails for three reasons only: not enough memory is available, the requested size exceeds the limit, or the process memory manager is corrupted.

The deallocator free() returns a segment to the list of free segments that is kept by the process memory manager. The functions realloc() and free() can each cause problems (including corruption of the process memory manager) if the pointer supplied is not pointing to a segment previously allocated by `malloc()`, `calloc()`, or `realloc()`, or if the segment it points to has meanwhile been freed.

There is not much to do about memory allocation errors, and a program should be promptly terminated if it runs into such an error. Detailed information (e.g., a log entry) about the error and its localization within the program should be provided so that the nature of the problem can be determined later. Safety-critical and fault-tolerant software systems should avoid dynamic memory allocation in their critical sections, possibly do their own memory management, or even be able to work with disk (instead of main) memory if allocation errors occur during execution of a critical section.

Exercises

4.1 What is the system heap and what it is used for?

4.2 Suppose our program requests just one memory allocation of a certain number of bytes. Checking the memory usage by our program during its execution shows that the dynamic memory increased more than we requested. Is this a sign of memory leaking?

4.3 Consider a simple program:

```
#include <stdio.h>
#include <string.h>

int main()
{
  char* p;

  p = malloc(20);
  strcpy(p,"hello");

  printf("%s\n",p);
  return 0;
}
```

The C compiler gives the strange warning message "line 8: warning: assignment makes pointer from integer without a cast", yet the program works correctly when executed. What is your explanation, considering that C compilers should allow `void*` to be stored in `char*` without complaining?

4.4 What is wrong with the following program?

```
#include <stdio.h>
#include <stdlib.h>
#include <string.h>

int main()
{
  char* p;
  p = realloc(p,100);
  strcpy(p,"hello");

  p = realloc(p,200);
  strcat(p," and good bye");
  return 0;
}
```

4.5 In a program we allocated 20 bytes of memory using p = malloc(20), yet we only need 10. For efficiency we decided to "return" a portion of the segment to the memory manager using free(&p[10]). What will happen? Will it compile? If so, will the program execute correctly and cause memory segment fragmentation? Or will it not work as intended – the memory manager will not "accept" the memory and the program will continue executing? Or will the program be terminated?

4.6 Will the following program crash? Always, sometimes, or never?

```
#include <stdio.h>
#include <stdlib.h>
#include <string.h>

int main()
{
  char *p, *q;

  p = malloc(20);
  strcpy(p,"hello");

  q = p;
  printf("%s\n",q);

  p = realloc(p,1000);
  printf("%s\n",q);
  return 0;
}
```

4.7   In the following program we allocate a memory segment of 20 bytes. What will happen to the memory segment after the program terminates?

```
#include <stdlib.h>
#include <string.h>

int main()
{
  char *p;

  p = malloc(20);
  strcpy(p,"hello");
  return 0;
}
```

4.8   Can we use free(p) if previously p was set by a call to realloc() via p = realloc(p,...)?

4.9   The allocators malloc(), calloc(), and realloc() and the deallocator free() work in a close relationship with the operating system. So how can a program using them be compiled by various compilers and executed on various machines?

4.10   How would you allocate a completely empty memory segment?

References

For general aspects of dynamic memory allocation, see the operating systems texts listed in Chapter 2. For a basic description of the C allocators and deallocators, see the C texts listed in Chapter 3.

Wilson, P. R., Johnstone, M. S., Neely, M., and Boles, D., *Dynamic Storage Allocation: A Survey and Critical Review*, Proceedings of the 1995 International Workshop on Memory Management (Kinros, Scotland, September 1995), Lecture Notes in Computer Science, 986, Springer-Verlag, New York.

For the programming point of view, see the following articles from the C/C++ Users Journal:

Allison, C., "Code Capsules – Dynamic Memory Management", part 1, *C/C++ Users Journal*, October 1994.

Allison, C., "Code Capsules – Dynamic Memory Management", part 2, *C/C++ Users Journal*, November 1994.

Halladay, S., "malloc-Related Errors", *C/C++ Users Journal*, May 1992.

Hogaboom, D., "A Flexible Dynamic Array Allocator", *C/C++ Users Journal*, November 1990.

Jaeschke, R., "Doctor C's Pointers – The Memory Management Library",
 C/C++ Users Journal, January 1990.
Sutter, H., "Sutter's Mill: Containers in Memory: How Big Is Big?", *C/C++ Users
 Journal,* January 2001.

*For programmatic details and debugging versions of the allocators and
deallocators, see the following websites:*

"Debugging Tools for Dynamic Storage Allocation and Memory
 Management", http://www.cs.colorado.edu/homes/zorn/public_html/
 MallocDebug.html.
"The Hoard memory allocator",
 http://www.cs.utexas.edu/users/emery/hoard/.
Lea, D., "A Memory Allocator",
 http://gee.cs.oswego.edu/dl/html/malloc.html.
"Malloc/Free and GC Implementations",
 http://www.cs.colorado.edu/~zorn/Malloc.html.
Watson, G., "Dmalloc – Debug Malloc Library", http://dmalloc.com/.

CHAPTER FIVE

FUNCTIONS AND FUNCTION CALLS

System stack, activation frame, activation frame as the storage for local auto objects and for function arguments. Passing arguments by value as opposed to by reference. Calling sequence. Recursion and its relation to activation frames and the system stack. The price of recursion.

Any program of even modest complexity must be modularized for many reasons: readability, testability, validation, extendibility, maintainability, and many others, all outside the scope of this book. However, we assume that the reader understands that any reasonable programming language must allow for some modularization; C and C++ are no exceptions. Besides modularization on the level of source files, virtually the only modularization feature of C consists of structuring a program into separate functions. The object orientation of C++ allows for a more complex and far better-controlled modularization.

A C/C++ function is a programming module with a precisely defined interface that consists of the function's *header,* which specifies the function's name, the data types of the *arguments* (the input to the function – though it is possible for a function not to have any arguments), and the data type of a single return value (the output of the function; again, it is possible for a function to return nothing at all). Let us observe that computer scientists prefer to speak of *procedures* (if no value is returned) and *functions* (if a value is returned and the execution has no "side effects", meaning that it does not modify any data not local to the function). However, we shall employ the usual C/C++ terminology and call them all functions regardless of whether or not a value is returned or any side effects occur. Similarly, the input to procedures and functions are generally called *parameters,* yet we will use the more traditional C/C++ term *arguments.*

In this chapter we take a detailed look at the mechanism underlying the function calls, with our customary focus on the role of memory.

The most important aspect of a function call is the sequence of activities that take place or (more properly) the *flow of control.* This sequence can be described in broad terms as:

(a) the instruction just before the call is executed,
(b) the function is called and its body is executed, and
(c) the instruction following the function call is executed,

and the execution of the program then continues in its customary top-down fashion. During a function call, control is passed to the *callee* (the function being called) and returned back to the *caller* (the function doing the calling) upon termination of the callee. This flow of control requires that the "execution environment" of the caller is somehow preserved and that the "execution environment" of the callee is somehow installed and used for the execution of the callee's body. On the termination of the callee, the execution environment of the callee is somehow disposed of and the previously preserved execution environment of the caller is reinstated. The flow of control during function calls is illustrated in Figure 5.1.

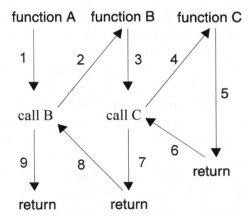

Figure 5.1   Flow of control during function calls

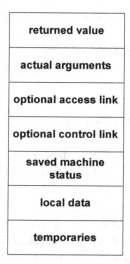

Figure 5.2   A general activation frame

We are very much interested in the "execution environment" part, for it is intimately tied to memory. The data structure to hold the information of this environment is called an *activation frame* (or *activation record*), since each call to (or *invocation* of) a function represents an activation of the function. A schematized activation frame is depicted in Figure 5.2.

The *returned value* field is reserved for the value the function is returning, and this is where the value is stored prior to termination of the function. The *actual arguments* field holds the values of, or references to, "objects" being passed to the function. The *optional control link* field, if used, points to the activation frame of the caller, and the *optional access link* field, if needed, is used to refer to nonlocal data stored in other activation frames. The *temporaries* field holds temporary values (such as those arising from the evaluation of expressions); the *saved machine status* field holds the values of system registers (e.g., program counter) at the moment of the call; and, most interesting to us, the *local data* field is where all local "objects" are stored. The precise nature and layout of the activation frame depends on the particular compiler and is not really important to us.

Before we embark on a detailed discussion of the steps involved in a function call, the *calling sequence* and *return sequence,* we will discuss general allocation strategies for activation frames. Generally, there are three ways to allocate (create) the activation frames.

1. Static allocation – lays out storage for the activation frame at compile time.
2. Dynamic allocation on the system heap – each activation frame is dynamically allocated on the system heap at run time during the actual function call.
3. Dynamic allocation on the system stack – same as above but with the system stack rather than the heap.

There are some trade-offs associated with each strategy. The static allocation has the advantage in the performance it facilitates: the compiler creates "empty" activation frames at compile time and, during the actual function call, only the relevant data are stored there, so the overhead of the function call remains low and thus enables very fast execution. The downside of static allocation is that multiple activations of the same function are not possible; in particular, recursion is not permitted. Fortran (up to the Fortran77 standard) allowed only static allocation of activation frames, but the later standards (Fortran87, 88, 89, now known under the umbrella term of Fortran90) allow the programmer to choose whether a procedure is static or recursive. However, computationally intensive applications of an iterative nature (e.g., weather modeling or fluid dynamics modeling), colloquially referred to as "number crunching", benefit from a low-overhead strategy; this is why languages with static allocation have their place in such applications.

Dynamic allocation on the system heap may cause the activation frame to "outlive" activation of the function itself or even the caller's activation. Yet for such languages the activation trees – which depict the way control enters and leaves activations or (more roughly) the entering and exiting of functions during execution – do not correctly depict the flow of control, so this strategy is generally not used.

Allocation on the system stack benefits from the system stack functioning as a control stack of the function calls: the activation frame is pushed onto the stack when the function is invoked and popped from the stack when the function terminates. Thus, the top of the stack correctly reflects the flow of control and this approach neatly facilitates not only multiple activations of functions but also recursion in its most general form. The disadvantage of this approach lies in the significant overhead associated with (a) the dynamic creation of a new activation frame, (b) pushing it onto the system stack at the beginning of a function call, and (c) popping it from the stack upon termination of the function. Nonetheless, in most cases the trade-off is worthwhile: the slowdown in execution is more than compensated by the problem-solving power gained.

We can now reward the patient reader and reveal that C and C++ are languages that follow the third strategy of dynamic allocation of the activation frames on the system stack. As such, C/C++ allows multiple invocation of functions and, in particular, recursion. Unfortunately, we are still not ready to discuss the C/C++ calling and return sequences. We have one more topic to cover, namely, how arguments are passed to functions. Again, we first discuss general strategies.

In essence, the simplest possible method is *call-by-value*, or passing the arguments *by value*. Here the caller evaluates the arguments prior to the call and passes the values (copies) to the callee as the actual arguments. The advantage of this method is in the safety of "information hiding", for operations performed on the actual arguments do not affect the values in the activation frame of the caller. The disadvantage is the memory required for copies of values requiring large storage, such as complex structures and objects. The C language passes arguments exclusively in this way (well, almost exclusively – see the discussion of arrays in Chapters 6 and 7); C++ also uses call-by-value as its default call method.

In *call-by-reference* (also known as *call-by-address* or *call-by-location*), arguments are passed *by reference* (also known as passing *by address* or *by location*). In this case a reference (address, location, pointer, etc.) of the argument is passed to the function. Of course, this means the argument must have a reference and, if an expression, the argument must evaluate to a reference. The advantage of this method is lower overhead for the call (no need to copy the values) and lower memory requirements, especially if we are passing arguments requiring large storage. The disadvantage is that the callee can modify data from the caller's activation frame, with possibly serious implications. (See Chapters 6 and 7 for a discussion of why arrays are in fact passed by reference.) In C++ the programmer is allowed to state explicitly that an argument should be passed by reference.

The other two generally used methods are *copy-restore* and *call-by-name*. We may briefly describe copy-restore as follows: First, use copies of arguments as in call-by-value; then, at termination of the function, use the newly computed values as replacements for the values of the original arguments. This "feels" like a call-by-reference, but it poses some quirky and subtle problems. The call-by-name method has probably been encountered by the reader in C/C++ *macro-expansion* or in ANSI C and C++ *inlining*. Both of these calling methods lie outside our present interests.

We are finally ready to tackle the calling and return sequences. The actual details depend on the compiler being used (as does the detailed structure of the activation frame), but for our purposes a broad description will suffice. Some of the steps are performed by the caller, whereas others are performed by the callee. This division is to some degree arbitrary and may depend on such factors as the operating system, the target platform, and so forth. However, in our discussion, "who does what" is less important than "what must be done".

Here is the calling sequence.

1. The activation frame for the callee is created by the caller.
2. The arguments are evaluated by the caller. For an argument, if passing by value is required, then the value of the argument is stored in the "actual arguments" field; if if passing by reference is required, the pointer to the argument is stored there.
3. The callee saves the machine's status in its activation frame – in particular, the value of the program counter that indicates which instruction should be executed next (i.e., the one right after the call).
4. The callee initializes its local data and starts executing.

The return sequence proceeds as follows.

1. The callee stores the return value in the "returned value" field in its activation frame.
2. The callee uses the information from the "saved machine status" field and restores the registers for the caller; this includes popping the system stack.
3. The callee branches to the return address of the caller.
4. The caller copies the returned value from the activation frame of the callee. Even though the system stack was "popped", the data is still there because we do not deallocate the memory but only manipulate the register that points to the top of the stack.
5. If a value is returned, then the caller uses it for evaluation of an expression and continues with its normal execution.

The reader may now better appreciate the overhead associated with dynamic function calls and start wondering whether recursion is really worth the trouble. In the rest of this chapter we will examine recursion in more detail and attempt to persuade the reader that it is worth the cost.

FUNCTIONS AND FUNCTION CALLS

Let us consider a simple C++ program:

```cpp
#include <iostream.h>

#define dot 1
#define id   2
#define error 3

int A(char*,int&);
int B(char*,int&);
int Next(char*,int&);

// function main ----------------------------
int main()
{
int sp = 0;
   char s[]="..a..";

   if (A(s,sp))
     cout << "syntax correct\n";
   else
     cout << "syntax error\n";
   return 0;
}//end main

// function A -------------------------------
int A(char* s,int& sp)
{
   if (!B(s,sp))
     return 0;
   if (Next(s,sp) != id)
     return 0;
   if (!B(s,sp))
     return 0;
   return 1;
}//end A

// function B -------------------------------
int B(char* s,int& sp)
{
   int sp1 = sp;

   if (Next(s,sp) != dot) {
     sp = sp1;
```

```
      return 1;
   }
   if (!B(s,sp)) {
      sp = sp1;
      return 1;
   }
   return 1;
}//end B

// function Next ----------------------------
int Next(char* s,int& sp)
{
   if (s[sp]=='.') {
      sp++;
      return dot;
   }else if ('a'<=s[sp] && s[sp]<='c') {
      while('a'<=s[sp] && s[sp]<='c') sp++;
      return id;
   }else
      return error;
}//end Next
```

The program is a *recursive descent parser* for a language that consists of strings in the form "a sequence of dots, possibly empty, followed by a sequence consisting of characters 'a', 'b', and 'c', followed by a sequence of dots, possibly empty". For instance, "..a.." is a such a string. The input to the parser is a character string s (see more on strings in Chapter 6), and sp is the *string position* variable, which keeps track of how much of the input has been consumed. The function Next() is the "scanner" of this parser, and it returns:

- a "token" dot if it has recognized and consumed '.' on the input;
- a "token" id if it has recognized and consumed a string consisting of characters 'a', 'b', and 'c' on the input; or
- a "token" error in all other cases.

If the input string is from the language, the program displays a syntax correct message and exits; otherwise, it displays a syntax error message and exits.

Let us discuss the program as it is running. We will take "snapshots" of the system stack at various times to illustrate how the stack controls the execution and keeps track of the recursion. All the functions involved, except main(), have two arguments passed by reference: the input string s and the string position indicator sp. The function B() has, in addition, a local variable sp1. Hence these three arguments are depicted in the schematic activation frames.

In the function main(), a local variable s (a character array) is initialized and holds a string "..a.." while another local variable sp is set to 0. Then A() is called:

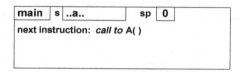

The activation frame for A() is created and pushed on the system stack (the arrows indicate the "reference"), and A() calls B():

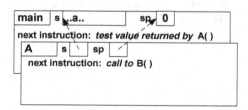

B() saves sp in sp1 and calls Next():

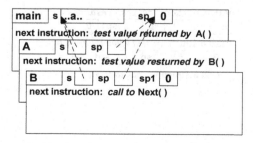

Next() consumes s[0] (the first '.'), updates sp (in the activation frame of main() as sp is passed by reference), and returns dot:

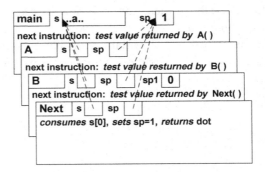

Back to B(), B() calls B():

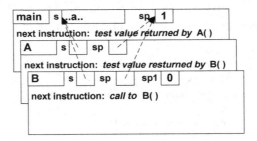

B() saves sp in sp1 and calls Next():

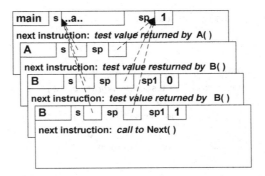

Next() consumes s[1] (the second '.'), updates sp, and returns dot:

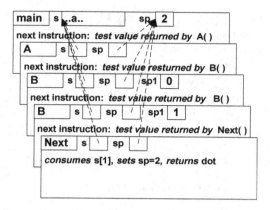

Back to B(), B() calls B():

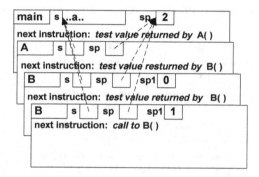

B() saves sp in sp1 and calls Next():

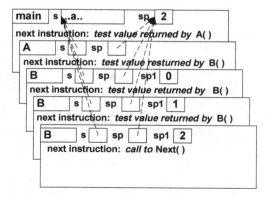

Next() consumes s[2] ('a'), updates sp, and returns id:

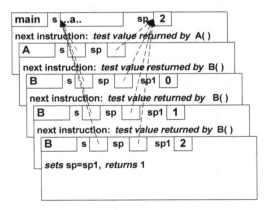

B() does not like id returned by Next(), restores sp to 2, and returns 1:

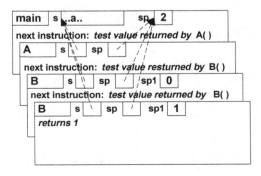

Back to B(), it has finished its job and returns 1:

Back to B(), it has finished its job and returns 1:

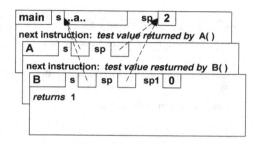

Back to A(), A() calls Next():

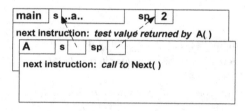

Next() consumes s[2] ('a'), updates sp, and returns id:

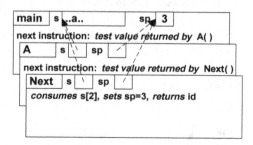

Back to A(), A() calls B():

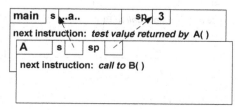

B() saves sp in sp1 and calls Next():

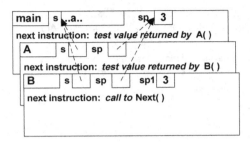

Next() consumes s[3], updates sp, and returns dot:

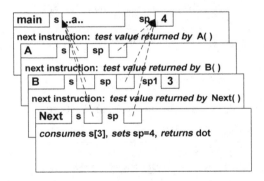

Back to B(), B() calls B():

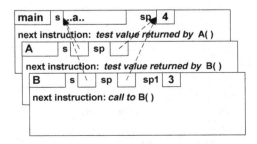

B() saves sp in sp1 and calls Next():

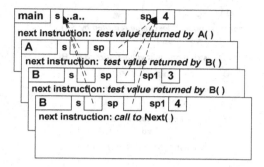

Next() consumes sp[4], updates sp to 5, and returns dot:

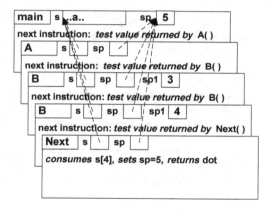

Back to B(), B() calls B():

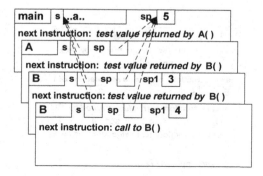

B() saves sp in sp1 and calls Next():

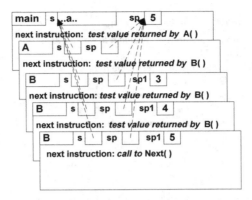

Next() consumes s[5], updates sp to 6, and returns error:

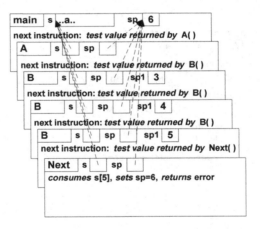

Back to B(), B() does not like the value error returned by Next(), restores sp to 5, and returns 1:

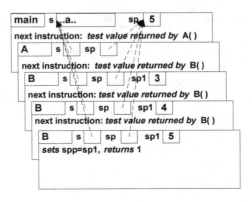

Back to B(), B() returns 1:

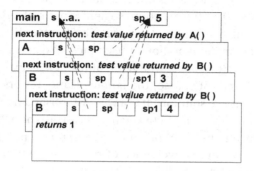

Back to B(), B() returns 1:

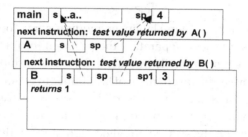

Back to A(), A() returns 1:

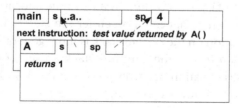

Back to main(), main() displays syntax correct and exits:

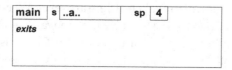

The execution of the program is over.

So, is recursion worth the trouble? Obviously yes, for otherwise the programming language and compiler designers would not bother. We are not really trying to beg the question, so here is our real answer. There are many areas in which recursion is a powerful and convenient tool: recursive descent parsers; implementation of backtracking algorithms; algorithms for data structures (this alone would be sufficient reason to use recursion; see Chapter 9); and, of course, the famous Hanoi towers puzzle and its (infamous?) recursive solution. It is a well-established mathematical fact that whatever can be achieved by recursion can also be achieved by plain old iteration (if you do not mind complex and messy programs). It is the clarity, simplicity, and convenience of recursive solutions that compel us to implement recursion in most general-purpose programming languages, including C and C++.

Review

Any reasonable programming language requires some form of modularization. By this we mean separating the program into well-defined and smaller modules that mutually interact in a precise fashion. Toward this end, C/C++ provide the mechanism of functions. In general, a data structure known as an activation frame is used to store all relevant information for the function to execute. A function call can be implemented in various ways, depending on the strategy for allocation of the activation frame. If a static allocation is used (in Fortran, e.g.) then multiple activations of a function are impossible, but the function call overhead is significantly reduced, leading to faster execution. If a dynamic allocation is used, the activation frame can be allocated on either the system heap or the system stack. Allocation on the system stack is more generally used because it gives the stack a role as the "control" stack; in such cases, the top of the stack and the activation tree truly represent the flow of control. Since C/C++ features dynamic allocation on the system stack, recursion can be used.

During a function call, control is passed to the *callee* (the function being called) and returned back to the *caller* (the function doing the calling) upon termination of the callee. There are several ways that arguments can be passed to functions. The copy-restore was used by early Fortran compilers but seldom since. Call-by-name for C/C++ is seen in macroexpansion and inlining. Call-by-value is exclusively used by C and is the default for C++.

In call-by-value, the arguments are passed by value – that is, their copies are passed. Whatever the function does with the arguments has no effect on the originals' values, thus providing an environment that is safe in terms of the "information hiding" principle. In call-by-reference, the arguments are passed by reference (or by address or location), which really means passing a pointer to the argument. This facilitates direct access to the argument and thus allows the function to modify whatever is passed to it in this fashion. In C++, passing by reference of selected arguments is allowed (by explicit statement).

The activation frame also serves as the storage for all local objects of the function (that are not declared as static). Since the activation frame is "erased" after the function terminates, the values of local auto objects cannot be held between different activations.

Allowing multiple activations and hence recursion slows the execution, but the price is well worth it. Many problems have a convenient and relatively simple solution when recursion is used.

Exercises

5.1 What is the difference between *invocation* and *activation* of a function?

5.2 Where is storage for the "auto" variables located?

5.3 Does every local variable have the "auto" storage class?

5.4 Explain why the variables of a function f() cannot retain values between two consecutive activations of f().

5.5 What are the differences between the system stack and the system heap? Try to list all differences – in their roles and purpose as well as in their implementations.

5.6 Define the following terms: calling sequence, calling convention, return sequence, flow of control. How are they related to execution of functions?

5.7 If a local variable is defined as static, does this make it global?

5.8 Is there any difference between C and C++ with regard to calling functions and passing arguments to them?

5.9 Which of the calling methods discussed in this chapter are relevant for C? Which are relevant for C++?

5.10 Rewrite the following simple C function, which receives an integer parameter, so that it emulates receiving the parameter by "reference".

```
void doit(int x)
{
  printf("%d\n",x);
  x++;
  printf("%d\n",x);
}
```

5.11 Rewrite the recursive descent parser used in this chapter to display (in a schematic fashion) what the system stack "looks like" during the execution: when a function is entered, display the "new activation frame"; when the function is exited, display the "previous activation frame". Use indentation to indicate how the stack grows (moving the indentation to the right) and how it shrinks (moving the indentation to the left). Then execute the program with input string "..a..". Compare your result with the diagrams shown here.

5.12 Repeat Exercise 5.11 for the Hanoi towers puzzle program listed in Appendix A.

5.13 Rewrite the recursive descent parser used in this chapter so that s and sp are global variables.

5.14 The following recursive program generates and displays all bit combinations for a byte.

```
#include <stdio.h>

char byte[8];

void bits(int n,char byte[])
{
 int i;

 if (n == 8) {
   for(i = 0; i < 8; i++)
    putchar(byte[i]);
   putchar('\n');
   return;
 }
  byte[n] = '0';
  bits(n+1,byte);
  byte[n] = '1';
  bits(n+1,byte);
}
```

```
int main()
{
  bits(0,byte);
  return 0;
}
```

We now rewrite it using global variables instead of arguments being passed along. Will it work? Justify your answer.

```
#include <stdio.h>

char byte[8];
int n;

void bits()
{
 int i;

 if (n == 8) {
   for(i = 0; i < 8; i++)
    putchar(byte[i]);
   putchar('\n');
   return;
 }
  byte[n] = '0';
  n = n+1;
  bits();
  n = n-1;
  byte[n] = '1';
  n = n+1;
  bits();
}

int main()
{
  n = 0;
  bits();
  return 0;
}
```

References

A basic understanding of function calls and C or C++ calling conventions may be gleaned from the C and C++ texts listed in references for Chapters 2 and 3.

The flow-of-control aspects of function calls and use of the system stack are described in the operating system texts listed in Chapter 2.

Theoretical aspects of recursion:

Cormen, T. H., Leiserson, C. E., Rivest, R. L., and Stein, C., *Introduction to Algorithms*, McGraw-Hill, New York, 2002.

Felleisen, M., Findler, R. B., Flatt, M., and Krishnamurthi, S., *How to Design Programs – An Introduction to Computing and Programming*, MIT Press, Cambridge, MA, 2001.

Mendelson, E., *Introduction to Mathematical Logic*, 4th ed., Chapman & Hall / CRC Press, Boca Raton, FL, 1997.

Odifreddi, P., *Classical Recursion Theory*, North-Holland, Amsterdam, 1999.

Programmatic aspects of recursion:

Smith, O. J. A., "Stack Free Recursion",
http://www.olympus.net/personal/7seas/recurse.html.

Syck, G., "Removing Recursion from Algorithms", *C/C++ Users Journal*, February 1991.

CHAPTER SIX

ONE-DIMENSIONAL ARRAYS AND STRINGS

Static one-dimensional arrays and their representation as pointers. Array indexing as indirection. Why an array index range check cannot be performed in C/C++. The price of run-time array index range checking; "compile-time checking" versus "run-time checking" philosophies. Passing static one-dimensional arrays as function arguments. Definition versus declaration of one-dimensional arrays. Dynamic one-dimensional arrays. Strings as static or dynamic one-dimensional char arrays terminated with NULL. How to add a custom-made run-time index range checker in C++.

The most frequently used composite data structures in programming are arrays. Since their use is so ubiquitous, they are provided as almost built-in data types in C/C++. Unfortunately, the emphasis is on "almost" and not on "built-in". On the one hand, "almost" here means that you need not provide any programmatic means of creating (building) and indexing the array and that any C/C++ compiler will provide both automatically. The array definition/declaration and access to the array items through indexing are thus integral parts of the C/C++ language. On the other hand, "almost" also means there is no innate data type array in C/C++ that is treated in its own special way, so each array is represented by an appropriate pointer pointing to an appropriate storage according to appropriate conventions. This has some unexpected consequences for "index out of range" run-time errors and for passing array arguments to functions.

The fundamental notion of an array is just an extension of the basic model of computer memory: an array of bytes accessible through indexes (their addresses). Thus an array of a data type D is a data structure where each array item is a "data container" of the same data type D and can be accessed through its index. This notion is taken to its most abstract form

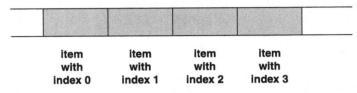

Figure 6.1   Concept of one-dimensional array

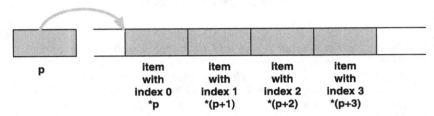

Figure 6.2   Accessing a one-dimensional array via a pointer

in C++, where you can define an indexing operator operator[] on any class and thereafter use the objects of the class as arrays.

Proper arrays in C/C++ are in fact even more "faithful" memory models, for not only does their indexing start from 0, also they really do consist of identical adjacent "data containers" (i.e., they reside in a contiguous memory segment); see Figure 6.1. It is quite natural (the reader may refer back to Chapter 3) to see the array items as "virtual data containers" accessed via the appropriate pointer. Thus, if a pointer p points to the very first item of an array, then we can see that *p represents the very first item in the array, *(p+1) represents the second item of the array, ..., *(p+i) represents the ith item of the array; see Figure 6.2.

Seeing how natural it is to access array items through a pointer, we cannot be surprised to learn that C/C++ treats one-dimensional arrays in this fashion. For instance, an int array x[] with six items defined by int x[6]; is thus represented by the C/C++ compiler as a constant pointer (meaning that the pointer cannot be reset) int* x and a statically allocated memory segment to accommodate six virtual data containers of the data type int, as indicated by Figure 6.3.

It also comes as no surprise that C/C++ compilers really do translate array indexing expressions like x[i] into indirection expressions like *(x+i). Moreover, pointers can be "indexed": If p is any pointer (except void*), then the expression p[i] makes sense when translated by the compiler to

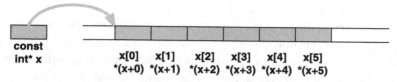

Figure 6.3   Representation of the int x[6] array

*(p+i) and so the program can be perfectly well compiled and executed. As we can see, arrays are treated as constant pointers, and the indexing mechanism is nothing but the dereferencing of these pointers. In fact, a static array is nothing but a constant pointer that points to a properly (statically) allocated memory segment.

This was rather convenient for the designers of C and also for the builders of C/C++ compilers in that there was no real need to deal with an innate data type array. However, it turns out that there are some unpleasant consequences.

The first of these concerns the "size" of an array. It is clear that, upon encountering a definition of an array, the compiler (a) creates a constant pointer, (b) allocates a sufficiently large memory segment (whose address is often referred to as the *base* of the array), and (c) points the pointer to it. Although the compiler knows the size of the array and the size of the allocated segment, the size is not *recorded* in any way and hence at run time the pointer holds only the base address, which is all that is known about the array; the knowledge of its size is gone. Unless the programmer remembered correctly the size of the array and worked with it properly in the rest of the program, all kind of problems can crop up during execution (as detailed in Chapter 3). There simply is no way a C/C++ program can make a run-time check of whether an array index is within the proper range.

This approach to arrays in C and C++ was deliberate. One of the aims of the C language designers was a language compiling to an object code that is as "lean" as possible. If one wants a language (e.g., Pascal) that facilitates run-time range checking, then arrays must be represented by special data structures that "remember" the range, increasing memory requirements. Moreover, every array access instruction of that language must be translated to a code that validates the range of the index *before* access to the array's storage, significantly increasing the size of the object code and memory requirements. (It is an interesting exercise to write two simple identical programs dealing with arrays, one in C and the other in Pascal, and – after compiling both – to compare the sizes of their respective object files.) Thus C and C++ compilers follow the philosophy of "compile-time checking": if you try to store more than the array can hold (e.g., during initialization of an array) or if some other "clear" violation of the index range occurs, the compiler will give you an error or a warning message. Run-time checking was deliberately omitted because of the associated costs. Consequently, the onus is on the programmer – which means you, the reader – to make sure that the range is not violated.

The second unpleasant consequence of having no array data type concerns passing of array arguments to functions during function calls. The C language professes to pass arguments exclusively by value, yet many a programmer has experienced (intentionally or unintentionally) a function call that somehow modified the array passed to it, as if it were passed by reference. In contrast, C++ is more flexible and gives you a choice between passing by value or by reference. Nevertheless, when passing an array by value, the program behaves as if it were passed by reference and when trying to pass it by reference, the compiler will not compile it! Consider the following simple program.

```
/* function doit --------------------------------------- */
void doit(int y[])
{
    y[0] = 0;
    y[1] = 1;
}/*end doit*/

/* function main --------------------------------------- */
int main()
{
    int i;
    int x[6]={10,11,12,13,14,15};

    doit(x);

    for(i = 0; i < 6; i++)
     printf("%d ",x[i]);
    putchar('\n');

    return 0;
}/*end main*/
```

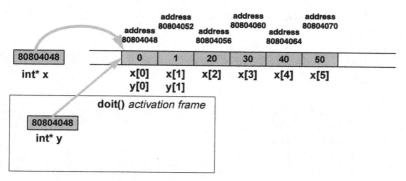

Figure 6.4 The array x is accessible from the function doit()

This program will display, as values of the array x after the call to doit(), the numbers 0 1 12 13 14 15; whereas we know that, prior to the call to doit(), they were 10 11 12 13 14 15. Definitely, x has been modified and hence not passed by value.

The truth is that C does pass x by value; doit() receives the base address via the pointer y and then modifies the first two items that pointer y points to – in effect, the first two items of array x. For instance, let us assume that the base of array x is 80804048. When passing the array x to doit(), instead the base address 80804048 is passed to doit() by *value*. Locally in doit(), then, y was set to 80804048. In fact, y[0]=0 is the indirection *y=0 and so an integer value of 0 is stored at the address 80804048. The address 80804048 happens to be the address of x[0]. Similarly y[1]=1 was translated to *(y+1)=1 and so an integer value of 1 is stored at the address 80804052, which happens to be the address of x[1] (see Figure 6.4). Case closed.

An interesting curiosity: C programmers sometimes use the struct construct to "wrap" the arrays and so protect them from being modified by functions if passed to them. The following sample illustrates this technique.

```
typedef struct { int array[6]; } wrap;

/* function doit ------------------------------------------- */
void doit(wrap y)
{
    y.array[0] = 0;
    y.array[1] = 1;
}/*end doit*/
```

```
/* function main ---------------------------------------- */
int main()
{
    int i;
    wrap x;

    x.array[0] = 10;
    x.array[1] = 11;
    x.array[2] = 12;
    x.array[3] = 13;
    x.array[4] = 14;
    x.array[5] = 15;

    doit(x);

    for(i = 0; i < 6; i++)
     printf("%d ",x.array[i]);
    putchar('\n');

    return 0;
}/*end main*/
```

This program will display values of the "wrapped" array x, after the call to doit(), which are unchanged (10 11 12 13 14 15). The explanation is simple: the object x (the reader will forgive us for borrowing this C++ terminology, which is not fully appropriate here) is passed to doit() by *value* and hence the object y has the same value as x (i.e., it is a copy of x). This copy gets modified, but the original x remains unchanged.

The reader should examine the header of the function doit(int y[]). The program would work equally well if it were defined either as doit(int* y) or as doit(int y[6]). This is the first meaningful example of a difference between a definition and a declaration that we have encountered in the book. A *definition* involves the "creation" of an object (data container) out of "raw" memory. A *declaration,* on the other hand, only introduces a symbol to the compiler together with what its type is and what it represents. Since we are passing an array to doit() as if by reference, no "creation" takes place; in reality, only a reference (pointer with the base address) is passed. Thus the expression used in the header of doit() is only a declaration, rather than a definition, because the compiler does not have to create the array. It is therefore perfectly acceptable to use either int y[6] (since conceptually we are passing an integer array of size 6 to doit()) or int *y (since we are really passing a pointer) or int y[] (since we are really passing an array reference).

The reader should now be comfortable with the notion that a static one-dimensional array is a pointer holding the base address and pointing to a (statically) allocated segment where the array items are stored. Similarly, readers should be comfortable with the idea that pointers can be indexed. In some sense, a pointer is like an array without a "body" – the segment to store the array items. It does not require a quantum leap of imagination to realize that we could provide the "body" dynamically during execution. This brings us to the concept of dynamic arrays.

A dynamic array is simply a pointer that is set to point to a dynamically allocated segment that will hold the array items. An illustration follows.

```
/* function main --------------------------------------- */
int main()
{
    int i;
    int* x;

    x = malloc(6*sizeof(int));
    if (x == NULL) exit(1);

    x[0] = 10;
    x[1] = 11;
    x[2] = 12;
    x[3] = 13;
    x[4] = 14;
    x[5] = 15;

    for(i = 0; i < 6; i++)
     printf("%d ",x[i]);
    putchar('\n');

    return 0;
}/*end main*/
```

The only difference from using a static array consists of the lines in which (i) the memory is allocated dynamically and (ii) the allocation is checked to see whether it has worked.

When should we use a dynamic rather than a static array? A static array is always preferable for two reasons: it is faster (dynamic memory allocation is a complex task; see Chapter 4) and it does not pose any danger of leaking memory. But if we do not know in compile time what would be a reasonable cap on the size of the array, or if the array needs to change to accommodate some more dynamically incoming data, then the safer and more efficient way is to use dynamic arrays. An obvious error (especially with novices) is to "forget" the allocation part. This leaves the pointer uninitialized, and any attempt to store anything in its direction may well lead to the ill effects discussed in Chapter 3. A more ominous error consists of failing to deallocate the dynamic array once it is no longer needed (especially when the array is frequently extended and when realloc(), with its implicit deallocation of the old segment, is not used for the task), which may result in memory leaking; more on this in Chapter 10.

Having covered static and dynamic arrays, we can now turn our attention to strings. Unlike arrays, which are almost innate data types for C/C++, strings are much less so. The C/C++ language does not provide any means of defining and working with strings, with one exception: literal strings. Yet strings are immensely useful and even more ubiquitous than arrays, so something must be done to facilitate their use. In C/C++ programs the compiler stores literal strings in memory as character arrays terminated by the NULL character ('\0'), so the same convention is used for all strings. Simply stated, a *string* is a char array terminated with NULL. Thus a string can be stored in a static array,

```
char x[30] = "hello";
```

or

```
char x[30];
strcpy(x,"hello");
```

as well as in a dynamic array,

```
char* x;
x = malloc(30);

strcpy(x,"hello");
```

In any case, a string is represented by a `char*` pointer that points to its beginning, and the string continues until NULL. All standard C functions dealing with strings (their prototypes are in the standard header file `string.h`) expect the strings to be represented by `char*` pointers and terminated by NULL. Of course, these functions are not a part of the C/C++ language – they are not terms in the language. For instance, `strcpy` is not a reserved keyword of C/C++, nor is it meaningful in any way. The compiler realizes only that it is a call to a function, and the linker will try to find the object code for it and link it with the program. However, any C/C++ compiler comes equipped with object libraries that ought to include the object code for `strcpy`. Thus the programmer's task is (a) to "tell" the compiler what `strcpy` is (by including the standard header file `string.h`), (b) to direct the compiler to the proper object libraries (automatic for the standard functions), and (c) to use the function properly.

For an illustration, we will examine two of the standard string functions: `strcpy()` and `strcat()`.

```
char* strcpy(char* dest,const char* src)

{
    char *dest1 = dest;
    while((*dest++ = *src++) != NULL);
    return dest1;
}
```

There are two interesting aspects of the function `strcpy()` that concern memory. First, it is the user's responsibility to provide sufficient memory for the string to be copied to (the pointer to points to it); this is often a source of overflow problems (see Chapter 3) when the memory provided is insufficient, or a source of memory access problems when the argument to is not set properly. Second, it neatly illustrates the essential role of the terminator NULL, since `strcpy()` will continue merrily copying until it reaches NULL. If NULL is not there, `strcpy()` will go through the whole memory (of course, the operating system will terminate it for memory access violation long before that). The sample program

```
int main()
{
    char* p;
```

```
    strcpy(p,"hello");
    return 0;
}
```

will exhibit the whole range of erratic behavior described in Chapter 3, for we are trying to store a copy of the string "hello" wherever p happens to point. Similarly, the following code may exhibit erratic behavior owing to overflow:

```
int main()
{
    char* p;
    p = malloc(4);
    strcpy(p,"hello");
    return 0;
}
```

The most frequent error is forgetting to allocate storage for the terminating character at the end of the string. Thus, when making a copy of a string q, we must not forget to add 1 to the length of q as computed by strlen() (which does not include the terminator NULL):

```
char* p;

p = malloc(strlen(q)+1);
strcpy(p,q);
```

The function strcat() is used to concatenate strings:

```
char* strcat(char* dest,const char* src)
{
    char* dest1 = dest;

    while(*dest++ != NULL);
    while((*dest++ = *src++) != NULL);
    return dest1;
}
```

As with strcpy(), it is the user's responsibility to provide enough memory after the end of the string dest to accommodate a copy of the string src. And again, if either of the strings is not properly terminated, the function will go through all memory until terminated by the operating system. Unfortunately, it is not always the case that the programmer is responsible for the allocation of memory; char* strdup(const char* src) will allocate the memory for a copy of the string src itself. This inconsistency may lead to programs with memory leaks (see Chapter 10).

The problem of when to use the static rather than the dynamic version of strings is the same as that for arrays, and likewise for the possible perils of using the dynamic version.

The final topic of this chapter will turn our attention to C++ and how we can provide arrays with run-time index range checking. Although we cannot provide this for the proper arrays, we can define a special class of such arrays. The following code illustrates a class of essentially int arrays that performs the index range checking (see the method Array::operator[]) for any access.

```
class Array {
  protected:
    int* body;
    int last_index;

  public:
    Array(int k) {        //constructor
      body = new int[k];
      last_index = k-1;
    }//end constructor

    //destructor
    ~Array() { if (body) delete[] body; body=0; last_index=-1; }

    //subscript operator
    int& operator[] (int i) {
      if (i < 0 || i > last_index)  // index is out of range
        exit(1); // exit or throw an appropriate exception
               // or take an appropriate action
      return body[i];
    }//end subscript operator
};//end class Array

// function main ------------------------------------------------
int main()
{
  Array x(4);
```

```
x[0] = 1;
printf("%d\n",x[0]);
return 0;
}//end main
```

Of course, the class could be defined as a template class and as such would allow us to have all kinds of arrays, not only int. Nor would it be too complicated to make the array grow dynamically if need be, but for the sake of simplicity we did not include these variations. For the same reason we did not include the copy constructor. We could have also defined body statically (for fixed-length arrays), but we wanted to include some dynamic memory allocation in the example. The reader should examine the destructor ˜Array(), which guarantees that once an object of this class (static or dynamic) is destroyed, all dynamic memory linked to it is deallocated as well. Hence no memory will leak on account of the Array objects.

In Chapter 9 we will discuss linked data structures and will also briefly focus on arrays as models of memory, showing how linked data structures can be created without pointers and pointer arithmetic.

Review

A static one-dimensional array in C/C++ is represented by a constant pointer, which holds the base address of the array and points to a statically allocated memory segment that stores the array items. The indexing expressions of type x[i] are translated by C/C++ compilers into indirection expressions of type *(x+i). For these reasons, the size of an array is unknown at run time and so a run-time index range check cannot be performed. Only a simple compile-time index range check is performed by C/C++ compilers (e.g., during initialization). This philosophy is deliberate, a response to the significant costs (as in Pascal) of run-time index range checking. Another consequence of the representation of arrays as pointers concerns passing of array arguments to functions. Though C can only perform passing by value and though the C++ default is also passing by value (passing by reference must be explicitly stated), it is actually the pointer *representing* the array that is passed by value, and this value (the so-called base address of the array) is then used to access the actual array. This results in the possibility of a function modifying the array that has been passed to it.

Because indexing expressions are translated into indirection expressions, all pointers (with the exception of void*) can be indexed. Pointers can therefore be regarded as "arrays without bodies" and hence a body can be provided dynamically. A dynamic one-dimensional array is a pointer that points to a dynamically allocated segment to store the array items. Such arrays behave in all respects as static ones, but they can be extended or reduced if need be. Common errors associated with the use of dynamic arrays include (a) using the pointer without allocating the segment to store the array items (discussed in Chapter 3 as "uninitialized pointer" error), (b) allocating insufficient storage (discussed in Chapter 3 as "overflow" error), and (c) forgetting to deallocate unneeded dynamic arrays or unneeded segments that may lead to memory leaks.

Strings are treated in C/C++ as character arrays terminated by NULL. They can be stored in either statically or dynamically allocated arrays. In either case, a string is represented by a char* pointer that points to the beginning of the string, and the string spans the memory from its beginning to the first NULL. Even though strings are not an innate data type of C/C++ and the language provides no means to deal with them, standard functions (declared in the string.h header file) that come with any C/C++ compiler cover the whole range of necessary operations with strings including copying, duplication, concatenation, length, and so on.

In C++ the programmer is allowed to overload the index operator operator[], which can thereby be defined for any class, and then treat objects of this class as arrays. These arrays may have all kind of properties; for example, they can dynamically grow and shrink as needed or can provide for run-time index range checking.

Exercises

6.1 Let x and y be two integer variables, and let int* p. Let x = p[0] while y = *p. Are the values of x and y the same? Under what circumstances may they differ?

6.2 Let int x[4] be an integer array. Let int *p and int *q be pointers. Let p = x and q = &x[0]. Are both pointers pointing to the same location or to different ones?

6.3 Let int *p and let int x[4] = {10,11,12,13}. Let p = &x[2]. What is the value of p[2]?

6.4 Once I saw the following problem in a C++ code. The programmer had a good idea for a "variable length dynamic array": as long as the array is not too big (10 in our example), store it in a static segment for efficiency;

but when it gets too long, use a dynamically allocated segment for the extra storage needed. The class definition is shown here:

```
class Array {
public:
 Array() { cont = 0; }
 ~Array() { if (cont) free(cont); }
 char& operator[] (int i) {
   if (i < 10)
     throw exception;
   if (i < 10)
     return base[i];
   i -= 10;
   if (cont == 0) {
     cont = (char*) malloc(i+1);
     length = i+1;
     return cont[i];
   }
   if (length <= i) {
     cont = (char*) realloc(cont,(i+1));
     length = i+1;
     return cont[i];
   }
   return cont[i];
 }
 void Strcpy(char* x) { strcpy(base,x); }

protected:

  char base[10];
  char *cont;
  int length;
};//end class Array
```

The program (not shown here) seemed to work fine, but once in a while it behaved erratically, sometimes crashing at the statement a.Strcpy(x); where Array a; and char* x. Can you explain why sometimes it works and sometimes it does not?

6.5 What will be the output of the following program?

```
int main()
{
  int i, a[3] = {0,1,2};
```

```
   doit(a,&a[1]);
   for(i = 0;  i < 3;  i++)
    printf("a[%d]=%d\n",i,a[i]);
   return 0;
}

void doit(int *a, int* b)
{
   a[0] = b[0];
   a[1] = b[1];
}
```

6.6 Will this compile? If so, will it run correctly?

```
char a[3] = {'('a),'('b),'('c)};
...
printf("%s\n",a);
...
```

6.7 We have a C program in two separate source files. In the first we define as a global variable a buffer char mybuf[100];. In the other source file we declare mybuf as external: extern char* mybuf;. When we compile and link our program using a C compiler, the program works correctly, but not when we compile and link it using a C++ compiler. What is your explanation?

6.8 We need a dynamic array of objects, and we expect frequent repetitions. Hence we keep a dynamic array with just one copy of each object and a dynamic array of pointers to the objects in the first array (see Figure 6.5). Because both arrays are supposed to be dynamic when needed, we extend them using realloc(). But sometimes this does not work. Why?

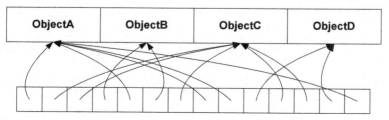

Figure 6.5 Dynamic array (Exercise 6.8)

References

All the C and C++ books listed in Chapters 2 and 3 treat arrays and strings quite adequately.

A bit of history:

Ritchie, D. M., "Variable-Size Arrays in C", *Journal of C Language Translation*, September 1990; also `http://cm.bell-labs.com/cm/cs/who/dmr/vararray.pdf`.

The following papers discuss topics from the programmer's point of view:

Marcok, Z., "Dynamic Arrays with Expression Templates", *C/C++ Users Journal*, July 1998.

Meyers, R., "The New C: Why Variable Length Arrays?", *C/C++ Users Journal*, October 2001.

Saks, D., "Stepping Up to C++ – Dynamic Arrays", *C/C++ Users Journal*, November 1992.

Web-based material concerning arrays:

"C On-line Tutorial", `http://cplus.about.com/library/blctut.htm`.

"C++ On-line Tutorial", `http://cplus.about.com/library/blcplustut.htm`.

"Ted Jensen's Tutorial on Pointers and Arrays in C", `http://home.netcom.com/~tjensen/ptr/cpoint.htm`.

"RedHat Course: Pointers and Arrays in C", `http://www.redhat.com/training/elearning/catalog/courses/c_pointers.html`.

Summit, S., "Pointers and Arrays", `http://www.eskimo.com/~scs/C-faq/s6.html`.

CHAPTER SEVEN

MULTI-DIMENSIONAL ARRAYS

Static multi-dimensional arrays and their representation. Row-major storage format and the access formula. Passing multi-dimensional arrays as function arguments. Dynamic multi-dimensional arrays.

It is natural and practical to extend the notion of one-dimensional arrays – that is, arrays accessible via a single index – to multi-dimensional arrays accessible through multiple indexes. We will illustrate the concepts on two-dimensional arrays, since the principles and issues are the same as for higher-dimensional arrays yet the notation and visualization are much simpler.

Consider a simple definition of a static two-dimensional int array x, where the first index ranges from 0 to 2 and the second index ranges from 0 to 3. For a better illustration, let us fill the array with some distinctive values using the C/C++ initialization:

```
int x[3][4] = {0,1,2,3,10,11,12,13,20,21,22,23};
```

A typical visualization of such an array is a table, as depicted in Figure 7.1.

Since memory is the focal interest of this book, the first question the reader must ask concerns the "dimension" of the visualization: the memory is dimensionless (or at best it is a one-dimensional array of bytes), so how is it that we can visualize the array x as a two-dimensional table? The second question ought to be: Why is the first index represented as rows of

0	1	2	3
10	11	12	13
20	21	22	23

Figure 7.1   Visualization of the two-dimensional array x

the table and the second index as columns? Moreover, is this really an accurate representation? The following simple program will "visualize" the array in both the row/column and the column/row manner.

```c
int main()
{
    int x[3][4] = {0,1,2,3,10,11,12,13,20,21,22,23};
    int i, j;

    for(i = 0; i < 3; i++) {
      for(j = 0; j < 4; j++)
        printf("%2d ",x[i][j]);
      putchar('\n');
    }
    putchar('\n');

    for(j = 0; j < 4; j++) {
      for(i = 0; i < 3; i++)
        printf("%2d ",x[i][j]);
      putchar('\n');
    }

    return 0;
}
```

producing output

```
 0  1  2  3
10 11 12 13
20 21 22 23

 0 10 20
 1 11 21
 2 12 22
 3 13 23
```

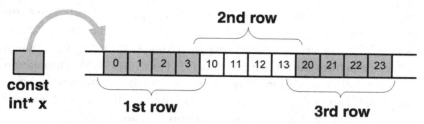

Figure 7.2 The row-major storing format of a two-dimensional array x

The answer to both questions is simple. The visualization has nothing to do with the physical dimensions of the storage. We are quite used to this; for example, a two-dimensional fax image is sent across one-dimensional phone wires. It is simply a convention to visualize two-dimensional arrays in this particular way. You could just as well visualize them in the column/row fashion (the second part of the program's output) and everything would be satisfactory, as long as you consistently worked with the same visualization. Hereafter, we shall work with the standard row/column visualization of two-dimensional arrays.

Now we can examine how a two-dimensional array is really stored in memory. The C/C++ language uses the *row-major* format, in which the array is (like the one-dimensional static array case discussed in Chapter 6) a contiguous statically allocated memory segment and the "rows" of the array are stored there one after another, as shown in Figure 7.2. And just as in the one-dimensional case, a single pointer suffices to hold the base address.

Access to the array items is performed according to the *row-major access formula*, which transforms a reference x[i][j] to an indirection expression *(x+i*n+j), where n is the row size of x. For example: x[0][0] is translated to *(x+0*4+0)=*x, hence the item with the value 0 is being accessed; and x[1][2] is translated to *(x+1*4+2)=*(x+6), hence the item with the value 12 is being accessed.

The reader should note a subtle difference between the indexing mechanism of one-dimensional arrays and that used for multi-dimensional arrays. For one-dimensional arrays, the indexing really is the indirection and so x[i]=*(x+i), whereas for multi-dimensional arrays the indexing is only based on the indirection with some additional information needed and so x[i][j]=*(x+i*n+j) (where n is the additional information in this example). Hence, we cannot simply view a two-dimensional array as a pointer with a "body" as we did for the one-dimensional case, even though

Figure 7.2 does not look that much different from Figure 6.3. The compiler represents the two-dimensional array x as depicted in Figure 7.2 and "knows" the row size of x (which happens to be 4) from the definition of x; thus it can translate any expression x[i][j] to *(x+i*4+j). Throughout the compilation, the compiler simply must treat the pointer int* x differently from "regular" int* pointers – unlike the one-dimensional case, for which the compiler treats int* x like any other pointer.

We have just illustrated that a multi-dimensional array is accessed at run time as a one-dimensional array, for the stored version of the array really is one-dimensional. The multiple indexes are transformed to proper single indexes via the row-major access formula. Thus, as in the one-dimensional case, in the multi-dimensional case the pointer representing the array is passed *by value*; this allows direct access to the actual array locally from within the function, as if the array were passed *by reference*. In order to facilitate access to array items through indexing, the compiler must have additional information (in the two-dimensional case, the row size) in order to translate the indexing to a proper indirection.

It is essential for the compiler to know the row size, but how does it obtain this value? While parsing the array's definition, the compiler extracts the row size – for instance, in int x[3][4], the last index limit (4) is the size it needs to know. However, in the previous chapter we learned that when declaring a one-dimensional array (most often as a function argument) we need not bother to specify the size. Can we do the same for multi-dimensional arrays? Clearly not, for the compiler must have this additional information in order to do its job. Thus, we may leave out the size of the first index but cannot leave out the size of any other index. We may therefore declare x either as x[3][4] or as x[][4].

We briefly consider the three-dimensional array int x[3][4][2]. The row-major format will store the items in the following order (we list only the indexes):

000,001,010,011,020,021,030,031,100,101,110,111,120,121,130,
131,200,201,210,211,220,221,230,231

The first eight entries constitute a two-dimensional array x_0[4][2] with the first index fixed at 0 (i.e., x_0[i][j]=x[0][i][j]), consisting of four rows of size 2: {000,001}, {010,011}, {020,021}, {030,031}. The middle eight entries constitute a two-dimensional array x_1[4][2] with the first index fixed at 1, consisting of four rows of size 2: {100,101}, {110,111},

{120,121}, {130,131}. Finally, the last eight entries constitute a two-dimensional array $x_2[4][2]$ with the first index fixed at 2, also consisting of four rows of size 2: {200,201}, {210,211}, {220,221}, {230,231}. The row-major formula comes to $x[i][j][k]=*(x+i*8+j*2+k)$.

In general, row-major storage is a recursive format that stores an n-dimensional array $x[i_1]..[i_n]$ as a contiguous sequence of L_1 arrays that are $(n-1)$-dimensional: $x_0[i_2]..[i_n], x_1[i_2]..[i_n], ..., $ and $x_{L_1}[i_2]..[i_n]$, where $x_k[i_2]..[i_n]$ denotes the array x with the first index fixed as k and where L_1 denotes the limit of the first index. The row-major formula in its generality is given by

$$x[i_1][i_2]..[i_n]=*(x+i_1*L_2*..*L_n + i_2*L_3*..*L_n +.. \\ + i_{n-2}*L_{n-1}*L_n + i_{n-1}*L_n + i_n)$$

where L_i denotes the size (limit) of the ith index, $i = 2, ..., n$.

The standard visualization of a three-dimensional array is a cube, where the first index is interpreted as the height (see Figure 7.3), the second index as the width (Figure 7.4), and the third index as the depth (Figure 7.5).

Even though it is simple and efficient, the treatment of multi-dimensional arrays as if they were one-dimensional poses some problems for the dynamic version. In the one-dimensional case we need only provide a "body" for a pointer and, voilà, we have an array. With multi-dimensional arrays we cannot do this, for the compiler cannot treat a pointer p as an array and translate $p[i][j]$ to $*(p+i*n+j)$. Not only is the compiler unaware of what n can possibly be – even the programmer might

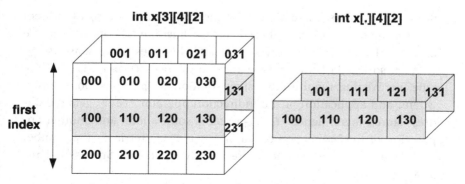

Figure 7.3 The "slice" when the first index is fixed as 1

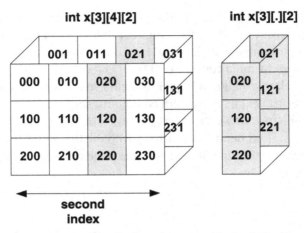

int x[3][4][2]   int x[3][.][2]

second
index

Figure 7.4   The "slice" when the second index is fixed as 2

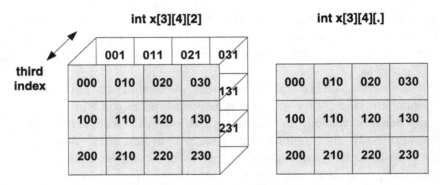

int x[3][4][2]   int x[3][4][.]

third
index

Figure 7.5   The "slice" when the third index is fixed as 2

not know. We must therefore rely on the automatic indexing as indirection for the one-dimensional case. Let us illustrate this on int** p. We have p[i][j]=*(p[i]+j)=*(*(p+i)+j) and this does make sense, since int** p, so *(p+i) is of the type int* and hence *(*(p+i)+j) is of the type int. We thus require a two-stage solution, for p+i must point somewhere, and application of the indirection operator *(p+i) gets the address stored there; hence *(p+i)+j points somewhere, and another application of the indirection operator *(*(p+i)+j) retrieves the number stored there. Here is a code to create a dynamic two-dimensional int array p[3][4]:

```
int** p;

p = malloc(3*sizeof(int*));
if (p == NULL) error();
for(i = 0; i < 3; i++)
 p[i]= malloc(4*sizeof(int));

/* let us put in values as sample accessing of the array items */
a = 0;
for(i = 0; i < 3; i++)
 for(j = 0; j < 4; j++)
  p[i][j] = a++;
```

Figure 7.6 illustrates the dynamic two-dimensional array p[2][3] created in this sample program.

Note that we have actually created four one-dimensional arrays. One is an array of pointers; let us call this the *row array,* as each item of this array is a pointer to a one-dimensional int array representing a row. The pointer p that represents the whole array points to the row array. In a sense we have created a dynamic one-dimensional array of dynamic one-dimensional arrays. For a three-dimensional dynamic array we would do exactly the same and create a one-dimensional dynamic array of two-dimensional dynamic arrays, and similarly for higher dimensions.

Let us now investigate exactly what (say) p[1][1] refers to in our previous sample code. The automatic indexing through indirection of p[1] refers to the pointer to the middle row, and hence the automatic indexing through indirection of p[1][1] refers the second item of the middle row

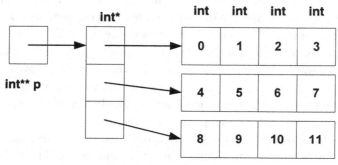

Figure 7.6   Dynamically created two-dimensional array p

(with value 5). Thus the structure exhibits the correct kind of behavior with respect to indexing.

It is interesting that – despite the high cost of their creation – dynamic multi-dimensional arrays may facilitate faster execution in comparison to static arrays. Access to a static array must always be calculated using the row-major formula and hence employs multiplication, an expensive operation. Yet access to a dynamic array is just a simple series of dereferencing, which is much less expensive. Thus, for a program with a large number of accesses to the array, the dynamic version may improve overall performance. For a program running in a system with constrained memory size and needing a large multi-dimensional array, it may be advantageous for the dynamic version of the array to consist of many unrelated smaller segments rather than a single large one as the static version requires. However, there are also potential drawbacks: a dynamic multi-dimensional array that spans a wide portion of the address space may complicate and slow down caching and/or paging and thus degrade performance.

Review

Multi-dimensional arrays are represented in the same way as one-dimensional arrays: by a pointer holding the base address and pointing to a contiguous statically allocated segment where all the array's items are stored. The array's dimension is a logical concept, not a physical one, and the compiler translates multi-dimensional access to the array items into ordinary one-dimensional access to the underlying one-dimensional array by using the so-called row-major formula. In other words, the array is stored as a one-dimensional array using the row-major format. For the two-dimensional case, the row-major format means that rows of the array are stored consecutively. In order to do this, the compiler must know the sizes of all indexes of the array (except for the very first one), and the programmer must deliver this information through appropriate definitions or declarations that include the explicit sizes of all indexes (save the first).

Because multi-dimensional arrays are actually stored and accessed as one-dimensional arrays, they exhibit the same behavior when passed to functions and so behave as if passed by reference.

For dynamic multi-dimensional arrays, we cannot rely on the automatic indexing that translates directly to indirection (as in the one-dimensional case), for the compiler lacks information about the explicit size of all indexes except the very first one. Thus, in the multi-dimensional case we create dynamic arrays of dynamic arrays in order to obtain the right kind of behavior with respect to indexing.

Exercises

7.1 We discussed static two-dimensional arrays (and their row-major storing) as well as implementation of two-dimensional dynamic arrays. Static and dynamic arrays both use the same "syntax" for access (e.g., x[2][3]); how is this possible given the totally different storage methods?

7.2 Write a simple C program in which a two-dimensional dynamic array is used. Now add a function that adds a new row to the array. How complicated was it?

7.3 Take the program from Exercise 7.2 and add a function that adds a new column to the array. How complicated was this in comparison to Exercise 7.2?

7.4 Implement a dynamic array of strings in the form of a dynamic array of pointers to strings. Use an implementation that is similar to a two-dimensional character array, where each string is stored in a row of different size.

7.5 In C, use the row-major approach to implement an integer dynamic two-dimensional pseudo-array that is always stored in a contiguous segment of memory. For access you must use two functions, Get(i,j) (to fetch a value) and Set(i,j,value); it is because you need these two access functions that we use the term *pseudo*-array. In C++, implement this as a class that allows the proper indexing x[i][j].

References

In addition to the references from Chapter 6:

Bavestrelli, G., "A Class Template for *N*-Dimensional Generic Resizable Arrays", *C/C++ Users Journal*, December 2000.
Connely, J., *C through Objects*, Scott/Jones, El Granada, CA, 2002.
Rahimi, A., "A Multidimensional Array Class", *C/C++ Users Journal*, July 1997.

A good website discussing multi-dimensional arrays:

http://www.csc.liv.ac.uk/~frans/COMP101/AdditionalStuff/
    multiDarrays.html.

CHAPTER EIGHT

CLASSES AND OBJECTS

Basic ideas of object orientation; the concepts of classes and objects. Operators new, new[], delete, *and* delete[], *and related issues. Constructors and destructors.*

In this chapter we will take the concept of "data container" introduced in Chapter 3 one step further. There we discussed some concepts concerning C++ objects; in particular, we mentioned that a structure defined by the struct construct is treated by C++ as the simplest class, with no explicit (user-defined) methods and with all (data) members being public. We will see that such a structure actually has a default constructor and destructor, but no other methods. We will describe these notions more precisely and will discuss them fully in the context of object-orientation as provided by C++.

Whether C++ is a "procedural language with classes" or rather a "real object-oriented" programming language is debatable. However, we shall neither discuss nor resolve the dilemma. We will simply work on the premise that – since it exhibits the three fundamental characteristics of object orientation (encapsulation, inheritance, and polymorphism) – C++ can be considered enough of an object-oriented language to call it so and hence to discuss some issues in an object-oriented context.

The *encapsulation* characteristic in C++ is facilitated by *data abstraction* and *data hiding*. The data abstraction is intended to shield the user of the abstract data types from implementation details. As long

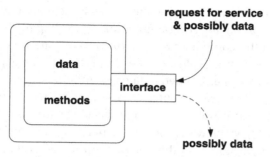

Figure 8.1   An object and its encapsulation

as the user knows how an abstract data type is supposed to behave, it is "safe" to use that type regardless of implementation. Data hiding (or information hiding) is a principle stipulating that a module should hide as much as possible of its innermost workings from other modules and should interact with them only through a specific and highly selective interface. The main objectives are safety (preventing accidental data corruption) and shielding users of the modules from implementation details.

In C++ the modules are objects. Thus encapsulation means that both the data and operations with the data – known as *methods* – are enclosed within the object itself and can only be used by others via requesting services from the object. The data abstraction part is provided by the mechanism of classes that can be viewed as "blueprints" for objects: for each class, the programmer defines the data and its behavior as well as the methods that can be performed on the data, including the services provided for other modules (see Figure 8.1). The reader is encouraged to compare this setting with the function concept; it is no coincidence that they are similar, since both are a form of modularization. However, the interface of a function is simple and rigid, and so is the conduit for the data passed to the function or returned by it. In contrast, the interface of an object can be as varied and flexible as desired, and likewise for the data "passed" to or from the object.

The *inheritance* characteristic in C++ is facilitated by subclasses (or, more properly, *derived classes*), which allow the programmer to "reuse" the definition of properties from one class in another class without any need to stipulate them explicitly. That is, an object from a subclass "inherits" all properties of objects from the superclass (or, more properly, the *base class*).

The *polymorphism* characteristic in C++ is facilitated by *overloading*, which allows: (a) having several functions (including methods) with the same name if the compiler can discern (from a call's unique signature) which function should really be called; and (b) extending any C++ operators to work with user-defined data types and in a way the programmer desires. In Chapter 6 we presented a class Array as an example of an array that provides for run-time index range checking with the subscript operator operator[], which we overloaded to perform the checking.

Because of our focus on the role of memory, we will concentrate on creation and destruction of objects – activities much more complex than creation and destruction of the variables, arrays, and structures discussed so far.

Static variables, arrays, and structures in a program are "pre-created" at compile time as a part of the program's address space (see Chapter 3). Hence their creation coincides with the beginning of the execution of the program when the address space is mapped to memory, and their destruction coincides with termination of the program. Automatic variables, arrays, and structures in a function are created automatically as a part of the activation frame of the function when the function is activated and are destroyed when the activation frame is destroyed at function termination (see Chapter 5). A dynamic construction of any kind of data requires a two-step process fully under the control of the programmer: first "raw memory" is allocated, and then it is filled with required values (see Chapter 4). The destruction is thus a direct responsibility of the programmer and is accomplished via explicit use of the deallocator free().

Since activation frames are allocated on the system stack whereas dynamic allocation uses the system heap, some authors simply state that the allocation of variables, arrays, and structures in C is either static, on the stack, or on the heap. The neat thing about this classification is its use of the "exclusive or" – that is, an array is either static, or on the stack, or on the heap. It is not possible for part of it to be static while some other part is on the heap or with yet another part on the stack. For *objects*, however, this complex situation is quite possible. This gives the programmer enormous flexibility but is fraught with dangers, especially with respect to memory leaks.

As just discussed, the situation in C is simple: the programmer need not worry about the destruction of static or automatic entities yet is fully responsible for the destruction of dynamic data. With C++ objects, the programmer must now worry about dynamically allocated parts of automatic objects. It comes as no surprise that automatic objects with dynamically allocated parts are the largest cause of memory leaks.

The construction of an object of a class (in some literature you may find the terms *instantiation* for creation and *instance* for object) proceeds according to the "blueprint" of one of several possible constructors. Let us consider a C++ program fragment featuring a simple class Sample with a single constructor Sample(char*). The constructor expects the object to be initialized with a string:

```
class Sample {
  public:
    char* salutation;
    Sample(char* c) {    //constructor
      if ((salutation=(char*)malloc(strlen(c)+1))==0) {
        cerr << "memory allocation error\n";
        exit(1);
      }
      strcpy(salutation,c);
    }//end constructor Sample
};//end class Sample

Sample sample("hey"); // static object of class Sample

// function main -----------------------------------
int main()
{
   cout << sample.salutation << '\n';
   return 0;
}//end main
```

The execution of the program displays hey on the screen. Figure 8.2 illustrates that the static object sample's location "spans" the static and dynamic memory both.

How has this come to be? Is not the object sample a static one? Is it not created by the compiler? Yes, but it is the "static" part of the object – in this case, the pointer salutation – that is created by the compiler and is a part of the static memory. But this is only the first step in creating the object.

Prior to the C99 standard, C required a strict separation of executable and nonexecutable statements in each block. Each block had to start with nonexecutable statements (mostly declarations and definitions) and

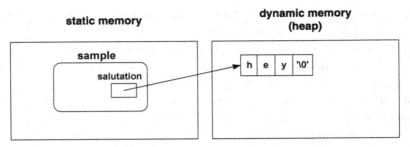

Figure 8.2 Memory allocation for `sample`

then be followed by executable ones. It made sense, since the nonexecutable statements are intended mainly for the compiler and only executable statements play a role during execution. Although simple and effective, this separation was rather rigid. Hence C99 and C++ allow significantly more flexibility in freely mixing executable and nonexecutable statements. For instance, with C++ it is possible to define the object `sample` as in our example program fragment: a kind of "classical" definition that is also an executable statement. The creation of `sample` is therefore finished at the beginning of the execution, when the constructor `Sample("hey")` of the object `sample` is executed. This execution allocates the dynamic memory segment, stores its address in `salutation`, and copies the string `"hey"` to that address.

We will discuss the operators `new` and `new[]` later in this chapter, but they were not used in our sample program because we did not want to distract the reader from focusing on the concept of object creation. Besides, it is perfectly valid (though not recommended) to use C allocators in C++.

To underscore some more subtle aspects of object creation, let us examine the same program and create one more extra global object, `sample1`. The definition of `class Sample` is the same:

```
class Sample {
 ..

 ..
};//end class Sample

Sample sample("hey");
Sample sample1("good bye");
```

```
// function main ------------------------------------------
int main()
{
    cout << sample.salutation << '\n';
    cout << sample1.salutation << '\n';
    return 0;
}//end main
```

The program will display hey on one line and good bye on the other. Figure 8.3 illustrates the memory allocation for the two objects. When the creation of sample is concluded by executing the constructor Sample("hey"), it only works with the data of the object it was invoked for – in this case, sample. At this point, sample1 is still only half-created. Then the creation of sample1 is concluded by executing Sample("good bye") on the data of sample1.

Now imagine that we are running our original program with just one object sample under a strange operating system: one that reclaims static memory after termination of the program but for some reason does not reclaim dynamic memory. Hence the static memory is reclaimed whereas the dynamic memory is still "allocated" to programs that have already finished. After executing our program repeatedly, the system will run out of dynamic memory. The memory is leaking.

We don't really need to posit a strange operating system. Instead, we can present our program in a slightly different setting and still arrive at the same outcome:

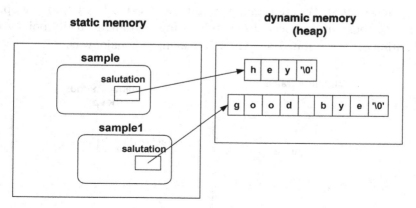

Figure 8.3   Memory allocation for global sample and sample1

```
class Sample {
  ..

  ..
};//end class Sample

// function doit ------------------------------------
void doit()
{
  Sample sample("hey");
  cout << sample.salutation << '\n';
}//end doit

// function main ------------------------------------
int main()
{
  while(1) doit();
  return 0;
}//end main
```

Every time `doit()` is called, `sample` is created as a part of the activation frame and – at the beginning of the function's execution – the creation is completed by executing the constructor. The constructor allocates dynamic memory and copies the initialization string therein. The situation is almost identical to the "strange" one described previously, with the activation frame of `doit()` playing the role of the static memory (see Figure 8.4).

Every time the function `doit()` terminates, its activation frame is destroyed and hence the object `sample` with it – but not the dynamic string "attached" to it. We are running the function `doit()` in an infinite loop. Hence these undeallocated dynamic strings cumulate to the point of halting the execution. The memory is leaking in a major way.

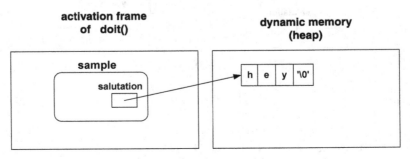

Figure 8.4 Memory allocation for local `sample`

If we only used the object `sample` a few times in our program, no serious harm would ensue. The problem manifests itself only when we use `sample` many, many times. However, when designing a class, we might not be able to anticipate how often it will be used and in what contexts. It therefore makes sense to provide a blueprint not only for construction but also for destruction. This is the role of yet another special method, the destructor. Let us illustrate:

```
class Sample {
public:
    char* salutation;
    Sample(char* c) { // constructor
      if ((salutation=(char*)malloc(strlen(c)+1))==0) {
        cerr << "memory allocation error\n";
        exit(1);
      }
    }//end constructor Sample
    ~Sample() { free(salutation); } // destructor
};//end class Sample

// function doit ------------------------------------
void doit()
{
  Sample sample("hey");
  cout << sample.salutation << '\n';
}//end doit

// function main ------------------------------------
int main()
{
  while(1) doit();
  return 0;
}//end main
```

The destructor for class `Sample` is the method `~Sample()`. As you can see, it has only one task: to deallocate the dynamically allocated part (if any) of the object. Now our program will run forever. Every time the function `doit()` terminates, the objects in its activation frame must be destroyed; for that purpose, the destructor is called and it deallocates the string. Then the whole activation frame is deallocated, a process that destroys the automatic parts of the object. Thus, the object is completely obliterated, memory is not leaking, and our rather uninteresting program can continue unimpeded and run for as long as we like.

We have established the need for both a constructor and a destructor for each class. Of course, it stands to reason that the programmer may want to have many constructors, each corresponding to a different way of initializing an object. The possible multitude of constructors does not cause any problems, since the programmer explicitly controls which of the constructors ought to be used by specifying it in the object's definition. However, we cannot have multiple destructors: the object's destruction is implicit, and the compiler would have no way of deciding which of the many destructors to use. If a constructor or a destructor is not provided explicitly by the programmer, the compiler will provide its default version. However, the compiler cannot anticipate the programmer's intentions with objects of the class. The default constructor is therefore rather simple, merely making sure that all data items of the object that are themselves objects have their appropriate constructors called; the default destructor is equally simple in just making sure that the appropriate destructors are called. It is customary to refer even to an explicitly given constructor that has no arguments as the default constructor.

In our previous example of the class Sample (with one explicit constructor and no destructor), the compiler provides a default destructor. However, since there is only one data item, a pointer salutation, the default destructor does nothing and so does not prevent memory from leaking.

An important issue regarding classes and objects is control of access to the data items and the methods, but since this does not concern memory we shall not delve into it. Suffice it to say that any class *member* (a data item definition or a method) can either be *public,* which allows access to it from outside the object (any constructor or destructor must by its nature be public), or *private* or *protected*, which allows access only from within the object or from other objects declared as *friends*. The only difference between "private" and "protected" class members concerns inheritance: the latter can (whereas the former cannot) be inherited.

Before we embark upon a discussion of memory handling operators, let us summarize the basic properties of constructors and destructors. Like other methods, constructors and destructors are declared within a class definition. Constructors and destructors do not have return types, nor can they return values. For obvious reasons, unions cannot contain objects that have constructors or destructors, for the size of such objects cannot be ascertained at compile time. Constructors and destructors obey the same access rules as all other methods. For instance, if a constructor is declared with the keyword "protected", then only derived classes and friends can use it to create class objects. You can call other class methods from constructors or destructors, which is often used to modularize complex constructors and destructors. Typically, memory allocation should be the last activity of a constructor after all other computations have successfully taken place; we do not want the memory to leak if the construction fails at some point.

A subtle yet critical fact that is seldom fully appreciated by programmers concerns inheritance: derived classes do not inherit constructors or destructors from their base classes; instead, they have their own. The default constructor of the base class may be invoked implicitly, but if all base constructors require arguments then they must be specified in the derived class constructor and the base constructor must be invoked. Similarly, the base destructor is not inherited but will be called implicitly:

```
class C {
public:
  char* salutation;
  C() { salutation=0; }
  C(char* c) {
    salutation=new char[strlen(c)+1];
    strcpy(salutation,c);
  }//end constructor
  ~C() {
    if (salutation) delete[] salutation;
    cout << "~C() invoked\n";
  }//end destructor
};//end class C

class CC : public C {
public:
  char* name;
  CC() { name=0; }    // C() will be invoked implicitly
  CC(char* s,char* n) : C(s) {    // C(s) invocation requested
    name=new char[strlen(n)+1];
    strcpy(name,n);
  }//end constructor
  ~CC() {          // ~C() will be invoked implicitly
    if (name) delete[] name;
```

```
    cout << "~CC() invoked\n";
  }//end destructor
};//end class CC

// function main ---------------------------------------------
int main()
{
  CC* x = new CC("hey","Joe");

  cout << x->salutation << ',' << x->name << '\n';
  delete x;

  return 0;
}//end main
```

The program will display hey, Joe and then (the main purpose of this illustration) ~CC() invoked followed by ~C() invoked. Notice the reverse order in which the destructors are called.

The C memory allocators malloc(), calloc(), and realloc() and the deallocator free() (see Chapter 4) are treated as standard functions from the programmer's point of view. In C++ their role is taken on by the more sophisticated memory operators new (and its array version new[]) and delete (and its array version delete[]). Calling them more sophisticated is warranted: they do more than simply allocate or deallocate segments of raw memory as their "plain vanilla" C cousins do; these operators are active and often main participants in the processes of object creation and destruction.

First of all, C++ allocators and deallocators are treated as operators and as such they can be overloaded. Thus, each class may have its own class-specific version of a memory operator. This is useful when dealing with memory leaks (as we discuss in Chapter 10) or when allocating from a specific arena (see Chapter 9). Besides these user-defined memory operators, there also exist the innate (often referred to as *global*) versions of the memory operators. As far as the management of raw memory is concerned, new behaves like malloc() and delete behaves like free. The main difference is in the interaction between new and constructors and between delete and destructors. Let us illustrate: the C++ code

```
  int* x;
  x = new int;
```

does not essentially differ from the C version,

```
int* x;
x = malloc(sizeof(int));
```

beyond using a more succinct and comprehensible notation. The same result will ensue, and a suitable segment of raw memory will be allocated. We may notice the first difference when we try to check for a possible failure of the allocation:

```
int* x;
x = new int;
if (x==0) error(....);
```

in comparison with the C version,

```
int* x;
x = malloc(sizeof(int));
if (x==NULL) error(....);
```

The C++ version may not actually work. Even though the original C++ required new to return a null pointer on failures, later versions included handling of the failure through a special handler, in essence giving two different ways of handling the allocation failures: (i) if new_handler was defined and the allocation failed, new called the function new_handler to handle the situation (which usually involved throwing an exception and catching it somewhere else in the program); (ii) if new_handler was not set, a null pointer was returned. Ever since acceptance of the 1998 C++ standard, new either handles the failure by new_handler or throws an exception of type bad_alloc. It thus depends on the implementation whether or not new returns a null pointer on failure. Therefore, a prudent approach prescribes handling allocation failures either by explicit new_handler, or through the exception mechanism, or by defining new_handler to return a null pointer.

There are other aspects to new that differ more remarkably from the C allocators. The first and most significant is the deep involvement of new in the process of object creation: the code

```
class X {
 public:
 X(..)  ....  // constructor
 ..
};//end class X


 ..
X* ptr;
 ..
ptr = new X(..);
```

will not only allocate raw memory for the object referenced via the pointer ptr, it will also call the constructor X(..) and thus complete construction of the object. Observe that the object is completely allocated on the heap. If some of data items of the object being created are themselves objects, their respective constructors will be called, and so on. In short, new is as involved with the creation of dynamic objects as the compiler is with the creation of static or automatic objects.

Additional arguments can be supplied to new using *placement syntax*. If placement arguments are used, a declaration of operator new with these arguments must exist. For example:

```
#include <new>
 ..
class X {
public:
 void* operator new(size_t,int,int) ...
 ..
 ..
};//end class X

// function main -------------------------------------
int main ()
{
  X* ptr = new(1,2) X;
  ..
  return 0;
}//end main
```

results in a call of operator new(sizeof(X),1,2). The additional arguments of placement syntax can be used for many specialized tasks. For instance, if we do not have a compiler that supports nothrow (a placement parameter that suppresses throwing an exception on allocation failure), then we can easily emulate it:

```
//in our custom header file "mynew.h"
struct nothrow { }; // dummy struct
void* operator new(size_t, nothrow) throw();
..
..
// implementation in a program
#include "mynew.h"
..
void* operator new(size_t s, nothrow) throw()
{
  void* ptr;
  try {
    ptr = operator new(s);
  }
  ..

  catch(...) { // ensure it does not propagate the exception
    return 0;
  }
  return ptr;
}//end new
```

If ptr = new X is used in a program, it results in a call of the "normal" operator new (the one that throws exceptions on failure), whereas if ptr = new(nothrow) X is used, it results in a call to the specialized new that is guaranteed to return a pointer and throw no exceptions.

The term "placement syntax" comes from the most intended use of the extra argument(s): to be used to "place" an object to a special location. This particular overload of new can be found in the Standard Library. It takes a void pointer to a segment of memory as an additional argument, and is intended to be used whenever memory for the object has already been allocated or reserved by other means. This so-called placement-new does not allocate memory; instead, it uses the memory passed to it (the programmer is responsible for ensuring the memory segment is big enough) and then calls the appropriate constructor. We will discuss some of the applications of placement-new in the next chapter.

The operator new is intended for dynamic creation of individual objects. For creation of arrays of objects, the operator new[size_t] must be used. Everything we have discussed so far for new applies equally to new[] with one exception: new[] can only be used for classes that have a default constructor and can only be used in conjunction with that default constructor (this just means that objects in an array cannot be initialized). The additional argument in [] is the number of objects in the array we want to create. The placement syntax as described for new can be used with new[] in the same way.

```
class C {
public:
  char* salutation;
  C() { salutation=0; }  // explicit default constructor
  void Mod(char* c) {
    // allocation failure handled by exception, not in this example
    salutation=new char[strlen(c)+1];
    strcpy(salutation,c);
  }
};//end class C

// function main ---------------------------------------------------
int main()
{
  C* x = new C[5];
  x[2].Mod("hey");
  cout << x[2].salutation << \n;
  return 0;
}//end main
```

Just as new is more than simply a memory allocator (it is involved in object construction by calling the appropriate constructor), delete is more than simply a memory deallocator. Though memory deallocation is an important aspect of delete, object destruction is another important aspect. Thus, when a dynamic object is to be deleted, the operator delete should be used, whose responsibility it is to call the appropriate destructor. Note that there is no need for any explicit calls to destructors in a C++ program; all the calls ought to be implicit and performed by delete. Whatever memory was allocated using new[] must be deallocated using delete[].

```
class C {
public:
```

```
    char* salutation;
    C(char* c) {
      salutation=new char[strlen(c)+1];
      strcpy(salutation,c);
    }//end constructor
    ~C() { if (salutation) delete[] salutation; }
};//end class C

// function main ---------------------------------------------
int main()
{
  C* x = new C("hey");

  cout << x->salutation << \n;
  delete x;   // calls ~C()

  return 0;
}//end main
```

The operators delete and delete[] can each be used with the placement syntax described previously for new under the same rules and with the same meaning. But there is one important difference. Unlike placement-new, placement-delete cannot be called explicitly, so why bother to have it at all? For one and only one purpose: if the construction of an object fails through an exception, the partial construction is rolled back. The compiler is aware of all allocations so far and by whom they have been done. To undo the construction, the compiler calls the corresponding deallocators and so, if some allocation during the construction has been done by a placement-new, the corresponding placement-delete will be called. We will expand on this topic in Chapter 10 when discussing memory leaks and their debugging.

Here are a few guidelines to make sure that the process memory manager does not become corrupted.

■ Never pass a pointer to free() that has not been returned previously by malloc(), calloc(), or realloc().
■ Deallocate segments allocated by malloc(), calloc(), and realloc() using exclusively free().
■ Never pass a pointer to delete that has not been returned previously by new.

- Deallocate segments allocated by new using exclusively delete.
- Never pass a pointer to delete[] that has not been returned previously by new[].
- Deallocate segments allocated by new[] using exclusively delete[].
- If your program uses placement-new, it should have a corresponding placement-delete (even though it will be only called implicitly by the compiler when an exception is thrown during the construction of an object).

Besides constructor(s) and a destructor, a class may need two more specialized methods that also deal with the construction of the objects of the class. The first – usually called the *copy constructor* – is a special kind of constructor necessary when an object is passed by value to a function. A value of an object is the object itself and hence copying the value of the object to a function's activation frame requires making a copy of that object (see Chapter 5). If the copy constructor is missing, the compiler just copies all data items of the object with their values (this is known as *memberwise* copy). If the object has some dynamically built parts then they will not be copied. Let us illustrate:

```
class C {
public:
  char* salutation;
  C() { salutation=0; }    // explicit default constructor
  C(char* c) {             // initializing constructor
    salutation=new char[strlen(c)+1];
    strcpy(salutation,c);
  }//end constructor
  C(const C& c) {          // copy constructor
    salutation=new char[strlen(c.salutation)+1];
    strcpy(salutation,c.salutation);
  }//end constructor

  ~C() { if (salutation) delete[] salutation; }   // destructor
};//end class C

// function doit ------------------------------------------------
void doit(C d)
{
  cout << d.salutation << '\n';
}//end doit
```

```
// function main -------------------------------------------------
int main()
{
    C c("hey Joe");

    doit(c);
    return 0;
}//end main
```

This program will work fine, displaying hey Joe on the screen. The object c created in main() using the constructor C(char*) will be copied to the activation frame of doit() using the copy constructor C(const C&). When doit() terminates, the object d – as built in the activation frame of doit() – is destroyed using ˜C().

On the other hand, had we not provided the copy constructor, our sample program would have crashed. It is most interesting to see why. When a copy of the object c is made in the activation frame of doit(), the data items are copied with their values. Hence d.salutation in doit() has the same value (i.e., points to the same string) as c.salutation in main(). Hence we will see the proper message on the screen (hey Joe), but then d is destroyed using ˜C(). During the destruction, the string "hey Joe" is deallocated. Function doit() terminates, function main() continues its execution, and when it terminates, the object c is destroyed via ˜C(). Then ˜C() will try to deallocate the string "hey Joe", most likely causing a memory access violation error.

An error I have seen many times occurs along these lines: A class C is defined without the copy constructor. A function doit() is first defined as getting the argument by reference – for example, doit(C& d). Everything works fine. Then somebody (perhaps even the original designer) worries about the object being passed by reference (which is unsafe from the standpoint of data protection) and, since the object is not modified in the function, the function is modified to receive the argument by value: doit(C d). From that moment on, the whole program does not work correctly, but the problem is subtle and usually leads to the kinds of erratic behavior described in Chapter 3. And the culprit is – the missing copy constructor. Let as remark that for greater efficiency a complex object should be passed by reference, and that protection of the passed object should be achieved by other means (e.g., using the const declaration).

The other specialized method involved somehow in the "business" of object construction is *assignment* or, more precisely, the operator=. This method specifies how to perform assignments of type o1=o2 between two objects (which is, in a sense, a form of copying, from o1 to o2). In the absence of an explicit assignment, the *memberwise assignment* is performed, and the same problems as discussed for the missing copy constructor may ensue. However, a missing assignment is even more dangerous because it can lead to memory leaks:

```
class C {
...
...
};//end class C

// function doit ---------------------------------------------
int doit()
{
  C c1("hey Joe"), c2;

  c1=c2;
  return 0;
}//end doit
...
...
```

Here c1 is created and c1.salutation points to a dynamically created string "hey Joe". Then c2 is created using the default constructor and so the value of c2.salutation is set to NULL. When the c1=c2 assignment is made, the memberwise copy is performed (because no assignment method was explicitly defined for the class C) and thus c1.salutation is set to NULL. When c1 and c2 are destroyed, neither is linked to the string "hey Joe" and so that string is never deallocated and "leaks".

The difference between assignment and copying is that the latter is concerned with "forming raw memory into an object" whereas the former must deal with a "well-constructed object"; thus, in essence the assignment must deconstruct the object before copying can proceed:

```
class C {
public:
  char* salutation;
  C() { salutation=0; }    // explicit default constructor
  C(char* c) {             // initializing constructor
```

```
    salutation=new char[strlen(c)+1];
    strcpy(salutation,c);
  }//end constructor
  C& operator=(const C& c) {          // assignment
    if (c!=this) {                    // don't copy itself
      if (salutation) delete[] salutation;           // deconstruct
      salutation=new char[strlen(c.salutation)+1];  // reconstruct
      strcpy(salutation,c.salutation);
    }
    return *this;
  }//end operator=
  ~C() { if (salutation) delete[] salutation; }      // destructor
};//end class C

// function main ----------------------------------------------
int main()
{
  C c1("hey Joe"), c2;

  c1=c2;
  return 0;
}//end main
```

The program now does not leak any memory.

Review

The two aspects of object orientation – encapsulation and inheritance – are facilitated in C++ by classes. Classes can be viewed as "blueprints" for objects. In a class, the programmer thus defines all data items that each object of the class should have (the so-called data members of the class) and also defines all operations with the data that can be performed and how (member methods). By stipulating which of the data members can be accessed from outside the object and by whom – as well as which of the member methods can be called from outside the object and by whom – the programmer manages both the encapsulation and the interface to the outside word. Though the concept of "object" is not very different from the concept of "function" (both are a form of modules), the C++ "class" approach allows for a much more flexible and controlled specification of the interface and of data transfer.

Every class is supposed to have one or more specialized methods that include constructors. A constructor is a blueprint of how to build an object and how to initialize it once it has been built. A constructor with no arguments is called a default constructor. If a class does not have an explicit constructor, the compiler builds a default constructor of its own. A derived class does not inherit the constructor(s) of its base class, yet they may need to be invoked explicitly in the definition of the derived class constructs. Each class is supposed to have a single destructor; if one is not explicitly specified, the compiler provides a default one. A derived class does not inherit the destructor of its base class, which nonetheless is called at the onset of executing the destructor of the derived class.

The operator new is used both to allocate raw memory for a dynamic object and to call the appropriate constructor that actually creates the object. Its counterpart, delete, is used both to call the appropriate destructor and to deallocate the memory. In order to create arrays of dynamic objects, the new[] operator must be used. The operator new[] can only be used in conjunction with the default constructors. Arrays created using new[] must be destroyed using the operator delete[]. The operator new[], in conjunction with innate data, functions just as a raw memory allocator; for example, x = new char[1000]; simply allocates 1000 bytes. All C++ memory operators can be used with the so-called placement syntax when additional arguments are passed to them. Unlike their global versions, placement-syntax versions must be explicitly defined by the programmer. A particular version of memory allocators using placement syntax (placement-new and placement-new[], with a single additional argument void* pointer) are in the C++ Standard Library; their task is not to allocate any memory but rather to construct an object (or objects) in memory secured by other means. All memory operators can be overloaded, and thus a class may have its own versions of memory operators.

If an object needs to be copied (passed by value to a function), an explicit copy constructor ought to be provided in the definition of the class. In its absence, a memberwise copy is used by the compiler, which may lead to subtle memory problems as discussed in Chapter 3.

If an object needs to be assigned to another object, an explicit assignment (operator=()) ought to provided in the definition of the class. In its absence, a memberwise copy is used by the compiler, which may lead to the same kind of problems as in the missing copy constructor case; moreover, memory leaks can thereby be created.

Exercises

8.1 Consider the following C++ class:

```
class A {
public:
  int a;
  char b;
  A() { a = 0; b = '\0'; }
};//end class A
```

Is it a problem that this class does not have a destructor? Is it a problem that the class does not have a copy constructor? Is it a problem that the class does not have an assignment?

8.2 Consider a C++ class:

```
class A {
public:
  B* b;
  A() { b = new B(1,2); }
  ~A() { delete b; }
  void* new(size_t size) {
    ...
  }
};//end class A
```

When an object of class A is being constructed, which new is being used to create the object of class B: the class-A specific new, or the class-B specific new, or the global new?

8.3 What is wrong with the following class, and what kind of problems might it cause during execution?

```
class A {
public:
 A() { string = 0; }
 A(char* x) {
  string = new char[strlen(x)+1];
   strcpy(string,x);
 }
 ~A() { if (string) free(string); }
```

```
A& operator= (const A& a) {
  string = new char[strlen(a.string)+1];
  strcpy(string,a.string);
  return *this;
}
```

8.4 The C++ compiler is complaining about "no appropriate default constructor for class A" but points to the B b; statement. Why? How would you fix this problem?

```
class A {
public:
  char string[10];
  A() { strcpy(string,"good bye"); }
  A(char* s) { strcpy(string,s); }
};//end class A

class B : public A {
public:
  int x;
  B(char* s) : A(s) { }
};//end class B

int main()
{
  A a("hello");
  printf("%s\n",a.string);

  B b;
  printf("%s\n",b.string);

  return 0;
}
```

8.5 The following program is leaking memory. Find where and correct it.

```
#include <iostream>

extern "C" {
  #include <stdio.h>
  #include <string.h>
  #include <stdlib.h>
}
```

```
class A {
public:
  char* string;
  A(char* s) { string = strdup(s); }
  A& operator=(const A& a) {
    string = a.string;
    return *this;
  }
};//end class A

int main()
{
  A a("hello");
  printf("%s\n",a.string);
  A b("good bye");
  printf("%s\n",b.string);
  b = a;
  printf("%s\n",b.string);

  return 0;
}
```

8.6 Having used placement-new in our program, we should also define a corresponding placement-delete. Can we call it explicitly within our program?

8.7 Write a C++ program in which an object is created that has some static data, some data on the stack, and some data on the heap. Do not peek at the next exercise. Designing programs like this is not advisable in real life!

8.8 What will happen in the following C++ program if the display statement in main() is uncommented and the program is recompiled and executed? Can you describe the output?

```
class A {
public:
  char* heap_string;
  char* stack_string;

  A() { heap_string = stack_string = 0; }
  void AttHStr(char* x) { heap_string = x; }
  void AttSStr(char* x) { stack_string = x; }
  friend ostream& operator << (ostream& os,const A& a) {
```

```
      os << "heap string=" << a.heap_string << "\n";
      os << "stack string=" << a.stack_string << "\n";
      return os;
    }
};

A a;

void doit()
{
    char s[] = "..stack..";
    a.AttSStr(s);

    cout << a << '\n';
}

int main()
{
    a.AttHStr(strdup("..heap.."));
    doit();
    //cout << a << '\n';

    return 0;
}
```

References

All C++ texts listed for Chapters 2 and 3. In addition:

Horstmann, C. S., *Mastering Object-Oriented Design in C++*, Wiley, New York, 1995.

Milewski, B., *C++ in Action: Industrial-Strength Programming Techniques*, Addison-Wesley, Reading, MA, 2001.

Stroustrup, B., *The Design and Evolution of C++*, Addison-Wesley, Reading, MA, 1994.

Stroustrup, B., *C++ Programming Language, Special Edition*, Addison-Wesley, Reading, MA, 2002.

Sutter, H., *More Exceptional C++: 40 New Engineering Puzzles, Programming Problems, and Solutions*, Pearson, Harlow, U.K., 2001.

Objects and the operators new *and* delete *from the programmer's point of view:*

Allison, C., "What's New in Standard C++?", *C/C++ Users Journal,* December 1998.

Becker, P., "The Journeyman's Shop: Wrapping up Error Handling Techniques", *C/C++ Users Journal,* February 1999.

CLASSES AND OBJECTS

Glen McCluskey & Associates LLC, "C++ Tutorial, Operators new and delete", http://www.glenmccl.com/bett_003.htm.

Saks, D., "C++ Theory and Practice – Class-Specific new and delete", *C/C++ Users Journal*, March 1997.

Saks, D., "C++ Theory and Practice: Thinking Even Deeper", *C/C++ Users Journal*, July 1999.

Sutter, H., "Sutter's Mill: To New, Perchance to Throw" (part 1 of 2), *C/C++ Users Journal*, March 2001.

Sutter, H., "Sutter's Mill: To New, Perchance to Throw" (part 2 of 2), *C/C++ Users Journal*, May 2001.

Some interesting polemics on the design of C++ operators new *and* delete*:*

Mazières, D., "My Rant on C++'s Operator new", http://www.scs.cs.nyu.edu/~dm/c++-new.html.

Some web-based material:

"Constructors and Destructors Overview", http://www.cascv.brown.edu/compute/cxxmanual/language/concepts/cncdovvu.htm.

Some discussion about object orientation:

Wise, G. B., "Object Orientation and C++" (part I), ACM Crossroads, http://www.acm.org/crossroads/xrds1-2/ovp.html.

Wise, G. B., "Object Orientation and C++" (part II), ACM Crossroads, http://www.acm.org/crossroads/xrds1-3/ovp.html.

CHAPTER NINE

LINKED DATA STRUCTURES

Fundamentals, advantages, and disadvantages of linked data structures. Moving a linked data structure in memory, or to/from a disk, or transmitting it across a communication channel – techniques of compaction and serialization. Memory allocation from a specific arena.

Linked data structures are intimately related to memory, where they are created, located, and processed. Naturally for this book, this relationship with memory is our principal focus in this chapter. It is not our intention to provide a comprehensive presentation of linked data structures in C or C++ and their applications. There are many excellent books on the topic of algorithms and data structures, particularly in C and C++.

Linked data structures and their applications are one of the great successes of the early decades of computer science. The reader can easily imagine how useful software would be if it worked solely with numbers and arrays. But how then would we model and program such things as lists, graphs, stacks, queues, charts, diagrams, and many other abstract notions that are needed to deal with today's complex programming tasks?

Philosophically, a linked approach to data structures is used for any of the following reasons: the data structure must be created dynamically; each part of it is created at a different time; the mutual relations of the parts change in time. Sometimes links are used as a "physical" implementation of "logical relations" (the best example would be databases and the use of foreign keys as "links"). Technically, linked data structures are built in a simple sequence: (i) create a part and (ii) link it with the structure. This simple sequence is repeated many times, often in a recursive manner. A typical example would be a linked list, but it is a bit too simple for some of the aspects we wish to discuss. Hence we have decided to use trees – as ubiquitous and well-understood as lists, and nicely treatable in recursive ways.

We will illustrate the issues using simple *binary search trees* for characters. Such a tree is a binary tree (each node has at most two children), each node stores a character value, and the value stored in the left (resp., right) child is smaller (resp., larger) than the value stored in the parent node. Among the nice properties of such a tree are: a search for a value has the average-case complexity $O(\log n)$, where n is the number of elements stored in the tree; and in-order traversal of the tree lists the characters stored in the tree in an ascending order.

Let us consider a classical recursive function Insert(), which inserts (creates and links) a new node for a given character c, and a recursive function Show() performing in-order traversal of the tree:

```c
struct NODE_STRUCT {
  char value;
  struct NODE_STRUCT* lch;    /* link to left child */
  struct NODE_STRUCT* rch;    /* link to right child */
};

typedef struct NODE_STRUCT NODE;
typedef struct NODE_STRUCT* PNODE;

/* function Insert --------------------------------------------- */
NODE Insert(PNODE n,char c)
{
  if (n == NULL) {  /* at the end of path, or tree not built yet */
    if ((n = malloc(sizeof(NODE))) == NULL) merror();
    n->value = c;
    n->lch = n->rch = NULL;
    return n;
  }
  if (c < n->value)   /* go left */
    n->lch = Insert(n->lch,c);
  else                /* go right */
    n->rch = Insert(n->rch,c);
```

```
  return n;
}/*end Insert*/

/* function Show -------------------------------------------- */
void Show(PNODE n)
{
  if (n == NULL) return;
  Show(n->lch);
  printf(" %c",n->value);
  Show(n->rch);
}/*end Show*/
```

For the sake of simplicity, we made Insert() return the "root" every time so we do not have to pass the root by reference (which in C can only be emulated). Thus, every time a character c is to be inserted in the tree with root tree, one must use tree = Insert(tree,c). (To keep the sample code as simple as possible, we also skipped dealing with insertion of a value already stored in the tree.) Show(tree) will display the list of characters stored in the tree in ascending order.

The first topic we would like to discuss is the nature of links. In the previous example we used pointers, which are quite suitable to the task. However, we may use something else. In our next example we have Insert1() and Show1() do likewise – build a search tree and traverse it, displaying the nodes visited in order – while using arrays and array indexes instead of pointers.

```
    #define null -1
    typedef int PNODE1;     /* a node */
·   char value[100];        /* value */
    int lch[100];           /* left child links */
    int rch[100];           /* right child links */
    int mem = null;         /* fake top of memory */

    /* function Insert1 ----------------------------------- */
    PNODE1 Insert1(PNODE1 n,char c)
    {
      if (n == null) {
        n = ++mem;
        value[n] = c;
        lch[n] = rch[n] = null;
```

```
    return n;
  }
  if (c < value[n])
    lch[n] = Insert1(lch[n],c);
  else
    rch[n] = Insert1(rch[n],c);
  return n;
}/*end Insert1*/

/* function Show1 ---------------------------------------- */
void Show1(PNODE1 n)
{
  if (n == null) return;
  Show1(lch[n]);
  printf(" %c",value[n]);
  Show1(rch[n]);
}/*end Show1*/
```

For a tree with up to 100 nodes, this will work as well as Insert(). In Chapter 6 we mentioned that arrays are such faithful models of memory that they can actually be used as memory, which is exactly what we have done here. However, using the arrays is rather a "static" approach – if the tree has only a few nodes then most of the memory is wasted, and if the tree needs more than 100 then it cannot be accommodated – unless the arrays themselves are dynamic (see Chapter 6). Nevertheless, we might consider this approach if we needed a simple and natural way to serialize the tree. We will discuss that topic later in the chapter.

The function Insert() (in the first example of this chapter) builds the tree completely on the heap. However, it is possible to build a linked data structure on the stack, as our next example demonstrates. Building on the stack is not usually advisable, but for some special cases it may be considered. In the code of the next example, List() is basically a recursive descent parser for a list of characters separated by commas. The function Next() (its scanner) returns the character it scanned, or –2 if it scanned a comma, or –1 when the end of the input string s is reached. Here sp – the *string position* indicator – is passed by reference for the sake of simpler code; only for that reason are we using C++ rather than C. List() builds the tree from multiple versions of the node n, which is a local auto variable, and so the tree is completely built on the system stack. The tree is used only at the bottom of the descent, when the whole input has been parsed. This is the point at which the whole tree is available and can be traversed by Show() as before. For this reason, the insertion of each new node is done via iteration rather than recursion (as in the previous examples). The advantage of such a linked data structure can be summarized simply: no explicit memory allocation is needed and hence there is no need for memory deallocation – unwinding of the stack will take care of the deallocation. The disadvantage is that such a data structure is only available to the bottom activation of List(). I have used such an approach only for a specialized class of problems: enumeration of combinatorial objects (like graphs or designs) in a recursive implementation of backtracking. In such problems you are only interested in the object when it is completely finished, and all you want to do with it is count it, display it, or store it in a file. Moreover, during enumeration, there may be many false starts and the partially constructed objects need to be destroyed. Building the objects entirely on the stack relieves the programmer from dealing with these issues. However, I cannot imagine another class of problems where such an approach would be useful.

```
// function List ---------------------------------
void List(PNODE tree,char* s,int& sp)
{
  NODE n;
  PNODE p;

  n.value = Next(s,sp);
  n.lch = n.rch = NULL;
  if (tree == NULL)
     tree = &n;
  else{
    p = tree;
    while(1) {
      if (n.value < p->value) {
        if (p->lch == NULL) {
          p->lch = &n;
          break;
        }else
          p = p->lch;
      }else{
        if (p->rch == NULL) {
```

```
            p->rch = &n;
            break;
         }else
            p = p->rch;
      }
    }//endwhile
 }

 if (Next(s,sp) == -1) {   // we parsed the whole string
    Show(tree);            // display the characters
    putchar('\n');
 }else
    List(tree,s,sp);
}//end List
```

The foregoing two examples serve as a reminder that linked data structures need not necessarily be linked through pointers, nor do they have to be completely built in dynamic memory. That being said, for the rest of this chapter we will assume the most common type of linked data structures: those built in dynamic memory and linked by pointers.

We have mentioned and illustrated the flexibility of linked data structures. One can easily add a piece, remove a piece, or reshuffle the pieces, for most of these activities require only some modifications of the links. But this "rubbery" nature of the links poses three major problems.

1. How can we move the whole structure to a different location in memory?
2. How can we record such a structure in a file and recreate it from the record?
3. How can we to transmit such a data structure across a communication link?

The first problem could be "solved" by simply recreating the structure and deleting the original one. But it would be impossible to control the placement of the new structure (except by using placement-new, if you were programming in C++). Nevertheless, such a solution would not work for problems 2 and 3. Possible solutions are compaction or serialization of the structure. By *compaction* we mean creating the data structure in a single contiguous segment of memory with a simultaneous "relativization" of addresses with respect to the beginning of the segment. By *serialization* we mean creating the data structure so that it consists of several compacted segments. For an illustration of serialization, take the tree we built in the three arrays value[], lch[], and rch[]. If we move the arrays (which is easy to do – just copy their contents byte by byte to a new location) then at the target location we will find the tree intact. If we record the arrays in a file, byte by byte, then we can later read them byte by byte from the disk and recreate them – and thus the tree. Similarly, we can transmit each array byte by byte in a serial fashion across a communication channel, recreating the arrays (and hence the tree) on the recipient side. All these scenarios are plausible because the links are array indexes, and an array index is essentially a relative address with respect to the beginning of the array.

Our binary search tree is rather simple and so it was easy to build it already serialized, as we did in the three-arrays example. It would be more complicated for more complex structures; it may even be unfeasible to conceive of some data structures as serialized right from the beginning. Moreover, unless you really need to move, record and restore, or transmit the data structure, there is no need to embark on a complex serialization of the initial construction. We will discuss instead the taking of a given data structure and then compacting or serializing it.

Compaction requires the data structure to be stored in a single segment, so it would be possible to build the structure in compacted form only if we had a reasonable cap on its size before construction began. The appropriate raw memory segment could be allocated and forged into the data structure. Of course, we could embark upon dynamic extension of a given segment if more memory were needed, but that would slow processing and bring costs up significantly (since all the links must be updated when the segment is extended) and thus is not very practical. In contrast, for serialization we may have many segments as long as the addresses are properly relativized. This allows the building of serialized data structures directly and with little overhead.

The next example of serialization incorporates a strategy called *memory allocation from a specific arena,* which is implemented using the class-specific operators NODE::new and NODE::delete as well as overloads of the operators new and delete. Therefore, any dynamic object of class NODE is created by using the operator NODE::new and not the global one. The case is similar for destruction: we use the class-specific NODE::delete that does not do anything, for if we want to deallocate the memory then we will deallocate the whole arena. Note that each object of class NODE has a static item, ARENA* arena, a pointer to the arena assigned to the whole class. This is set by a public method TREE::SetArena(), which invokes a protected method NODE::SetArena() (it can do so because it is a "friend"). Each object of class TREE or class NODE points to the same object of class ARENA.

The arena allocates memory from segments – in our example, segments of an unreasonably small size of 24 bytes, a size chosen to force the arena to allocate several segments even for a small tree. The operator NODE::new uses the memory allocated from its arena. Thus, when a tree is created, it is built completely in several segments of the arena. Note that the arena can accommodate any allocation by dynamically creating more segments as needed. Even though the tree is stored in these segments, it is not serialized yet, for the addresses are still actual addresses and not relative to the beginning of each segment. The public method TREE::Relativize() starts a recursion of the protected method TREE::Relativize1() that replaces each address in the tree by a pair of two short integers: the first is the index of the segment the address happens to come from; the second is the offset from the beginning of the segment. For technical reasons the index of the segment is shifted upward by 1, since otherwise the relativized address of the very first byte in the very first segment would be 0 (segment 0, byte 0) and then we could not tell a genuine NULL pointer from the one that pointed to the beginning of the arena before relativization. (Note that this did not bother us in the example of the tree stored in three arrays, for we were using null = -1 as a fake null "pointer".)

After relativization, the segments of the arena represent a serialized version of the tree. To illustrate this, in main() we make a copy of the arena (b = arena;) using the method ARENA::operator= (i.e., ARENA-specific assignment) and absolutize the addresses in the copy – a kind of reverse process to relativization, where each address interpreted as a pair (*segment* + 1, *offset*) is replaced by the actual address. Using TREE::Show() on the re-created tree demonstrates that we indeed have the same tree. It is not hard to see that, had we stored the segments on a disk and then read them from the disk again (or transmitted them across a communication channel), after reassembling them and absolutizing the addresses we would have a perfect copy of the original linked tree.

The code presented next is simplified as much as possible in order to focus on allocation from arena and on relativization and absolutization of addresses. Hence all inessential checking is omitted, and the memory alignment is handled by passing the appropriate parameter to ARENA() during the instantiation (4 in our example) rather then being obtained for each platform in a more independent way.

```
class ARENA
{
public:
  ARENA(int ss,int a) {
    arena = NULL;
    last_segment = -1;
    segment_size = ss;        //arena segment size
    align = a;                //memory alignment boundary
  }

  ~ARENA() {
    for(int i = 0; i <= last_segment; i++)
     delete[] arena[i];
    delete[] arena;
  }

  ARENA& operator= (const ARENA& ar) {
    int i, j;

    for(i = 0; i <= last_segment; i++)  // destroy old data
      delete[] arena[i];
    delete[] arena;
    arena = NULL;

    segment_size = ar.segment_size;      // copy new data
    next_ind = ar.next_ind;
    last_segment = ar.last_segment;
    align = ar.align;

    arena = new char* [last_segment+1];
    for(i = 0; i <= last_segment; i++) {
      arena[i] = new char[segment_size];
      for(j = 0; j < segment_size; j++)
        arena[i][j] = ar.arena[i][j];
    }
    return *this;
  }

  void* Alloc(size_t s) { //alloc. memory of size s from its segment
    char** a;             //obtains a new segment if need be
```

```
      int i;
      void* ret;

      if (arena == NULL) {                         //alloc 1st segment
        arena = new char*[1];
        last_segment = 0;
        arena[0] = new char[segment_size];
        last_segment = 0;
        next_ind = 0;
      }else if (s > (size_t) segment_size-next_ind) {
        last_segment++;
        a = new char*[last_segment+1];
        for(i = 0; i < last_segment; i++)
          a[i] = arena[i];
        delete[] arena;
        arena = a;
        arena[last_segment] = new char[segment_size];
        next_ind = 0;
      }
      ret = (void*) &arena[last_segment][next_ind];
      next_ind += s;
      // align next_ind for future use
      while(((long)&arena[last_segment][next_ind]%align)! = 0)
        if (next_ind >= segment_size) break;

      // if next_ind runs to the end of the segment, no problem
      // on next Alloc() a new segment will be enforced
      return ret;
  }

void* Relativize(void* s) {      //relativizes address s with respect
    short segment, offset, *ip; //to the segment that s belongs to
    void* res;

    if (s == NULL) return NULL;

    for(segment = 0; segment <= last_segment; segment++) {
      if (s < arena[segment])
        continue;
      if (s >= arena[segment]+segment_size)
        continue;
      // so we have the right segment
      offset = (short) ((long)s - (long)arena[segment]);
      segment++;              // shift segment by 1 so the beginning
      ip = (short*)&res;  // does not get relativized to NULL
```

```
        *ip++ = segment;
        *ip = offset;
        return res;
      }
      return NULL;
  }

void* Absolutize(void* s) {  //absolutize relative address s
    short *ip, segment, offset;
    void* r;

    if (s == NULL) return NULL;
    r = s;
    ip = (short*) &r;
    segment = *ip++;
    segment--;                  // undo the shift
    offset = *ip;
    return (void*)&arena[segment][offset];
  }

protected:
  char** arena;
  short last_segment;
  short segment_size;
  short next_ind;
  short align;

};//end class ARENA

class TREE;

class NODE
{
  friend class TREE;
public:

  NODE() { value = 0; lch = rch = NULL; }
  NODE(char c) { value = c; lch = rch = NULL; }

  NODE& operator = (NODE& n) {
    if (lch) delete lch;
    if (rch) delete rch;
    value = n.value;
    lch = n.lch;
```

```
      rch = n.rch;
      arena = n.arena;
      return *this;
   }

protected:
   char value;
   NODE *lch, *rch;
   static ARENA *arena;

   //the following methods are only for arena allocation
   static void* operator new(size_t s) { return arena->Alloc(s); }

   // we will deallocate the whole arena instead
   static void operator delete(void* s) { return; }

   static void SetArena(ARENA* a) { //set the arena for NODE object
     static int first = 1;
     if (first) {
       arena = a;
       first = 0;
     }
   }
};//end class NODE

ARENA* NODE::arena = NULL;

class TREE
{
public:
   TREE() { root = NULL; }

   void Insert(char c) {    //start recursive insertion
     NODE* p;
     p = new NODE(c);
     p->lch = NULL;
     p->rch = NULL;
     if (root == NULL) {
       root = p;
       return;
     }else
       Insert1(root,p);
   }
   void Show() {
```

```
   if (root == NULL) return;
   Show1(root);
   cout << '\n' << flush;
}
void SetRoot(NODE* r) { root = r; }
NODE* GetRoot() { return root; }

static void SetArena(ARENA* a) {  //set arena for TREE object
   static int first = 1;
   if (first) {
     arena = a;
     NODE::SetArena(a);
     first = 0;
   }
}

void Relativize() {          //start recursive relativization
   Relativize1(root);        //at the root
   root = (NODE*)arena->Relativize(root);
}

void Absolutize() {          //start recursive absolutization
                             //at the root
   root = (NODE*)arena->Absolutize((void*)root);
   Absolutize1(root);
}

protected:
  NODE* root;
  static ARENA* arena;

void Insert1(NODE* n,NODE* p) { //continue recursive insertion
    if (p->value < n->value)
      if (n->lch == NULL)
        n->lch = p;
      else
        Insert1(n->lch,p);
    else
      if (n->rch == NULL)
        n->rch = p;
      else
        Insert1(n->rch,p);
  }
```

```
  void Show1(NODE* p) {
    if (p == NULL) return;
    Show1(p->lch);
    cout << ' ' << p->value;
    Show1(p->rch);
  }

  void Relativize1(NODE* n) {  //continue recursive relativization
    if (n == NULL) return;
    Relativize1(n->lch);
    Relativize1(n->rch);
    n->lch = (NODE*)arena->Relativize((void*)n->lch);
    n->rch = (NODE*)arena->Relativize((void*)n->rch);
  }

  void Absolutize1(NODE* n) {  //continue recursive absolutization
    if (n == NULL) return;
    n->lch = (NODE*)arena->Absolutize(n->lch);
    n->rch = (NODE*)arena->Absolutize(n->rch);
    Absolutize1(n->lch);
    Absolutize1(n->rch);
  }
};//end class TREE

ARENA* TREE::arena = NULL;

// function main ------------------------------------------------
int main()
{

  ARENA arena(24,4), b(0,0);
  TREE t, t1;

  t.SetArena(&arena);
  t.Insert('d');
  t.Insert('c');
  t.Insert('e');
  t.Insert('a');
  t.Insert('b');
  t.Show();
  t.Relativize();

  b = arena;
  t1.SetArena(&b);
  t1.SetRoot(t.GetRoot());
```

```
t1.Absolutize();
t1.Show();

return 0;
}//end main
```

Let us now visualize the arena after each stage of the process. After node for 'd' is created:

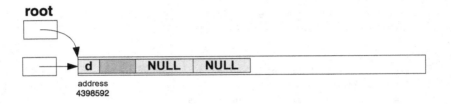

After node for 'c' is created:

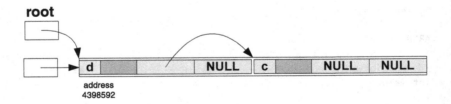

After node for 'e' is created:

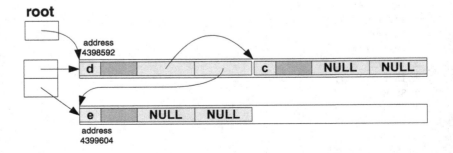

After node for 'a' is created:

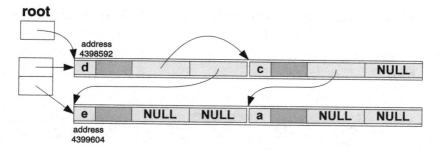

And finally, after the last node for 'b' is created:

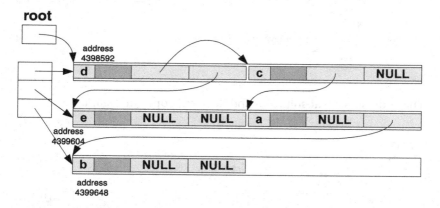

This clearly shows how the arena allocation keeps the tree quite "compact", even though it is a fully linked data structure and all pointers hold actual addresses.

In the following diagram we indicate the relativized addresses as pairs of (*segment*+1, *offset*) values. The tree is relativized:

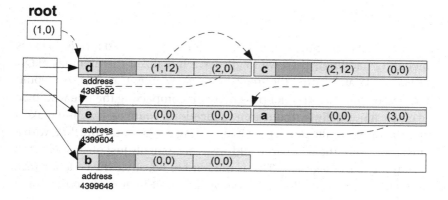

The arena is copied into a different location. The data kept in the arena (and so the relativized tree) is the same as in the original one:

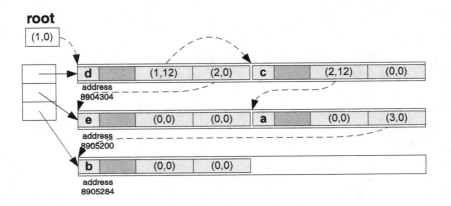

The addresses are absolutized and the tree "pops out" again:

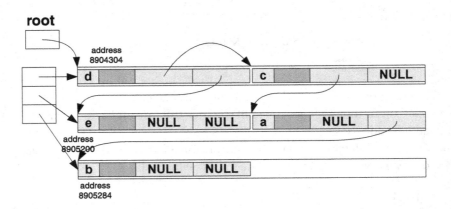

If we had known the size of the tree before we created it (it is 60 bytes including padding), then we might have initialized the arena as ARENA arena(60,4) and stored the tree in a single segment; in fact, we would have compacted it. Another possibility for compacting the tree would be to create it normally (without arena allocation), count its size, and make a copy using arena allocation to fit it into a single segment. Note that, with a single segment, the relativized addresses are actually just offsets from the beginning of the segment. This is not hard to do, since the code for TREE and NODE will work perfectly well if we just omit references to the arena

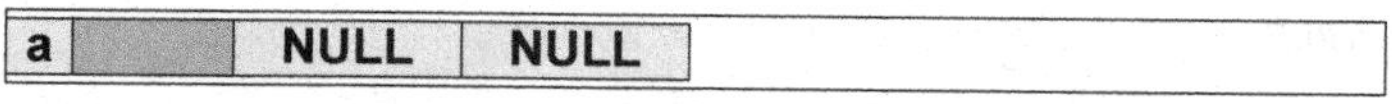

Figure 9.1   A node with 'a' stored in it

Figure 9.2   A compacted node with 'a' stored in it

there and in the overloaded new and delete. But it may be complicated to establish the size of an existing tree that includes padding, since the size may depend on such elusive aspects as the order in which items are defined. The only reasonable approach to counting the size of a linked data structure is doing so during construction – allocate some memory and add it to the count.

Our approach to serialization preserves padding. This may or may not be desirable. If we preserve padding then all the items remain "justified" and hence can be accessed (before relativization and after absolutization) in the normal way; for instance, the usual pointer notation works correctly. If we intend to move the data structure (either via a disk or across a communication channel) to a different platform, then there is no reason to preserve the padding and transmit all that junk. We could compact the tree without the padding, but then we might not be able to use the convenient pointer or membership notation for accessing the individual items.

We deliberately designed the structure/class NODE so that it has size of 12 bytes, but 3 bytes are wasted on padding (see Figure 9.1). If we compact it without the padding then the space is saved – but now we cannot use p->lch or p->rch to refer to the pointers to the child nodes; see Figure 9.2.

In order to work with such a compacted structure, we must have our own custom-made functions for accessing items that are not properly aligned. The following example creates a regular tree, computes its size without padding, and creates a compacted version of the tree that can only be accessed using the specialized access functions; then the compacted version is relativized. The resulting relativized compacted version can be transferred to a machine with a different memory alignment, absolutized, and accessed by again using the specialized access functions. For the sake of simplicity we have omitted the code dealing with different "endianess" (see Chapter 3). Class NODE remains the same as before.

```
class TREE
{
public:
  TREE() { root = NULL; }

  void Insert(char c) {
    NODE* p;
    p = new NODE(c);
    p->lch = NULL;
    p->rch = NULL;
    if (root == NULL) {
      root = p;
      return;
    }else
      Insert1(root,p);
  }

  void Show() {
    if (root == NULL) return;
    Show1(root);
    cout << '\n'<< flush;
  }

  int Size() {
    return Size1(root);
  }

  char* Compact(char*& croot) {
    char* segment;
    int ind = 0;

    segment = (char*) new char[Size()];
    croot = Compact1(ind,segment,root);
    return segment;
  }

  void CShow(char* segment,char* cnode) {
    if (cnode == NULL) return;
    CShow(segment,GetLch(cnode));
    cout << ' ' << GetValue(cnode);
    CShow(segment,GetRch(cnode));
  }

  char* Relativize(char* segment,char* croot) {
    char* p;
```

```
      if (croot == NULL) return NULL;
      p = GetLch(croot);
      if (p != NULL) {
        Relativize1(segment,p);
        PutLch(croot,(char*)(p-segment+1)); // shift by 1 to
                                            // distinguish from NULL
      }
      p = GetRch(croot);
      if (p != NULL) {
        Relativize1(segment,p);
        PutRch(croot,(char*)(p-segment+1)); // shift by 1 to
                                            // distinguish from NULL
      }
      return ((char*)(croot-segment+1));    // shift by 1 to
                                            // distinguish from NULL
    }

  char* Absolutize(char* segment,char* croot) {
    if (croot == NULL) return NULL;
    // undo the shift
    croot = ((char*)(segment+((unsigned long)croot)-1));
    Absolutize1(segment,croot);
    return croot;
  }

protected:
  NODE* root;

  void Insert1(NODE* n,NODE* p) {
    if (p->value < n->value)
      if (n->lch == NULL)
        n->lch = p;
      else
        Insert1(n->lch,p);
    else
      if (n->rch == NULL)
        n->rch = p;
      else
        Insert1(n->rch,p);
  }

  void Show1(NODE* p) {
    if (p == NULL) return;
    Show1(p->lch);
    cout << ' ' << p->value;
```

```
    Show1(p->rch);
}

int Size1(NODE* p) {
  if (p == NULL)
    return 0;
  return p->Size()+Size1(p->lch)+Size1(p->rch);
}
char GetValue(char* p) { // use instead of p->value
  return *p;
}
void PutValue(char* p,char c) { // use instead of p->value
  *p = c;
}
char* GetLch(char* p) {  // use instead of p->lch
  char *q, *q1, *q2;
  int i;

  q2 = (char*)&q;
  q1 = p+sizeof(char);
  for(i = 0; i < sizeof(char*); i++)
    *q2++ = *q1++;
  return q;
}
void PutLch(char* p,char* addr) {  // use instead of p->lch
  char *q, *q1, *q2;
  int i;

  q = addr;
  q2 = (char*)&q;
  q1 = p+sizeof(char);
  for(i = 0; i < sizeof(char*); i++)
    *q1++ = *q2++;
}
char* GetRch(char* p) {  // use instead of p->rch
  char *q, *q1, *q2;
  int i;

  q2 = (char*)&q;
  q1 = p+sizeof(char)+sizeof(char*);
  for(i = 0; i < sizeof(char*); i++)
    *q2++ = *q1++;
  return q;
}
```

```
void PutRch(char* p,char* addr) {  // use instead of p->rch
  char *q, *q1, *q2;
  int i;

  q = addr;
  q2 = (char*)&q;
  q1 = p+sizeof(char)+sizeof(char*);
  for(i = 0; i < sizeof(char*); i++)
    *q1++ = *q2++;
}

char* Compact1(int& ind,char* segment,NODE* n) {
  char *lch, *rch, *ret;

  if (n == NULL) return NULL;
  lch = Compact1(ind,segment,n->lch);
  rch = Compact1(ind,segment,n->rch);
  //copy n to segment to location segment[ind]
  ret = &segment[ind];
  PutValue(&segment[ind],n->value);
  PutLch(&segment[ind],lch);
  PutRch(&segment[ind],rch);
  ind += n->Size();
  return ret;
}

void Relativize1(char* segment,char* cnode) {
  char* p;

  p = GetLch(cnode);
  if (p != NULL) {
    Relativize1(segment,p);
    PutLch(cnode,(char*)(p-segment+1)); // shift up by 1 to
                                        // distinguish from NULL
  }
  p = GetRch(cnode);
  if (p != NULL) {
    Relativize1(segment,p);
    PutRch(cnode,(char*)(p-segment+1)); // shift up by 1 to
                                        // distinguish from NULL
  }
}

void Absolutize1(char* segment,char* cnode) {
  char* p;
```

```
    if ((p = GetLch(cnode)) != NULL) {
      // undo the shift
      p = ((char*)(segment+((unsigned long)p)-1));
      PutLch(cnode,p);
      Absolutize1(segment,p);
    }

    if ((p = GetRch(cnode)) != NULL) {
      // undo the shift
      p = ((char*)(segment+((unsigned long)p)-1));
      PutRch(cnode,p);
      Absolutize1(segment,p);
    }
  }
};//end class TREE
```

After a tree is built in the normal way, it can be compacted using croot = Compact(segment,croot). Note that char* croot must be initialized to NULL prior to the call. The function Compact() will allocate a contiguous segment of the correct size, will make segment point to it, and will then store the tree in a compacted form; it also returns a pointer to the root, which need not be the very first node in the segment. The compacted tree cannot be accessed normally, but it can be viewed using CShow() – show compacted tree. We can then relativize it, absolutize it, and show it again using CShow() to verify that the program has worked properly. Again, we must ensure that a genuine NULL pointer can be distinguished from the very first byte in the segment.

In Figure 9.3, the compacted tree (as built and compacted in the previous example) is shown. Figure 9.4 illustrates the compacted tree after relativization.

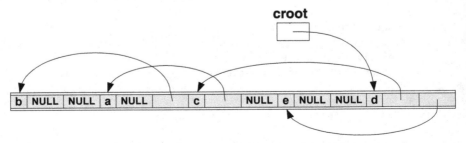

Figure 9.3 Compacted tree from the example

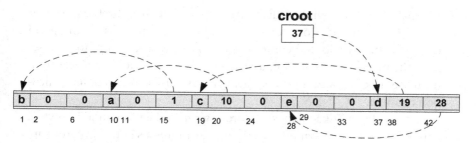

Figure 9.4 Compacted tree from the example: after relativization

It is clear that many other methods could be used to serialize or compact linked data structures. In real life, an ad hoc method pertinent to a particular structure is normally used. However, in this chapter we have tried to provide some insight into the issues and furnish the reader with some ideas of how to go about resolving them. In our age of networking and distributed computing, moving data structures among different machines and different platforms is fast becoming commonplace.

Allocation from a specific arena can be used for problems other than serializing linked data structures. Any application that needs to perform a lot of allocation/deallocation of small chunks of memory may have its performance dramatically improved if the allocation is handled through a specific arena. Some authors claim that the time spent by a running program on allocation and deallocation is by far the most significant component in overall performance, so any improvement in these functions should yield welcome dividends.

Review

Linked data structures are extremely useful in both C and C++ programming, and they are employed for modeling many diverse aspects of real systems. They are used in situations where the data structure must be built dynamically, or where its parts are built at different times, or where the mutual relationships among the constituent parts change in time. They are extremely flexible, making it easy to add, remove, or modify a part of the data structure. They can also be fashioned to provide maximally efficient access to the data they store. Usually, linked data structures are created on the heap (dynamic memory), and pointers are used as the links. However, it is also possible to build linked data structures on the system stack and/or without pointers.

The flexibility of linked data structures, though desirable and welcome, is an obstacle to three increasingly common tasks in an age of networks and distributed computing: (a) moving a structure to another place in memory; (b) storing a structure in a disk file and restoring it from the disk file; and (c) transmitting a structure across a communication channel.

We say that a linked data structure is *serialized* if it is stored in several contiguous memory segments and if all the addresses in the structure are relative to the beginning of the segment in which they are located. We use the term *relativization* to denote the process of replacing the actual addresses by these "relative" ones. The reverse process, which restores the relative addresses back to actual addresses, is called *absolutization*. We have shown by example how to serialize a binary tree using the technique of memory allocation from a specific arena and properly overloading operators `new` and `delete`. A handy aspect of this approach is the need to append just slightly to the existing code for the data structure, code that otherwise remains intact. Besides that, our approach preserves padding and so the usual referencing of items by pointers or as members works well. A serialized structure can be easily moved, recorded/restored, or transmitted as long as source and destination places have the same memory alignment.

We call a linked data structure *compacted* if it is stored in a single contiguous memory segment and if all the addresses in the structure are relative to the beginning of the segment. We gave an example of compacting a search tree. In our approach, the padding is intentionally not preserved. A compacted structure can be easily moved, recorded/restored, or transmitted even if the source and destination places have different memory alignments. However, items in a compacted structure cannot be accessed through the usual referencing by pointers or members. Specialized access functions allowing retrieval and storage in locations not properly aligned must be provided.

Allocation from a specific arena can greatly improve the performance of any program that does a lot of allocation and deallocation of small chunks of memory. In the arena approach, only the whole arena is allocated via a call to the process memory manager (`malloc()`, `new`) and deallocated as a whole when no longer needed; the allocation and deallocation of smaller items is handled within the arena much faster and more efficiently.

Exercises

9.1 Why is it that linked data structures cannot be copied to a disk and then later read from the disk and reinstalled? For instance, take a search tree and write each node to a disk. Then just read it back, and store it in the memory. Don't we get the same tree?

9.2 Write access functions that can retrieve or store a `float` value at any memory location without regard to memory alignment.

9.3 Write a program that compacts a structure (including an `int` array, a `float`, a `double`, and a `char`) and then relativizes the segment where the structure is compacted. Write access functions that can access (store or retrieve) the relativized compacted form of the structure.

9.4 Write a program that creates a linked tree in which each node has an arbitrary number of children. Then write a function that uses the allocation from arena strategy to create the tree in a serialized way. Relativize the serialized tree, copy the segments somewhere else in the memory, absolutize the tree, and check that it is the same tree. You may modify the code presented in this chapter.

9.5 Modify the code from Exercise 9.4 for some other linked data structure.

9.6 Redo Exercise 9.4 to obtain a serialized version of the tree.

9.7 Redo Exercise 9.5 to obtain a serialized version of the data structure.

9.8 Using two arrays of size N, implement a serialized version of a doubly linked list of integers in the range `0..N-1`.

References

Data structures in C and C++:

Dale, N., *C++ Plus Data Structures*, Jones & Bartlett, Sudbury, MA, 1999.

Ford, W., and Top, W., *Data Structures with C++*, Prentice-Hall, Englewood Cliffs, NJ, 1996.

Kirch-Prinz, U., and Prinz, P., *A Complete Guide to Programming in C++*, Jones & Bartlett, Sudbury, MA, 2002.

Standish, T. A., *Data Structures, Algorithms and Software Principles in C*, Addison-Wesley, Reading, MA, 1995.

Weiss, M. A., *Data Structures and Algorithm Analysis in C++*, Benjamin/ Cummings, Redwood City, CA, 1994.

Allocation from arena:

Austern, M., "The Standard Librarian: I/O and Function Objects: Containers of Pointers", *C/C++ Users Journal,* October 2001.

Hanson, D., "Fast Allocation and Deallocation of Memory Based on Object Lifetimes", *Software Practice and Experience,* January 1990.

Milewski, B., *C++ in Action: Industrial-Strength Programming Techniques,* Addison-Wesley, Reading, MA, 2001.

Stroustrup, B., *C++ Programming Language, Special Edition,* Addison-Wesley, Reading, MA, 2002.

Some web-based material:

`http://users.bestweb.net/~ctips/tip049.html`.

CHAPTER TEN

MEMORY LEAKS AND THEIR DEBUGGING

Classification of the causes of memory leaks. Tracing memory leaks in C programs using location reporting and allocation/deallocation information-gathering versions of the C allocators and deallocators. Tracing memory leaks in C++ programs: overloading the operators new *and* delete *and the problems it causes. Techniques for location tracing. Counting objects in C++. Smart pointers as a remedy for memory leaks caused by the undetermined ownership problem.*

As mentioned previously, I do not like the terms "memory leaks" or "leaking memory". They somehow put the onus on memory, as if it were the memory's inadequacy that caused the problem. Every time I hear a project manager or a student explain in a grave tone of voice that "the project is delayed because we have memory leaking", I feel like retorting "OK, find a better memory that doesn't leak". In truth, it's not the memory but rather the program that is inadequate. We should be talking about leaking programs, not about leaking memory. In this chapter we will classify the most common problems leading to memory leaks and discuss how to identify and locate them. We will start with trivial and obvious problems and proceed to more subtle ones that are harder to deal with.

The first class of memory leaks is called *orphaned allocation* and is characterized by allocation of a memory segment whose address is not preserved for later deallocation. This is seldom intentional and usually results from insufficient knowledge of the C or C++ language. We present a few classic examples with strings (though any kind of object could be involved). First,

```
char* p;
...
p = malloc(strlen(s)+1);
p = s;
```

The memory for a copy of the string s is allocated, yet the pointer p is merely set to point to the same place as the pointer s. Even if free(p) is subsequently invoked, it does not free the segment previously allocated. The program may seem to work (at least p seems to be the "correct" string), but trying to free p and then s may induce a crash because some operating systems (like LINUX) will terminate a program that is trying to free a segment not currently allocated. A similar situation holds for

```
char* p;
...
p = malloc(4);
p = "abc";
```

The next class of memory leaks is referred to as the *hidden allocation* problem. It is characterized by a call to another function to deliver an object without realizing that the object has been created on the heap. As an example, consider the standard function strdup(). It duplicates a string and returns a pointer to it. The duplicated string is created on the heap. If not deallocated later, the memory leaks. However, shouldn't all C/C++ programmers know what a standard function such as strdup() does? Of course, but do they all know everything that standard functions do? And how about their knowledge of the particular operating system being used? Very often we need the services of external procedures, as in particular system calls. For instance, consider the UNIX system call

```
struct group *getgrnam(const char *name)
```

Is the structure group allocated on the heap or somewhere else (say, in the kernel of the operating system)? Should it be deallocated by the user when no longer needed? Or consider the following Windows example:

```
HBRUSH br;
...
br = CreateSolidBrush(RGB(255,255,255));
```

Here br is a handle to a brush. We created a solid brush of certain color and captured the reference to it in br. Is the brush an object on the heap? Do we need to deallocate it? A diligent and thorough programmer would find answers to these questions, but often the questions are simply not asked. It's almost as if the programmer is behaving according to the principle "I am not responsible for what I have not done explicitly". The consequences of implicit actions are too often ignored.

The third class of memory leaks is a close relative to the previous one of hidden allocation; we call it the *undetermined ownership* problem. When discussing resources and their allocation, it is customary to refer to the entity responsible for "releasing" an unneeded resource as the "owner" of the resource. Thus the owner of a memory segment is (as far as we are concerned) the module that is responsible for deallocating it. The undetermined ownership problem is characterized by a module obtaining a memory segment without realizing that it is now the owner and therefore responsible for its deallocation. A typical scenario runs along the following lines. A module A requests a module B to provide an object. The object is created dynamically and thus it cannot be owned by B. But the programmer of module A is not aware of the ownership issue – thinking perhaps that the object will be deallocated by some other module somewhere else, for the programmer is just "using" the object here. This confusion is usually compounded by the path of an object being more complex; for example, an object might have been created by a module D, which passed it to C, which passed it to B, which passed to A. Hence the programmer responsible for the design and/or coding of A may not even know the object's origin, let alone its intended future or who should deallocate it. The further apart the place where a dynamic object is created and the place where it is used, the more likely the object will be forgotten and undeallocated. Because objects are sometimes – for the sake of efficiency – passed in static "containers" (e.g., a function returns a pointer to a string that was not created dynamically but was stored in a static buffer), the problem cannot be avoided by following some simple rule like "always deallocate the object you received if you do not pass it along".

The fourth class of memory leaks, which is specific to C++, are those caused by an incorrect or missing destructor (as discussed in Chapter 8). We call this the *insufficient destructor* problem, and it arises when an object has some dynamic parts that are created by constructor(s) or other means yet are not specifically deallocated in the destructor. If an explicit destructor is omitted, the default destructor may be insufficient for the task.

Similar to the insufficient destructor problem is the fifth class of memory leaks (again, particular to C++ and detailed in Chapter 8), known as the *incorrect assignment* problem. When assigning new values to all the various members of an object, if any member is a dynamically allocated segment then it must be explicitly deallocated prior to assigning a new value. Most often this situation occurs when an explicit assignment is missing and so a default memberwise assignment is used instead.

The sixth class of memory leaks is also specific to C++; we call it the *exception-unsafe code* problem. It can be described as the following scenario:

```
void doit()
{
   TYPE *t = new TYPE;
   ...
   ...      // the code here can throw an exception
   ...      // that is caught outside of doit()
   ...
   delete t;
}
```

If an exception is thrown by the code in the middle of the function doit() then the fully formed dynamic object that t points to will *not* be deallocated, because dynamic objects can be explicitly deallocated only by delete or delete[] (though delete or delete[] themselves may be called implicitly by a destructor).

Exceptions thrown in a constructor are not a problem, since all objects that have been created up to the throw point are automatically destroyed when the system stack is unwinding. In this case a memory leak could occur only if some raw memory had been allocated using the C allocators. Automatic objects are always destroyed when they go out of scope, no matter what the reason. Thus, they will also be destroyed during the stack unwinding.

The real problem is with exceptions in destructors: if an exception is thrown in a destructor, the deallocation that was to take place after the throw point does not happen. However, exceptions in destructors can be prevented by adhering to a simple principle: *do not use any code that can throw an exception in a destructor.* No matter how careful we are in the design of constructors and the destructor, the function doit() in the previous code will still leak memory if an exception is thrown.

Writing code that is exception-safe must be implemented in a design that is centered on the safety issue. Exception safety is an important programming issue in C++, and many excellent texts are available that deal with the whole range of its aspects. Let us simply mention that, in its abstract form, "exception safety" refers to making sure that no resources have leaked and that certain invariants are preserved when an exception is thrown. In broader, colloquial terms: after an exception has occurred, a thorough housecleaning is performed that brings the system back to the state before the "offending" module was activated. Later in the chapter we will discuss some possible solutions, but for now let us illustrate how insidious the problem can be. If you think that the offending code can easily be modified along lines like this:

```
void doit()
{
    TYPE *t = new TYPE;
    try {
    ...       // the code here can throw an exception
    ...       // that used to be caught outside of doit()
    }
    catch(...) {
      ...
      delete t;
      throw;   // re-throw the same exception so it can be caught
    }          // at the original site outside of doit()
    ...
    delete t;
}
```

then beware of the same problem in a much more innocuous setting. The order of evaluation of subexpressions in an expression (or of arguments to a function) are not specified by the language, in order to allow some flexibility in the design of compilers. Thus an exception thrown by a TYPE2 constructor in the call

```
    void doit(TYPE1*,TYPE2*);   // prototype
    ...
    doit(new TYPE1,new TYPE2);  // call
```

cannot be rectified because we do not know whether the object of TYPE1 has been constructed yet. This is just poorly designed code. Another example:

```
class COMP_NUMB {  //complex numbers
...
    friend COMP_NUMB& operator+(COMP_NUMB&,COMP_NUMB&);
...
...
};//end class COMP_NUMB
...
p = p + (*(new COMP_NUMB(2,3)) + *(new COMP_NUMB(3,5)));
```

If new COMP_NUMB(3,5) throws an exception, we do not know whether COMP_NUMB(2,3) has been created yet.

In neither of the previous two examples can we rectify the problem by placing an extra try{ } and catch{ } to provide the opportunity for a housecleaning. Instead, such code should simply be otherwise designed in the first place.

Finally, the last class of memory leaks is labeled the *external component* problem. It is quite conceivable that a memory leak occurs in an external component we are using (e.g., some operating system function or class, or some commercial software for distributed computing, or some database system, etc. – just search the Internet to see how common this actually is). With the complexity of software rapidly increasing, more and more software systems use components that come from external sources and not from where the software system is being developed.

Let us summarize our classification of memory leaks by stating to what language each type applies, identifying the usual cause, and assessing how difficult it is to rectify the problem.

1. *Orphaned allocation* (C and C++) – caused by poorly developed programming skills; can easily be rectified when detected and located.
2. *Hidden allocation* (C and C++) – caused by insufficient knowledge of the modules being used; can be rectified when detected and located, though changes in the code could be significant.
3. *Undetermined ownership* (C and C++) – caused by poor design and integration; can be rectified when detected and located, though changes in the code could be significant.

4. *Insufficient destructor* (C++) – caused by poor design and/or poor programming skills; can be relatively easily rectified when detected and located (it's the detection that is difficult).
5. *Incorrect assignment* (C++) – caused by poor design and/or poor programming skills; can be relatively easily rectified when detected and located (it's the detection that is difficult).
6. *Exception-unsafe code* (C++) – caused by poor design and/or poor programming skills; rectification requires a significant redesign of the code (this problem is difficult to detect and localize).
7. *External component* (C and C++) – caused by tough luck; not too much you can do about it except contact the external source or work around the problem.

In the following we will turn our attention to tracing memory leaks resulting from C allocators and from C++ operators. By my own reckoning, the undetermined ownership problem is the most prevalent cause of memory leaks in C-based software; whereas in C++ software the undetermined ownership, insufficient destructor, and incorrect assignment problems (in that order) are the most prevalent causes of memory leaks. I believe that there is a lot of exception-unsafe code out there, but the memory leaks associated with such software manifest themselves rarely, so finding them is crucial only for fail-safe and mission-critical applications. The only remedy for memory leaks associated with exception-unsafe code is to redesign the software, which of course is beyond the scope of this book. Similarly, memory leaks associated with the insufficient destructor and incorrect assignment problems are evidence of poor programming and must be rectified by providing or fixing the constructors and/or assignments. This is also outside the scope of this book, yet we hope that the material in Chapter 9 provides sufficient understanding of these issues to help the reader avoid the leaks. At the end of this chapter we shall deal with the undetermined ownership problem by discussing a possible C++ remedy in the form of so-called safe or smart pointers.

Tracing Memory Leaks in C

Allocation of memory using the C allocators `malloc()`, `calloc()`, and `realloc()` was covered in Chapter 4. The C approach to allocation presents a slight problem because the allocation is not type-safe; for instance, `p = malloc(sizeof(NODE))` will yield a totally different result than `p = malloc(sizeof(NODE*))`, an easy error to make. On the other hand, all C allocators are standard functions and hence are not tied to the compiler – by which we mean that, unlike in C++, the compiler need not be aware that any allocation or deallocation is taking place. It is thus extremely simple to use replacement versions of these functions that can provide much more than just the allocation/deallocation. This is an invaluable tool for tracing memory leaks in C programs. For simplicity we will discus only `malloc()` and `free()`, though the same remarks may be applied to `calloc()` and `realloc()`. The basic idea is to have `malloc()` record what was allocated, who (i.e., which piece of the code) requested the allocation, and when it was allocated; likewise, we use `free()` to keep track of what has been deallocated, by whom, and when. We want to do this with the least effort and without significantly modifying the program.

The simplest approach utilizes the ANSI C preprocessor. If we merely add to our program the preprocessing directive

```
#define malloc(size) debug_malloc(__FILE__,__LINE__,size)
```

then (for example) an occurrence of `p = malloc(sizeof(NODE));` in the source file `source.c` on line 321 will be expanded prior to compilation to `p = debug_malloc("source.c",321,67);`. We link with the program our debugging version of `malloc()` using the prototype

```
void* debug_malloc(const char* src,int line,size_t size)
```

Besides allocating the requested amount of memory (through a call to ordinary `malloc()`), `debug_malloc()` can record the information in a log file and/or keep it in a private data structure that is accessible only by `debug_malloc()` and `debug_free()`. Similarly, we can add the preprocessing directive

```
#define free(ptr) debug_free(__FILE__,__LINE__,ptr)
```

and, for instance, an occurrence of `free(p);` in the source file `source.c` on line 457 will be expanded to `debug_free("source.c",457,p);`. Our debugging version of `free()` with prototype

```
void debug_free(const char* src,int line,void* ptr)
```

must also be linked to the program; this version can log the information (in the same log file as debug_malloc() or in a separate log) and/or remove the information from the private data structure. Of course, debug_free() deallocates the requested memory using the ordinary free().

We can also have statistics – on what remains undeallocated – printed out or logged at program termination. The least intrusive method is to add (to the beginning of main() of our program) an *atexit registration* of a function that prints or logs the statistics; the ANSI C function atexit() provides the registration. A function registered "atexit" will be automatically executed by the ANSI C function exit() used to terminate programs – unless the program uses some other means of termination (e.g., _exit() under UNIX) that bypasses atexit.

By examining the log or the exit statistics after program execution, we can determine whether all dynamically allocated memory has been deallocated – that is, whether memory is leaking. Information concerning what has not been deallocated and which part of the code requested the offending allocation can help determine if there really is a memory leak.

If debug_malloc() and/or debug_free() log the information in a file, it is prudent to execute fflush(log) after each entry to the log so that the log will be current if a crash occurs. (If our program spawns multiple processes or executes in a multithreaded fashion then the logging becomes more complicated, because some form of file locking must be provided in order to prevent two processes or two threads from writing into the log simultaneously; we will touch upon this topic in Chapter 11.) As Figure 10.1 illustrates, our approach to tracing memory leaks requires just small changes to the program.

The localization provided by __FILE__ and __LINE__ may not be sufficient. Consider a service function doit() that is called in a large number of lines of the code of the program. We may determine that the leaks occur in doit() based on the data passed to doit() by its caller. But which caller is it? There is a solution, but it must be built into the coding practice; it cannot be just "magically added on" when we need to trace memory leaks as we did with debug_malloc() and debug_free(). It is always prudent in serious software development – especially if network-based – to require programmers to denote entry into modules in some standard way and so enable extensive logging in test versions of the system. For instance, we may use something like

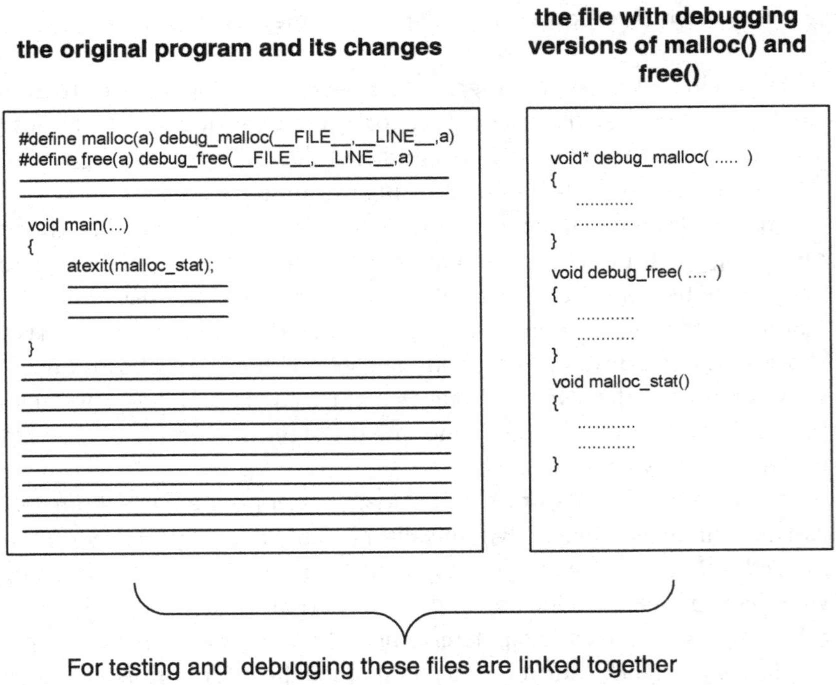

the original program and its changes

the file with debugging versions of malloc() and free()

```
#define malloc(a) debug_malloc(__FILE__,__LINE__,a)
#define free(a) debug_free(__FILE__,__LINE__,a)


void main(...)
{
        atexit(malloc_stat);
```

```
void* debug_malloc( ..... )
{
    ............
    ............
}
void debug_free( .... )
{
    ............
    ............
}
void malloc_stat()
{
    ............
    ............
}
```

For testing and debugging these files are linked together

Figure 10.1   Modifying a C program in order to trace memory leaks

```
void doit(....)
{
   TRACE(doit)
   ...
   ...
   ...
   RETURN
}
```

where TRACE is defined through a macro to set some global variable with the unique designation of the function doit() upon its activation. This can provide run-time localization of the log entry. Similarly, RETURN is defined as a macro as needed. Logs with such entries are easier to read and examine than mere references to lines in the source files. If desired for more detailed debugging (as a compilation option), the macro TRACE is defined to actually stack the function references during execution and the macro RETURN is defined to pop the stacked function references, thus providing the means to trace a whole thread of execution for debugging. For a production build, RETURN is simply defined as return (a more detailed treatment of this topic may be found in the following section on tracing memory leaks in C++ programs).

There are many reasons for *not* using macros. The most important reason is that they may change the "common sense" semantics of the code – for example, #define add(a,b) subtract(a,b) (purposefully an extreme example) will confuse everyone reading the program, since they would naturally think that add(a,b) in the code actually adds the values. However, enabling detection of leaks is one of the few cases for which I recommend using macros to alter the code. Using macros to define TRACE() and RETURN for tracing (as illustrated previously) is similarly justified. It does not confuse anybody because it is not used in any context other than designating the entry or exit of a function. Macros provide a speedy and efficient way to handle certain tasks, and they can be of great help if used sparingly and cautiously.

The approach described here works well for C programs developed in-house, but is not very helpful if the system includes external C-based object code where the leak may have occurred. All calls to malloc() and free() in the object code linked with our program will be linked with the *system* malloc() and free(), not our debugging versions. In this situation we must use some replacement versions of malloc() and free(), say rmalloc() and rfree(). We also need intimate knowledge of the compiler being used.

First we need a new function malloc() that does essentially the same job as debug_malloc() but gets its location information from global variables (rather than arguments) and uses rmalloc() for the actual allocation. Second, we now need a new debug_malloc() function: it has the same prototype as the previous version but now merely sets the global variables for malloc() and calls malloc(). Similarly, our new deallocator free() does essentially the same job as debug_free() did previously, getting its location information from the global variables and using rfree() for the actual deallocation. The new debug_free() sets the global variables and calls free(). Prior to each call to a function from the offending object code, we add instructions setting the localization global variables accordingly. We link with our program the object codes of malloc() and free() (avoiding the standard malloc() and the standard free(); this is where we

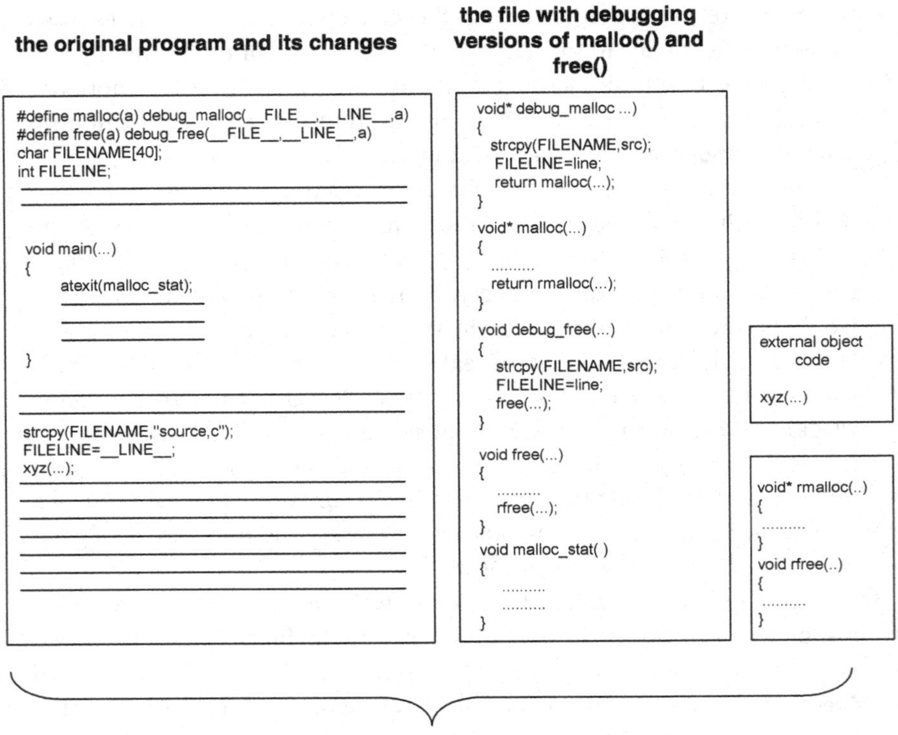

the original program and its changes   **the file with debugging versions of malloc() and free()**

```
#define malloc(a) debug_malloc(__FILE__,__LINE__,a)
#define free(a) debug_free(__FILE__,__LINE__,a)
char FILENAME[40];
int FILELINE;
```
```
void main(...)
{
    atexit(malloc_stat);



}
```
```
strcpy(FILENAME,"source.c");
FILELINE=__LINE__;
xyz(...);
```

```
void* debug_malloc ...)
{
   strcpy(FILENAME,src);
   FILELINE=line;
   return malloc(...);
}

void* malloc(...)
{
   .........
   return rmalloc(...);
}

void debug_free(...)
{
   strcpy(FILENAME,src);
   FILELINE=line;
   free(...);
}

void free(...)
{
   .........
   rfree(...);
}
void malloc_stat( )
{
   .........
   .........
}
```

```
external object
code

xyz(...)
```

```
void* rmalloc(..)
{
   .........
}
void rfree(..)
{
   .........
}
```

For testing and debugging these files are linked together

Figure 10.2   Modifying a C program that has an external object code in order to trace memory leaks

need a good knowledge of the C compiler we are using), debug_malloc(), debug_free(), ... Thus we have a program in which every call to malloc() in the part programmed by us is a call to debug_malloc(), which sets the location global variables and calls our version of malloc(). Every call to malloc() within the external object code is now a call to our version of malloc(), and likewise for free(). As before, we can log or store the information about allocation and deallocation and use it to determine if (and where) memory leaks have occurred. See Figure 10.2.

There are many public-domain or commercial versions of malloc() and free() available. Many of those have debugging features along the lines described here. The decision of whether to obtain them or to use your own debugging versions of malloc() and free() depends on many factors outside the scope of this book. In any case, understanding how the debugging feature works is essential to a proper use of the debugging versions of malloc() and free().

Tracing Memory Leaks in C++

Unfortunately, the situation here is not as straightforward as with C programs; in fact, it is downright convoluted. Of course, we can overload the global operators new and delete as in the following sample code.

```
extern "C" {
 #include <stdio.h>
 #include <string.h>
 #include <stdlib.h>
}
#include <iostream>

//location new
void* operator new(size_t size,const char* src,int line)
{
  void *p;
  p = malloc(size);
  cout << "location new in " << src << " at line "
      << line << " size " << size << " alloc "
      << (unsigned int)p << '\n';
  return  p;
}


//location delete
void operator delete(void* p,const char* src,int line)
{
  cout << "location delete in " << src << " at line "
      << line << " alloc " << (unsigned int)p << '\n';
  free(p);
}


//overloaded delete
void operator delete(void* p)
{
  cout << "overloaded delete alloc " << (unsigned int)p << '\n';
  free(p);
}


#define new  new(__FILE__,__LINE__)
```

```
class X
{
public:
  int *val;
  char filler[2];
  X() { val=NULL; }
  X(int x) {
    cout << "CON\n";          //entering constructor
    val = new int;
    *val = x;
    cout << "EXIT CON\n";     //exiting constructor
  }
  ~X() {
    cout << "DES\n";          //entering destructor
    delete val;
    cout << "EXIT DES\n";     //exiting destructor
  }
};//end class X

void doit();

// function main -----------------------------------------
int main()
{
  doit();
  return 0;
}//end main

// function doit -----------------------------------------
void doit()
{
  X x(32);
  cout << "address of object x is " << (unsigned int) &x << '\n';

  X *p = new X(33);
  cout << "p = " << (unsigned int) p << '\n';
  delete p;
}//end doit
```

Execution of the program will output something like this (of course, we added the annotations in [brackets]).

```
CON          [entering constructor for the auto object x]
location new in x.cpp at line 43 size 4 alloc 4391008
             [allocated x.val]
EXIT CON     [exiting constructor for the auto object x]
address of x is 1244952
location new in x.cpp at line 69 size 8 alloc 4398224
             [allocated p]
CON          [entering constructor for the dynamic object *p]
location new in x.cpp at line 43 size 4 alloc 4390960
             [allocated p->val]
EXIT CON     [exiting constructor for the dynamic object *p]
p = 4398224
DES          [entering destructor for *p]
overloaded delete alloc 4390960
             [deleted p->val]
EXIT DES     [exiting destructor for *p]
overloaded delete alloc 4398224
             [deleted p]
DES          [entering destructor for x]
overloaded delete alloc 4391008
             [deleted x.val]
EXIT DES     [exiting destructor for x]
done
```

As you can see, the global operator new has been replaced by the location operator new (due to the macro #define new new(__FILE__,__LINE__)), but the location operator delete apparently did not participate though the overloaded delete did. Unfortunately, as discussed in Chapter 8, the operator delete cannot be called explicitly in a program with place-ment syntax. This is why the global (and overloaded) delete is called instead. So why have the location delete at all? During construction of an object of class X, the compiler keeps track of which new is used; when an exception is thrown during the construction, the pieces constructed so far are destroyed using the appropriate delete. However, once the construction is completed, the information concerning which new was used is erased; hence the compiler has no way of selecting the appro-priate delete and thus the global one is used by default. To summarize: we have the location delete there just for the case of an exception dur-ing construction, and any other delete is performed by the overload of the global delete. So here is our first disappointment with the approach that worked so well with C. There is no simple way to have delete announce its location. Our second problem involves placement of the macro #define new new(__FILE__,__LINE__). If placed after the definition of the class X, then the new used in the constructor of X would not be location new. The picture can get even murkier, for we might have a class-specific new that we do not want to "modify" to the location new. In a given class there can actually be mixed use of new: in some places the global new is used and elsewhere the class-specific new is used. We might not want to "change" the former, but we might want to "change" the latter.

On the other hand, if we want each new to report its location and if we want to log and keep track of what is allocated (as in the debug version of malloc()), we would have to "change" not only the global operators but also every new and delete in all classes in the program – not an easy task. Since new and delete are operators and not (as in C) standard functions, they cannot be "replaced" and thus you have no chance of detecting memory leaks in external object code that is written in C++. And we have not even discussed new[] and delete[] yet. All these troubles arise because new and delete are operators (and hence a part of the language) – unlike in C, where the allocators are simply standard functions that can be plugged in or unplugged at will.

By now the reader must be convinced that, without significant changes to the C++ program being debugged for memory leaks, the task cannot be done. However, we can certainly employ certain programming strategies to produce a C++ code that at least facilitates reasonable tracing.

Mark an entry to any function using TRACE(function name). If the program is already written, a simple preprocessor can provide this. Mark every exit from a void function using RETURN and from a nonvoid function using RETURN1(..), and do not let the code "fall off" at the end of a function; use either RETURN or RETURN1. (Again, if it has not been done, a simple preprocessor can do it.) Thus we have each entry and exit of any function marked in a special way. Introduce a global variable char* LOC. For a production build, use

```
#define TRACE(a) LOC=#a;
#define RETURN return;
#define RETURN1(a) return(a);
#define FILELOC(0) LOC
```

Thus, for instance, for a production run

```
void doit()
{
  TRACE(doit)

  .... RETURN

  ....
  RETURN
}
```

will be preprocessed to

```
void doit()
{
  LOC="doit";

  .... return;

  ....
  return;
}
```

In the program we can use FILELOC(0) as a location reference for logging (if our system is supposed to provide logging in production runs); this will report the function in which the report is being made. The overhead during execution is minimal.

For a debugging run we can define

```
#define TRACE(a) push_on_stack(#a);
#define RETURN {pop_stack(); return;}
#define RETURN1(a) {pop_stack(); return(a);}
#define FILELOC(n) show_stack(n)
```

which will modify our example to

```
void doit()
{
  push_on_stack("doit");

  .... {pop_stack(); return;}
```

```
    ....
    {pop_stack(); return;}
}
```

We must now link the program that is being debugged with our additional debugging functions void push_on_stack(char*), void pop_stack(), and char* show_stack(int n). The role of the first two functions is self-explanatory; the function show_stack(n) returns the string that is located n positions from the top of the stack. In the program we can use as location references FILELOC(m) ... FILELOC(0), which will report the sequence of the last m calls in the correct order. The overhead during execution is not trivial, but this is for a debugging run and so performance is not an issue. FILELOC(m) ... FILELOC(0) together with __FILE__ and __LINE__ will give us a decent location reference for debug_malloc() and for location overloaded new and delete, while FILELOC(m) ... FILELOC(0) will give us a somewhat less decent location reference for overloaded delete.

For each class suspected of leaking memory, we can employ two strategies. In the first we overload its class-specific new and delete (as we did for the global operators) and then check the logs and the final statistics to determine if memory is leaking in these objects. In the second strategy we implement an "object counting" approach to see if there exist some objects that remain undeallocated. Which approach is more suitable depends on the circumstances. Generally speaking, the first strategy should be used if you suspect that memory is leaking somewhere in the destruction of the objects, whereas the latter one should be used if you suspect that memory is leaking on account of whole objects not being deallocated. In the worst case, both approaches can be combined.

Doing all of this for a large program that is leaking memory may prove to be quite laborious. It is thus highly advisable to design the program with these debugging features right from the start and to have these features turned on or off based on compilation flags (in this way, the program may be compiled either for a production build or for debugging).

Counting Objects in C++

Every object of a class must be constructed using one of the constructors, so it is a simple idea to have some kind of a counter that is incremented by the constructors every time they construct a new object of the class. Similarly, the destructor can decrement the counter every time it destroys an object. At termination of the program we can display a count of the remaining objects to determine if they leak or not.

The idea is simple, but its realization is more complex. Providing such a counter for a single class – and modifying all its constructors and the destructor to work with the counter – is not too complicated. But we do not want to do this for each class separately, so we need an approach that is a bit more sophisticated. (Of course, as before, we would like to be able to turn the counting on or off in a simple way that entails minimal overhead during the program's execution when it is turned off.) There are basically two approaches that feature a special class OBCOUNT, which takes care of the counting business. In the first approach, an OBCOUNT object is embedded in the definition of every class; in the second approach, each class to be part of the counting process is derived from class OBCOUNT. The former technique is a bit easier to understand, but its implementation requires more memory during execution and it is a bit awkward to turn on and off, so I have decided to discuss the latter approach here.

We want the class OBCOUNT to be usable with any class in our program, so we parameterize it with a template class X. This will allow us to make OBCOUNT class-specific for any class.

```
#ifdef _COUNT_ON
  class X;  //just for the compiler so it can deal with the template

  template <class X> class OBCOUNT
  {
  public:
    OBCOUNT() { count++; }
    OBCOUNT(const OBCOUNT& c) { count++; }
    ~OBCOUNT() { count--; }
  protected:
    static size_t count;
  };//end class OBCOUNT
#endif //_COUNT_ON
```

We then modify every class definition of a class that we are interested in counting as follows:

```
#ifdef _COUNT_ON
 class ACLASS : private OBCOUNT<ACLASS>
#else
 class ACLASS
```

```
#endif
{
public:
  ACLASS() { ... }
  ... //all other constructors
  ~ACLASS() { ... }
  #ifdef _COUNT_ON
    static void ReportCount() {
      cout << "ACLASS::count=" << count << '\n' << flush;
    }
  #endif
  ...
  ...
};//end class ACLASS

#ifdef _COUNT_ON
 size_t OBCOUNT<ACLASS>::count=0;  // define and init ACLASS counter
#endif
```

You can see the coding is straightforward, and if the counting is turned off (_COUNT_ON is not defined) then the class ACLASS has no overhead due to counting. There are two comments to be made, though. First, the reader may ask why the class ACLASS is derived from the class OBCOUNT as private. The reason is rather simple: we want to prevent having anywhere in our program a statement like delete p where OBCOUNT *p. By deriving ACLASS from OBCOUNT as private, the compiler will not allow such a statement. Had we not done so, we would have to provide a virtual destructor for OBCOUNT and thus greatly complicate our program. However, since OBCOUNT is there only for debugging purposes when the count is turned on, such statements should not be in our program anyway, so this restriction is a price we gladly pay. The second comment concerns the actual definition of the counter for the class ACLASS. Here we placed it right after the class definition, but if the class definition is in a header file included in many source files of our program, the compiler would complain. It has to be simply defined only once in the body of the program.

It is clear from our discussion that tracing memory leaks in C++ programs is not an easy task, primarily because memory allocation and deallocation is handled by operators that are a part of the language and are not outside entities like the standard allocators in C. The question of whether this could be designed differently is still being discussed within the C++ community. There is no simple answer, since unwinding the system stack after exceptions requires the compiler to know about the allocations and deallocation during construction of an object. The finer points of this discussion are not part of this book's focus, but I encourage the interested reader to get involved in the debate. On the other hand, C++ provides some powerful techniques that can be employed to detect or prevent memory leaks, as our example of object counting illustrates. There is one more topic that fits in this chapter and has a reasonable solution in C++: the problem of undetermined ownership.

Smart Pointers and the Undetermined Ownership Problem

As mentioned previously, the undetermined ownership problem is characterized by a module obtaining a dynamic object from some other module without also obtaining the ownership (i.e., the responsibility of deallocating it). In most cases a dynamic object is acquired through a reference – that is, a pointer. In this discussion we will call the ordinary pointers *naked pointers*. From the ownership point of view, a naked pointer has the following property: the default state is to "preserve untouched" the object it references when it goes out of scope, and if the object is to be deallocated then this must be done explicitly before the pointer goes out of scope. In many situations we would like to reverse things and have as the default the "destruction" of the object being referenced; then by some explicit means we could achieve "preserving" the object untouched when the pointer goes out of scope. This is the main idea behind *safe* or *smart pointers.*

Let us illustrate the concept of smart pointers for a class ACLASS, a kind of "wrapper" around the naked pointer.

```
class ACLASSPtr
{
public:
 ACLASSPtr(ACLASS *a) : naked_ptr(a) { } //init naked_ptr
 ~ACLASSPtr() { delete naked_ptr; }       //delete the object *naked_ptr
 ACLASS* operator->() const {             //define ACLASSPtr->
  return naked_ptr;
 }
 ACLASS& operator*() const {              //define *ACLASSPtr
  return *naked_ptr;
 }
private:
 ACLASS* naked_ptr;
};//end class ACLASSPtr
```

Let as assume that A is an object of type ACLASS and that a naked pointer p points to it. The instruction ACLASSPtr smartp(p) creates and initializes a smart pointer smartp referencing the same object as p. From now on in the program p->... and smartp->... give the same result, and so will *p and *smartp. The behavior of p and smartp are undistinguishable with one significant difference: when smartp goes out of scope, the object A will be deleted.

We could easily add the counting of objects of the class ACLASSPtr (as discussed previously) and allow deletion in the destructor only if it is the very last smart pointer pointing to A. This would provide us with an automatic system, almost a garbage collector, where objects referenced via smart pointers are destroyed when no longer referenced by any smart pointer. The least intrusive implementation uses linking of the smart pointers that reference the same object, which adds two more pointers to each smart pointer (prev points to the previous smart pointer pointing to the same object, and next points to the next smart pointer pointing to the same object). A construction of such a smart pointer must insert it in the appropriate list of smart pointers, and its destruction must delete it from the list.

In the form just illustrated, the smart pointers would not be too helpful because there are no means of passing them across function boundaries (either up using return or down as arguments). For that we need to augment our definition of ACLASSPtr by the appropriate copy constructor and assignment. For reference-counting smart pointers, both the copy constructor and the assignment must properly update the linked list of pointers pointing to the same object.

In programs with large number of objects referenced through smart pointers, the processing and memory overhead associated with reference counting may be significant. The fundamental idea of smart pointers is of course fraught with perils. If a smart pointer is made referencing an object on the stack or a static object, then any attempt to delete that pointer when it goes out of scope will result in a crash. If a single smart pointer were to reference an object that never goes out of scope (either because it is static or is dynamic and never deleted), then no object of class ACLASS would ever be deleted through a smart pointer. Thus, rather than automatic deletion based on reference count, we more often prefer smart pointers that transfer ownership so that there is just a single owner at any given moment. Usually the ownership transfer is achieved by zeroing the transferor, so when the transferor goes out of scope there is no object to be deleted. If we had some need for the transferor still to reference the object, then we could add an extra member (the ownership flag owner) to the definition of ACLASSPtr in order to indicate who is the owner. However, in both cases the principle of ownership transfer is the same, so the interested reader can easily modify the following code, which uses zeroing for ownership transfer, to a code that uses ownership flags.

```
ACLASS* Transfer() {      //provides transfer of ownership
  ACLASS* p = naked_ptr;  //by zeroing the transferor
  naked_ptr = 0;
  return p;
}

//copy constructor with the transfer of ownership
//since Transfer() modifies the transferor, we cannot
//have the usual (const ACLASSPtr& p) declaration of  the argument
ACLASSPtr (ACLASSPtr& p) : naked_ptr(p.Transfer()) { }

//assignment with the transfer of ownership
//since Transfer() modifies the transferor, we cannot
//have the usual (const ACLASSPtr& p) declaration of the argument
ACLASSPtr& operator= (ACLASSPtr& p) {
  if (naked_ptr != p.naked_ptr)
    delete naked_ptr;
  naked_ptr = p.Transfer();
  return *this;
}
```

It does not matter if we use static or dynamic smart pointers – as long as these "never go out of scope" smart pointers transfer the ownership. But it still is true that, if a smart pointer that is going out of scope references a static object or an object on the stack, a crash will ensue. However, a smart pointer as a local variable going out of scope in any fashion (including via stack unwinding after an exception) will delete the object it owns and thus yield code that is far more exception-safe than if the naked pointers were used. Moreover, the transfer of ownership using zeroing prevents smart pointers from dangling.

Smart pointers as discussed here are in essence the auto_ptr<X> defined in the C++ Standard Library. There it is implemented using templates, so it can be defined for any class X.

Review

Memory leaks can be caused by a variety of problems. Some are easy to detect and can be remedied in a simple way; some are difficult to detect yet can be easily remedied; and some are extremely difficult to detect and remedy.

1. The *orphaned allocation* problem applies to both C and C++ programs. Here the pointer to an allocated segment is not stored for later deallocation, but this can be easily rectified when detected and located.

2. The *hidden allocation* problem applies to both C and C++ programs and is caused by insufficient knowledge of what is being used – usually in the form of obtaining an object from another module without knowing that the object was allocated on the heap and that it should be deallocated. This problem can be rectified when detected and located, though changes in the code could be significant.

3. The *undetermined ownership* problem applies to both C and C++ programs and is caused by poor design and integration – usually in the form of obtaining a dynamic object from another module without assuming the responsibility for its deallocation. This problem can be rectified when detected and located, though changes in the code could be significant.

4. The *insufficient destructor* problem applies only to C++ programs. In this case there is usually no explicit destructor provided for a class that has some of its members created dynamically. Though relatively easy to rectify when detected and located, this problem is difficult to detect.

5. The *incorrect assignment* problem also applies to C++ programs only and is usually caused by a missing assignment for a class that has some members created dynamically. This problem can be rectified fairly easily once detected and located, but again it is the detection that is difficult.

6. The *exception-unsafe code* problem applies only to C++ programs. It usually takes the form of code that, when interrupted by an exception, does not properly clean up whatever has been allocated prior to the exception. This problem is quite difficult to detect and localize, and rectification requires a significant redesign of the code.

7. The *external component* problem applies to both C and C++ programs. There is not too much you can do about it besides contacting the external source or working around the problem.

Tracing memory leaks in C programs is relatively easy. Using the pre-processor, all calls to the C allocators and the deallocator can be transformed to calls to their respective debugging versions. These versions can keep track of the location from which they were called and/or log this information, and upon program termination they may display or log statistics concerning what remains undeallocated. Together with the location information, this helps detect and localize memory leaks. For a simple location reference the preprocessing directives __FILE__ and __LINE__ can be used. For a more detailed location reference, the entrances and exits of all functions must be marked by specialized functions that keep a global stack of names of functions being called. With replacement allocators and a replacement deallocator, even leaks in an external C-based object code can be traced.

Tracing memory leaks in C++ programs is much more complex, for two reasons. First, the allocators and deallocators in C++ are not (as in C) standard functions and hence cannot be unplugged and replaced; they are operators and as such are part of the language. Second, C++ programs may use any mixture of C allocators and the deallocator, global new and delete, class-specific new and delete, their array versions (new[]...) and possibly overloaded versions of all of these. In essence, the first reason explains why you cannot trace memory leaks from an external object code that is written in C++. With regard to the second reason, an approach similar to that used for C programs may be used for C++ programs: news and some deletes may be overloaded so as to become location-sensitive and provide tracking and/or logging of what has been allocated/deallocated by whom. However, unlike in C, such an effort will probably require significant modifications to the program.

A simple aid in tracing C++ memory leaks – one that requires only modest changes in the program and that can easily be turned on and off – may be obtained using object counting. Upon termination of the program, we can display or log statistics of how many objects remain undeallocated. The counting can be made location-sensitive (i.e., keeping track not only of how many objects were created but also where and/or when they were created).

The flexibility of C++ can be used to remedy the problem of undetermined ownership through the use of so-called safe or smart pointers. These are implemented in the C++ Standard Library in the form of auto_ptr<X>. Smart pointers are objects that behave like pointers with the additional property that their destructors deallocate the object they reference when the pointers go out of scope. If used in a disciplined way, smart pointers can prevent the undetermined ownership problem and also provide for an exception-safe design.

Exercises

10.1 Create a minimal C++ or C-based program that exhibits the orphaned allocation problem.

10.2 Create a minimal C++ or C-based program that exhibits the undetermined ownership problem. Then rectify the problem by using smart pointers.

10.3 Create a minimal C++ program that exhibits the insufficient destructor problem and then correct it.

10.4 Create a minimal C++ program that exhibits the incorrect assignment problem and then correct it.

10.5 Write a simple C program that performs some allocation and deallocation of memory, and make sure that it uses `realloc()`. Then use the techniques from this chapter to make all the memory handling functions location-sensitive (using `__FILE__` and `__LINE__`) and write into a log all memory transactions (you can use the logging functions from Appendix D).

10.6 Extend the program from Exercise 10.5 to include localization tracing by using a stack for function names (see Appendix C).

10.7 Write a simple C++ program incorporating smart pointers that use nonintrusive reference counting, and have them written into a log (you can use the logging functions from Appendix D).

References

Levine, D. L., Gill, C. D., and Schmidt, D. C., "Object Lifetime Manager – A Complementary Pattern for Controlling Object Creation and Destruction", in L. Rising (Ed.), *Design Patterns in Communication*, Cambridge University Press, 2000.

Milewski, B., *C++ in Action: Industrial-Strength Programming Techniques*, Addison-Wesley, Reading, MA, 2001.

Stroustrup, B., "Programming with Exceptions", *InformIt*, 2001; also at http://www.research.att.com/~bs/eh_brief.pdf.

Sutter, H., *Exceptional C++*, Addison-Wesley, Reading, MA, 2000.

Sutter, H., *More Exceptional C++: 40 New Engineering Puzzles, Programming Problems, and Solutions*, Pearson, Harlow, U.K., 2001.

MEMORY LEAKS AND THEIR DEBUGGING

Memory leaks from the programmer's point of view:

Batov, V., "Extending the Reference-Counting Pattern", *C/C++ Users Journal*, September 1998.

Batov, V., "Safe and Economical Reference-Counting in C++", *C/C++ Users Journal*, June 2000.

Colvin, G., "Smart Pointers for C++ Garbage Collection", *C/C++ Users Journal*, December 1995.

Doe, R. B., "How to Leak Memory in C++", *C/C++ Users Journal*, March 1997.

Gareau, J. L., "Tracking Memory Leaks under Windows CE", *C/C++ Users Journal*, February 2000.

Guisado, E., "Debugging Component-Based Memory Leaks", *C/C++ Users Journal*, January 2000.

Koenig, A., and Moo, B. E., "C++ Made Easier: Handles and Exception Safety, Part 1: A Simple Handle Class", *C/C++ Users Journal*, August 2002.

Koenig, A., and Moo, B. E., "C++ Made Easier: Handles and Exception Safety, Part 2: Intrusive Reference Counting", *C/C++ Users Journal*, October 2002.

Koenig, A., and Moo, B. E., "C++ Made Easier: Handles and Exception Safety, Part 3: Non-Intrusive Reference Counting", *C/C++ Users Journal*, December 2002.

Meyers, S., "Counting Objects in C++", *C/C++ Users Journal*, April 1998.

Ngai, K., "A Template for Reference Counting", *C/C++ Users Journal*, August 1997.

Schmidt, B., "Uncaught Exceptions: Remembrance", *C/C++ Users Journal*, May 2000.

Sutter, H., "Using auto_ptr Effectively", *C/C++ Users Journal*, October 1999.

Sutter, H., "The New C++: Smart(er) Pointers", *C/C++ Users Journal*, August 2002.

Trudell, B., "The Application Watchman Class", *C/C++ Users Journal*, July 2002.

Vlasceanu, C., "Generalizing the Concepts behind auto_ptr", *C/C++ Users Journal*, August 2001.

Wagner-Krankel, A., "Smart Pointers in C++", *C/C++ Users Journal*, August 1992.

White, R. G., "Copy-on-Write Objects for C++", *C/C++ Users Journal*, August 1991.

A major web portal concerning tools for detecting memory leaks and their debugging:

Zorn, B., "Debugging Tools for Dynamic Storage Allocation and Memory Management", `http://www.cs.colorado.edu/homes/zorn/public_html/MallocDebug.html`.

All sorts of postings on detecting and debugging memory leaks:

`http://search.microsoft.com/`.

Some related web-based material:

"C++ Tips: Exceptions", http://cpptips.hyperformix.com/Exceptions.html.

Jelovic, D., "C++ without Memory Errors", http://www.jelovic.com/articles/
cpp_without_memory_errors_slides.htm.

Mazières, D., "My Rant on C++'s Operator new",
http://www.scs.cs.nyu.edu/~dm/c++-new.html.

Sharon, Y., "Smart Pointers – What, Why, Which?",
http://ootips.org/yonat/4dev/smart-pointers.html.

"Writing Exception Safe Classes",
http://www.infrasoft.co.at/hn/exceptions.txt.

CHAPTER ELEVEN

PROGRAMS IN EXECUTION: PROCESSES AND THREADS

Environment and environment variables, command-line arguments and command-line argument structure. A process and its main attributes – user space and process image. Spawning a new process (UNIX fork() *system call) from the memory point of view. Principles of interprocess communication; System V shared memory segments and "shared memory leaks". Threads and lightweight processes; advantages and disadvantages of threads over processes. The need to protect the "common" data in threads. Memory leaks caused by careless multithreading.*

In this chapter we will complete the circle that took us through Chapters 2 to 10. This tour of the memory-related aspects of C and C++ programs started with a discussion of programs in execution and how their address spaces relate to memory. Most of what was said in Chapter 2 is not specific to C/C++ programs – it applies to all programs no matter what programming language is used for their creation. However, all the discussions in subsequent chapters assumed a reasonable understanding of that material. Here we return to examining the run-time environment of programs, but now with particular emphasis on the notions of *process* and *thread*. As in Chapter 2, most of this material is not specific to C/C++ programs, but an understanding of processes and threads is essential for development of software based on the C/C++ language. The run-time environment of a program is really a matter of the operating system. Nevertheless, when discussing processes and threads, we will focus on the fundamental concepts that are common across various operating systems. For examples (and when we must take the OS into account), we will assume UNIX as the operating system because I am more conversant with it than with any other OS.

A program executes in an *environment,* which consists of a block of named *environment variables* with string values. Through system calls the program can access an environment variable to fetch or modify its value. In a sense, an environment variable has the same relationship to a program as a global variable has to a function. The primary purpose of environment variables is to be set up appropriately (i.e., to create an appropriate environment) prior to the start of program execution.

Let us give a simple example: Our program is to read a file "file1" from a specialized directory. However, on different systems the specialized directory may be installed in different places. We can solve the problem by using an environment variable. The information concerning where the specialized directory is located will be stored in an environment variable called SPECDIR.

```
#include <stdio.h>
#include <stdlib.h>
char* p;
FILE* fp;
char pathname[100];
...
p = getenv("SPECDIR");          //get the pathname of spec. directory
sprintf(pathname,"%s/file1",p);//create pathname for the file
fp = fopen(pathname,"r");       //open the file
...
```

It is clear that, had the environment variable SPECDIR not been created and set properly prior to execution of our program, an error would have ensued. Our example used the UNIX system call getenv() to obtain a value of the environment variable. A corresponding system call putenv() can be used to set a value of an environment variable or to define a new environment variable and set its value. With UNIX, environment variables can be used for "interprogram" communication whereby a sequence of programs is executed within the same process: program A executes and, based on its execution, sets environment variables appropriately for a program B to use.

Where and how the actual values of the environment variables are stored depends on the operating system. It is therefore better to assume that they are not stored within the user space of your program. Do not try to manage or access the space directly; use exclusively the system calls to fetch or modify the values of environment variables or to create them. In some UNIX systems, getenv() returns the value in a static buffer, so use only one call to getenv() at a time. The corresponding Windows system calls are GetEnvironmentVariable and SetEnvironmentVariable, which employ a user-defined buffer to receive or pass the values.

Besides these environment variables, a C/C++ program has additional means of receiving some information when it is starting up. This feature is called *command-line arguments* because values for the arguments are part of invoking the program, usually in the form of a command. To run a program called prog and supply it with two arguments Arg1 and Ar2, in UNIX you type the command prog Arg1 Ar2 and hit enter; in Windows you click on Run, type the command into the dialog box that pops up, and then click on OK (or use the command prompt window and type in the command). If we instead want to run the program with three arguments A, B2, and C45, we use the command prog A B2 C45.

The operating system creates a structure very much like the dynamic two-dimensional array we discussed in Chapter 7; the only difference is that the "rows" are not necessarily of the same length. In each of the "rows", one argument (a string) is stored. Thus, prior to startup of the program prog using the command prog Arg1 Ar2, the operating system creates a command-line argument structure as depicted in Figure 11.1. If we invoke the program using the command prog A B2 C45, the operating system creates a different command-line argument structure; see Figure 11.2.

How is the command-line argument structure made available to our program, and how can our program access it? This is accomplished by way of two special arguments of the function main(): one is the int argument argc and the other is the char** (or, equivalently, char* []) argument argv. The pointer argv points to the beginning of the command-line argument structure, and (as explained in Chapters 6 and 7) argv[0],

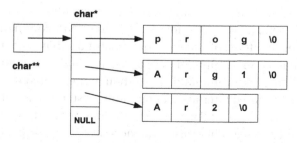

Figure 11.1   Command-line argument structure for prog Arg1 Ar2

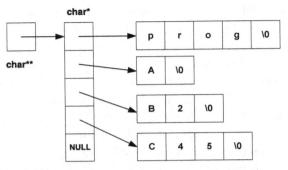

Figure 11.2   Command-line argument structure for prog A B3 C45

argv[1],... are strings in the individual "rows" of the structure. There are argc+1 rows in the structure, where the last one is empty to mark the end of the command-line structure even in the absence of argc. (It is traditional for the int argument of main() to be called argc and for the char** argument to be called argv, but of course they could be called anything.)

In some operating systems (e.g., Windows) the very first string is the pathname of the program; in some (e.g., UNIX) it is just the program name. In our diagrams we used the program name for simplicity. The second string is the first command-line argument, the third string is the second command-line argument, and so forth. The command-line argument structure thus always has at least two rows, the first one holding the name of the program being executed and the last one being empty. As far as storage for the command-line argument structure is concerned, whatever we have said for environment variables applies here as well. Therefore, you should not try to manage or access the memory directly; instead, treat it as read-only memory that is not really a part of your user space.

In an age of graphic user interfaces for operating systems, it is not clear why we need anything like command-line arguments, but it is clear from a historical perspective. Take for example the UNIX command cat file to display the contents of a file: it is quite natural to have the name of the target file passed to the program cat as a command-line argument, for it really is a part of the command. Even though it is rooted in the past era of character-oriented interfaces for operating systems, it is nevertheless a useful feature and so is still kept intact. Besides, it ought to remain intact for backward compatibility reasons alone – we still want our old programs to be executable under contemporary or future operating systems.

PROGRAMS IN EXECUTION: PROCESSES AND THREADS

What is a process and what is a thread cannot really be precisely defined without reference to the operating system. In UNIX, the process is the basic concept around which the operating system is built whereas the thread is a derived concept. In fact, UNIX features two kinds of threads: *lightweight processes,* which are threads scheduled and managed by the operating system; and *user threads* (or simply *threads*), which are scheduled and managed by the process itself and of which the operating system has no knowledge. On the other hand, for Windows the fundamental concept is the thread, and it is scheduled and managed by the operating system. For Windows the process is a derived concept – in fact, it is just a "bunch of threads" (possibly a single one) running within the same context (the same address space).

A popular definition of a process is "a program in execution". This is not very precise; for instance, UNIX distinguishes between a process and a program in execution because within a process you can switch to execute a different program. However, for our discussion the definition is reasonable and sufficient. The most important attributes of a process from our point of view are that (a) it has a unique user space in which the process image is stored and in which the process is running and (b) it has a unique *process ID.* In Chapter 2 we discussed the notion of program address space: the user space is the memory into which the address space is mapped, and the contents of that (i.e., the image of the address space) is often referred to as the process image. Thus every time the process is running on the processor, its process image is mapped to its user space; during context switching, the changes of the contents of the process image are recorded. Throughout the execution of a process, the exclusive relationships between the process and its image and its process ID are preserved.

In UNIX there is no system call to create a new process, so you can only duplicate the existing process through a system call fork(). Even though this may seem rather limiting, in fact it is more than sufficient. If we need two processes – one with behavior *A* and the other with behavior *B*, then we can write a program to create the desired variety of behavior along the following lines: function A() defines behavior *A*, and function B() defines behavior *B*. In main() we duplicate the process: one copy (the *parent process*) continues with the original process ID; the other copy (the *child process*) continues with an entirely new process ID. After fork() we put a test to determine whether A() is to be executed (if it is the parent process) or whether B() is to be executed (if it is a child). Until fork() there will only be a single process running, but after fork() there will be two processes running; the one with the original process ID will be exhibiting behavior *A* while the other exhibits behavior *B*. This technique can be used to create N different processes with N different types of behavior. This program could be coded as follows.

```c
#include <stdio.h>
#include <stdlib.h>
#include <string.h>
#include <sys/types.h>
#include <unistd.h>
#include "log.h"        //reporting and logging functions

void A();
void B();

/* function main --------------------------------------- */
void main()
{
  pid_t pid;

  printf("I am the process before fork(), my pid=%u\n",
         getpid());
  if ((pid = fork()) < 0)
    sys_exit("fork error");

  if (pid == 0)    // child process
    B();           // B does not return, it exits
  else             // parent process
    A();           // A does not return, it exits

}/* end main */

/* function A ------------------------------------------- */
void A()
{
  printf("I am doing A, my pid=%u\n",getpid());
  fflush(stdout);
  exit(0);

}/* end A */

/* function B ------------------------------------------- */
void B()
```

```
{
    printf("I am doing B, my pid=%u\n",getpid());
    fflush(stdout);
    exit(0);

}/* and B */
```

In this example we have used one of the reporting and logging functions presented in Appendix D, sys_exit(). If fork() did not work, then the program would be terminated and the error number (errno) would be translated to a corresponding error message. Here is some sample output from the program:

```
I am the process before fork(), my pid=8425
I am doing A, my pid=8425
I am doing B, my pid=8426
```

The careful reader may object that this approach is rather inefficient: even though the parent process is executing only the function A(), it still carries in its process image a complete code for the function B(), and the child process is executing only the function B() yet carries a complete code for A() in its process image. The objection is valid and, indeed, the program is inefficient with respect to storage requirements. Had the code for behavior A and behavior B been extensive, in real-world programming neither A() nor B() would carry a complete code for the alternate behavior. Instead, using one of the family of exec() system calls, A() would execute a program for behavior A and B() would execute a program for behavior B. The overhead would be minimal because the parent process would never execute the program for behavior B and the child process would never execute the program for behavior A. The exec() system calls replace the process image of the process currently running by the process image based on the address space of the program being executed.

Note how a process discovers whether it is the parent process or the child process: this is determined by the value returned by the system call fork(). For the child process, 0 is returned; for the parent process, the process ID of the newly created child process is returned.

From the memory point of view, fork() makes a copy of the process image of the current process and creates a new process with an identical copy of the process image as the original process. In the process image of the original process the return value of fork() is set to the process ID of the newly created process, while in the process image of the new process (otherwise a perfect copy of the original process image) the return value of fork() is set to 0. Hence all data values within the process image as computed up to the moment of fork() are the same for both processes; the only difference is the return value of fork(). Of course, after fork() each version of the process image has its own life, and what is happening in one is not happening in the other. An analogy of fork() as a photocopy machine and the process image as a picture might help. The existing picture is "photocopied". Then the original picture and the new copy are altered slightly (but in different ways). Though the pictures were identical immediately after photocopying, now they are slightly different. If the owner of the original picture (the parent process) makes some changes to his picture, they are not reflected in the copy (owned by the child process) and vice versa. Another way to visualize fork() is as if the original process image and the copy were running in physically separate sections of the memory. After fork(), they have no memory in common.

On the one hand, the total and physical separation of the user spaces of the two processes is a nice feature. We do not have to worry about the two processes trying to access the same memory location and work with the same data. If the parent process sets a variable to some value, we do not have to worry about the child process changing it. In OS terminology the two processes are not "sharing the memory as a resource". On the other hand, this separation prevents any straightforward communication (data exchange) between the two processes. How, for example, can the child process pass any data to its parent process? At best we can use the process image to pass some data from the original process (before it becomes the parent) to the child if the data is available prior to fork(), since the child "inherits" a perfect copy of the process image.

Interprocess communication is an important topic in operating systems. Although the actual implementation of each particular communication system is OS-dependent, they are usually based on similar ideas. The following brief overview of interprocess communication systems is based on these common approaches. It is most interesting for us that all (except the "signals") rely on memory as the medium facilitating the communication.

■ *Messages.* Both UNIX and Windows have this feature, and in Windows it is the fundamental approach to interprocess communication. The idea is straightforward: at some predetermined location in the memory that is accessible by all processes involved, a message is stored in a message queue. The recipient process (or processes) is "notified" and so can access the memory location and retrieve the message from there. Since the messaging system directly manages the memory for the message queues, this technique is not interesting from our point of view.

■ *Signals* – in UNIX, a kind of 1-bit message that cannot queue (simply a notification that some event has occurred). Because signals are defined by ANSI as a part of C, in Windows some signals are available: SIGABRT, SIGFPE, SIGILL, SIGINT, SIGSEGV, and SIGTERM. Since memory is not really involved, this technique also is not interesting from our point of view.

■ *Shared memory.* Again the idea is simple: a segment of memory is set aside and made available to both processes as an extension of their respective user spaces, and hence the image of its contents is an extension of their respective process images. So if one process stores some data in the shared memory segment, the other process will find it there. Of course, sharing a memory segment brings forth the problem of synchronization – for instance, we do not want a process to use data from the shared memory segment before the other process has finished its update. Most UNIX systems support the System V shared memory segments mechanism; in Windows, a similar effect can be achieved using memory-mapped files or memory-mapped page files. Since shared memory segments can "leak" profusely, we will discuss this topic in more detail later.

■ *Pipes.* Used in both UNIX and Windows for processes of common ancestry, this feature is based on a communication buffer created in a memory segment that is accessible to both processes. When the processes using the pipe terminate, the pipe "disappears" (such pipes are thus sometimes referred to as temporary pipes). When a pipe is established between two processes, one process writes into the pipe using the file system calls for writing while the other process reads the pipe using the file system calls for reading. In reality, the sender writes the data into the communication buffer of the pipe and the recipient reads it from the very same buffer. This creates some synchronization problems, including how long the recipient should wait on the pipe if there are no data (blocking versus nonblocking read), how long the sender should wait to write data into the pipe if the pipe is "full" (blocking versus nonblocking write), and how to emulate end-of-file. Pipes come in two varieties: duplex (bidirectional – the communication can flow both ways) and semi-duplex (unidirectional – the communication can flow only one way). Since the main issues in using pipes concern synchronization rather than memory, we will not discuss them any further.

■ FIFOs, or *named pipes*, are used in UNIX (and in some versions of Windows) for processes that may not be related. These are similar to pipes but have a fixed name that is used for access; they are usually implemented as communication buffers, one for each pair of communicating processes. As with pipes, both duplex and semi-duplex versions are available but neither is interesting from a memory standpoint.

Working with a shared memory segment exhibits some of the pitfalls of memory access discussed in previous chapters, most notably with respect to the overflow. If a program tries to store more data in a shared memory segment than can fit there and the boundary of the segment is exceeded, the whole spectrum of problems discussed in Chapter 3 can occur and result in an erratically behaving program. However, owing to the nature of the shared memory segments, the most likely outcome of the overflow is a memory access violation.

The main problem with shared memory segments is their "persistence". All memory dynamically allocated to a process is reclaimed by the operating system upon termination of the process. So even if a program has plenty of memory leaks, the system recovers immediately after program termination. This is not the case with shared memory segments. They remain until explicitly deallocated or until the next boot, and they can easily outlive the processes that created them. This leads to the most common problem with shared memory segments – the failure of a program to clean up. Shared memory segments can leak in a truly significant way. One real-world example is a database system under UNIX that relies on shared memory segments for communication with various clients. If the segments are not properly cleared away then eventually the system limit is reached and no new shared memory segments can be created; communication between the database system and its clients is no longer possible and the whole system grinds to a halt. I have seen this happen. It goes without saying that over the years my OS-course students have many times brought the entire system to a standstill through unremoved shared memory segments.

In the following example a shared memory segment is created, some data is stored in it, and some data is fetched from it. This is all simple. However, the reader should notice that – even prior to creating the shared memory segment – we took the care to remove it as long as the program terminates via exit(). The cleanup is provided by the atexit registered function cleanup.

```c
#include <stdio.h>
#include <stdlib.h>
#include <string.h>
#include <sys/types.h>
#include <unistd.h>
#include <sys/ipc.h>
#include <sys/shm.h>
#include "log.h"        //reporting and logging functions

void cleanup();

//variables for indexing of messages by logging functions
int logindex = 0;
int *logi = &logindex;

//variables for shared memory segments
int shmid = -1;             //id
void* shmaddr;              //address where it is attached
struct shmid_ds shmbuf;     //structure with info

/* function main ------------------------------------------- */
int main()
{

  int i;
  int *p;

  if (atexit(cleanup)<0)
    sys_exit("atexit error");

  if ((shmid = shmget(IPC_PRIVATE,100,S_IRUSR|S_IWUSR))<0)
    sys_exit("shmget error");
  else
    msg("shared memory segment of size 100 with id=%d created\n",
        shmid);
```

```
shmaddr = shmat(shmid,(const void *)0,S_IRUSR|S_IWUSR);
if (((int)(shmaddr)) == -1)
    sys_exit("shmat(%d,.....) error",shmid);
else
    msg("shared memory segment id=%d attached at address %u\n",
        shmid,shmaddr);

// store int 235 in it
p = shmaddr;
*p = 235;

//fetch the value from it
msg("int value stored in the shared memory segment is %d\n",*p);

exit(0);

}/* end main */

/* function cleanup ---------------------------------------- */
void cleanup()
{
 if (shmid >= 0) {
    if (shmctl(shmid,IPC_RMID,&shmbuf)<0)
        sys("shmctl(%d,IPC_RMID,...) error",shmid);
    else
        msg("shared memory segment id=%d removed\n",shmid);
 }

}/* end cleanup */
```

In UNIX, when a program is terminated by the operating system (colloquially speaking, the program has "crashed") it is always by means of a signal. It is possible to catch all signals and terminate the program through exit() in the signal handler. This strategy takes care of the cleanup of unwanted shared memory segments under almost all circumstances. Why "almost"? There are three signals that cannot be caught: SIGKILL, SIGSTOP, and SIGCONT. SIGSTOP makes the program pause, and SIGCONT wakes it up from the pause. Thus we need only worry about SIGKILL, which terminates the recipient process. If something terminates our program by sending it the SIGKILL signal, there is nothing we can do about it and the shared memory segment will remain in the system unremoved.

address space

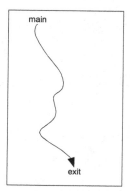

Figure 11.3   A single thread of execution

We observe (for the sake of completeness) that UNIX semaphores exhibit the same "persistence" as shared memory segments and should be treated similarly. The UNIX command `ipcs` allows the user to view statistics on all shared memory segments and semaphores of the whole system, while `ipcrm` allows users to remove manually the shared memory segments or semaphores that they own. Source code for the reporting and logging functions used within this chapter is presented and discussed in Appendix D. Since it utilizes shared memory segments, the code illustrates their use as well as some other UNIX programming concepts.

The term *thread* is short for *thread of execution*. When a program executes, the CPU uses the process program counter to determine which instruction to execute next. The resulting sequence of instructions is called the thread of execution. A thread is the flow of control in the process and is represented by the sequence of addresses of the instructions as they are being executed. We can visualize it as a path through the address space (see Figure 11.3).

In contrast to processes with their separate address spaces (process images), concurrency can be achieved within the same address space via the method of multiple threads. For illustration, imagine that the thread of execution of our process is a sequence $\{a_1, a_2, \ldots, a_{1000}\}$ of instruction addresses. Let us assume that the process is finished in three turns on the CPU: during the first turn, the process executes instructions with addresses $\{a_1, \ldots, a_{300}\}$; during the second turn, the process executes

address space

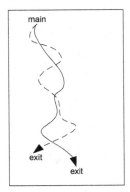

Figure 11.4   Two different threads of execution

the instructions with addresses $\{a_{301}, \ldots, a_{600}\}$, and during the third turn, the CPU executes the instructions with addresses $\{a_{601}, \ldots, a_{1000}\}$. This is single-thread executing. Now imagine that, at every turn, the process actually executes two different threads: in the first turn, the instructions $\{a_1, \ldots, a_{150}\}$ of thread A are executed and then instructions $\{a_1, \ldots, a_{150}\}$ of thread B; on the second turn, first the instructions $\{a_{151}, \ldots, a_{300}\}$ of thread A are executed and then instructions $\{a_{151}, \ldots, a_{300}\}$ of thread B; and so on – for six turns on the CPU. In essence, the same program is simultaneously executed twice with virtually no overhead for switching from one thread to another. If we ran the processes simultaneously, there would be a significant overhead in switching the context from one process to another. In a nontrivial program the flow of control is not simple, and the course of action is determined by the data being processed. It is thus clear that the two threads would actually differ, since the one executing slightly later would be encountering different data. For a visualization of multiple threads, see Figure 11.4.

The overhead for switching from one thread to another is virtually nil: we need only store the next instruction address of thread A somewhere and restore the program counter to the saved next instruction address of thread B. There is nevertheless a penalty for using threads – now, when two or more threads are using the same address space, we face real problems with the synchronization and protection of data integrity. Take the following simple example of a "for" loop:

```
...
for(i = 0; i < 100; i++) {
  ...
}
i = 0;
...
```

If we are not careful and hence thread A gets past the loop before thread B, it will reset the value of i before it reaches 100 in thread B and as a result the loop will start anew in thread B. In fact, as long as both threads can use the "same" i, the loop may end up a total mess.

Can careless multithreading lead to memory leaks? Let us examine the following simple multithreaded program:

```c
#include <stdio.h>
#include <stdlib.h>
#include <string.h>
#include <pthread.h>
#include "log.h"

//variables for indexing of messages by logging functions
int logindex=0;
int *logi = &logindex;
//thread mutex lock for access to the log
pthread_mutex_t tlock = PTHREAD_MUTEX_INITIALIZER;

void* doit(void*);
char* p = 0;
pthread_t tid1, tid2;

// function main  -----------------------------------------
int main()
{
  create_log("log.txt");

  Msg("going to create the first thread");
  pthread_create(&tid1,NULL,doit,NULL);

  Msg("going to create the second thread");
  pthread_create(&tid2,NULL,doit,NULL);
```

```
    Msg("going to wait for the first thread to exit");
    pthread_join(tid1,NULL);
    Msg("the first thread exited");

    Msg("going to wait for the second thread to exit");
    pthread_join(tid2,NULL);
    Msg("the second thread exited");

    exit(0);

}//end main

// function doit ------------------------------------------
void* doit(void* x)
{
    pthread_t me;

    me = pthread_self();
    Msg("I am thread %u (p=%u)",me,p);

    p = malloc(10);
    Msg("I am thread %u and I allocated segment %u",me,p);
    if (me==tid1)  // allow thread B to do the
      sleep(2);    // allocation and deallocation

    if (p) {
      free(p);
      Msg("I am thread %u and I deallocated segment %u",
          pthread_self(),p);
      p = NULL;
    }

    pthread_exit(NULL);
    return NULL;

}//end doit
```

Here is log.txt, the log created by the program:

```
message number = 0, process id = 19560, time and date = 21:39:16 01/12/03
 going to create the first thread
message number = 1, process id = 19560, time and date = 21:39:16 01/12/03
 going to create the second thread
```

```
message number = 2, process id = 19560, time and date = 21:39:16 01/12/03
  going to wait for the first thread to exit
message number = 3, process id = 19560, time and date = 21:39:16 01/12/03
  I am thread 4 (p=0)
message number = 4, process id = 19560, time and date = 21:39:16 01/12/03
  I am thread 4 and I allocated segment 151072
message number = 5, process id = 19560, time and date = 21:39:16 01/12/03
  I am thread 5 (p=151072)
message number = 6, process id = 19560, time and date = 21:39:16 01/12/03
  I am thread 5 and I allocated segment 151096
message number = 7, process id = 19560, time and date = 21:39:16 01/12/03
  I am thread 5 and I deallocated segment 151096
message number = 8, process id = 19560, time and date = 21:39:18 01/12/03
  the first thread exited
message number = 9, process id = 19560, time and date = 21:39:18 01/12/03
  going to wait for the second thread to exit
message number = 10, process id = 19560, time and date = 21:39:18 01/12/03
  the second thread exited
```

It is quite clear that the segment with address 151072 has never been deallocated; hence we have a memory leak.

Now let us make a simple change in our program and move the global definition char* p = NULL; inside the function doit(). As a result, p is no longer a global variable but rather a local variable in doit(). Let us run the program again and examine the log:

```
message number = 0, process id = 20254, time and date = 21:55:48 01/12/03
  going to create the first thread
message number = 1, process id = 20254, time and date = 21:55:48 01/12/03
  going to create the second thread
message number = 2, process id = 20254, time and date = 21:55:48 01/12/03
  going to wait for the first thread to exit
message number = 3, process id = 20254, time and date = 21:55:48 01/12/03
  I am thread 4 (p=0)
message number = 4, process id = 20254, time and date = 21:55:48 01/12/03
  I am thread 4 and I allocated segment 151024
message number = 5, process id = 20254, time and date = 21:55:48 01/12/03
  I am thread 5 (p=0)
message number = 6, process id = 20254, time and date = 21:55:48 01/12/03
  I am thread 5 and I allocated segment 151048
message number = 7, process id = 20254, time and date = 21:55:48 01/12/03
  I am thread 5 and I deallocated segment 151048
message number = 8, process id = 20254, time and date = 21:55:50 01/12/03
  I am thread 4 and I deallocated segment 151024
```

```
message number = 9, process id = 20254, time and date = 21:55:50 01/12/03
  the first thread exited
message number = 10, process id = 20254, time and date = 21:55:50 01/12/03
  going to wait for the second thread to exit
message number = 11, process id = 20254, time and date = 21:55:50 01/12/03
  the second thread exited
```

This time both segments have been deallocated and no memory is leaking. The explanation for the difference is simple. In the first run, the first thread allocated the segment and saved the address in the global variable p. Then we let it sleep for 2 seconds in order to mess up the synchronization and allow the second thread to do both the allocation and deallocation. After the second thread finished the deallocation, it set the pointer p to NULL. When the first thread woke up from sleep and got to the "if" statement, no deallocation took place because the value of p was NULL. In fact this problem is quite common (though of course not in such a simple form, but identical in principle), yet the memory leaks associated with it manifest themselves only occasionally. If the first thread succeeded in freeing p before the second thread allocated its segment, there would be no memory leak and all would be well (the purpose of the sleep(2) call in our program was exactly to keep it from accidentally running without a memory leak).

Should we not prevent such leaks by simply enforcing the rule "do not allocate/deallocate memory in more than one thread"? This might be too drastic and would limit the usefulness of multithreading. Besides, in the second run of our sample program, when p was a local variable, everything was in order and no memory leaked. The explanation is again rather simple: each thread requires its own system stack (else function calls would be a total mess) and thus all auto variables are private to each thread. The problem of simultaneous access to memory by different threads is a concern for static objects only.

In Chapter 10 we discussed the concept of smart pointers in C++ programs. It is not too complicated to include the thread ID in the ownership information. In such a form, thread-safe smart pointers can prevent the undetermined ownership problem from occurring even if one thread allocates something while another thread is using it. But it is always better not to design programs in such a convoluted way in the first place.

The rules of thumb for memory allocation and deallocation in a multithreaded program can be stated as follows.

- Never use static objects to reference dynamically allocated memory in a thread.
- If a thread A allocated memory that is supposed to be deallocated, then the deallocation should be the responsibility of the same thread A; otherwise, we can easily create the undetermined ownership problem (as discussed in Chapter 10).
- It is not a good idea to have a dynamic object created by thread A and used by thread B, since this too can easily create the undetermined ownership problem.

Review

A program executes in a particular environment that consists of environment variables, which have the same relationship to a program as global variables have to a function. The purpose of environment variables is to set up an appropriate environment for program execution, and they also represent a possible data input into a program. Most operating systems provide the programmer with system calls to create environment variables and to set or fetch their values.

Besides environment variables, C/C++ programs have other means of receiving small amounts of data upon startup in the form of command-line arguments. The operating system creates a dynamic structure that is akin to a dynamic two-dimensional array, and one of the command-line arguments (words) is stored as a string in each of the "rows" of the structure. The very first row carries the program pathname and the very last one is empty. A C/C++ program receives this structure via the char** (or equivalently the char* []) argument of the function main().

A process is a fundamental concept in UNIX, while in Windows it is a concept derived from the fundamental concept of thread. A simple definition of a process is "a program in execution", though in UNIX they mean slightly different things. The UNIX system call fork() is used to create a copy of a running process (of its process image) and install it as a new process. The original process is then called the parent process while the new process is called the child process. The respective process images are almost identical; the only difference is that in the parent process the return value of fork() is the process ID of the child process, whereas in the child process this value is 0. The return value of fork() is used to determine whether a given process is the parent or the child. Even though no new processes can be created directly in UNIX, this mechanism suffices for all practical purposes. In Windows, a new process can be created by a proper system call without being a copy of the parent process. The same effect is achieved in UNIX by using one of the exec() calls to switch to the execution of a different program within the same process. From our point of view, two attributes of a process – the uniqueness of the process image and the process ID – are of interest and are maintained throughout the life span of the process. Because the user spaces of the two processes are completely and physically separated, there is no reason to worry about simultaneous access of the two processes to data stored in the memory. However, this separation prevents the processes from communicating and exchanging data. For that purpose, special interprocess communication systems must be provided. These may be summarized as follows.

- *Messages* – message queues are used in both UNIX and Windows; they use memory to store messages where the recipient processes can find them. The memory for messages is explicitly controlled by the messaging system.
- *Signals* – a kind of 1-bit message that cannot queue; a notification that some event happened. No memory is involved.
- *Shared memory* – a memory segment is made available to several processes, and it becomes an extension of their respective user spaces and can be accessed like "ordinary" memory. The shared memory segments can be very persistent (i.e., can outlive the process that created them) and can leak in a significant way. Under almost all circumstances, simple programming techniques can be used to prevent the leaks.
- *Pipes,* or *temporary pipes* – usually are implemented as memory buffers accessible by two related processes; they allow one process to write into the pipe and the other process to read from the pipe. Besides the buffer residing in memory, no memory handling is involved. The pipes can be unidirectional or bidirectional.
- *FIFOs,* or *named pipes* – like the temporary ones, but these can be used for unrelated processes and are accessed (like files) using a fixed name.

The term "thread" is derived from "thread of execution", which is represented by a sequence of instruction addresses as they are being executed. It is possible to run more than one thread within the same context (the same address space). The flow of control depends on the data being processed, and two threads are usually not identical because the latter may encounter different data. In UNIX, the so-called lightweight process consists of threads that are scheduled and controlled by the operating system, whereas user threads are scheduled and controlled by the process and so the operating system is not aware of them. On the other hand, threads in Windows are scheduled and controlled by the operating system. Like processes, threads are used to implement concurrent processing. Two of the advantages of threads are (i) the virtually nonexistent overhead for switching from one thread to another and (ii) the fact that only one process image (address space) needs to be maintained, whereas for processes two images must be maintained at the possibly significant cost of disk space and/or memory. The disadvantage of threads is that all kinds of resources are shared by the threads, compelling us to synchronize the threads and to provide protection for both the code (critical sections) and the data (mutexes). Careless multithreading can lead to memory leaks, but a proper programming approach can easily prevent this.

Exercises

11.1 A shared memory segment cannot be extended. Write a C program that has, as an argument, an attached shared memory segment and some data. This program will create and attach a new and bigger shared memory segment. It will copy the data from the old shared memory segment to the new one and will also store there the additional data. It will then detach from the old memory segment and destroy it. It essentially does the same as `realloc()` when that function cannot physically extend a memory segment. Here, though, there are some synchronization problems that `realloc()` does not have to deal with. First, your program must "lock" the segment for the duration so that no other process can use it. Then it must make sure that all other processes know that the segment "has moved" and "where". Try to complete this exercise using semaphores and shared memory segments only.

11.2 Write a simple C program that forks one or more child processes. Use the logging functions from Appendix D, but do not create a shared memory segment for `logi`. Create a single log before the very first `fork()` so that all the child processes will inherit it. Check the log and the sequential numbers of messages from all the processes involved.

11.3 Repeat Exercise 11.2 with one change: let the program create a shared memory segment before the first `fork()` and let `logi` point to it.

Check the log and the sequential numbers of messages from all the processes involved. Compare this with the log from Exercise 11.2.

11.4   Repeat Exercise 11.2 with the following change: each child process will open its own and different log after the fork(). Compare the logs.

11.5   Write a simple multithreaded C program in which one thread creates a dynamic object and a different thread deallocates it. What kind of "communication" must take place?

11.6   Write a simple multithreaded C++ program using smart pointers that are "thread aware" – that is, deallocation takes place only in the thread that is the "owner".

11.7   Write a simple multithreaded C program in which some linked data structure is built and then the data structure is destroyed. Deliberately write the program so that a memory leak can occur. Your program should be a more sophisticated version of the example from this chapter.

References

Reeves, R. D., *C++/C# Programmer's Guide for Windows 2000*, Prentice-Hall, Englewood Cliffs, NJ, 2002.

Robbins, K. A., and Robbins, S., *Practical UNIX Programming, A Guide to Concurrency, Communication, and Multithreading*, Prentice-Hall, Englewood Cliffs, NJ, 1996.

Stevens, W. R., *Advanced Programming in the UNIX Environment*, Addison-Wesley, Reading, MA, 1992.

Stevens, W. R., *UNIX Network Programming, Interprocess Communications*, vol. 2, Prentice-Hall, Englewood Cliffs, NJ, 1999.

Tracing memory leaks, objects, processes, and threads from the programmer's point of view:

Broadman, A., and Shaw, E., "Executing a Class Member in Its Own Thread", *C/C++ Users Journal*, December 1999.

Calkins, C., "Integrating Threads with Template Classes", *C/C++ Users Journal*, May 2000.

Chaudhry, P., "Per-Thread Singleton Class", *C/C++ Users Journal*, May 2002.

Freda, W. J., "UNIX Interprocess Communications", *C/C++ Users Journal*, November 1990.

Freed, A., "Guidelines for Signal Processing Applications in C", *C/C++ Users Journal*, September 1993.

Halladay, S., and Wiebel, M., "A Practical Use for Multiple Threads", *C/C++ Users Journal*, January 1992.

Manley, K., "Improving Performance with Thread-Private Heaps", *C/C++ Users Journal*, September 1999.

Plauger, D., "Making C++ Safe for Threads", *C/C++ Users Journal*, February 1993.

Richards, E., "Adding Level-2 Thread Safety to Existing Objects", *C/C++ Users Journal*, February 1999.

Sutter, H., "Optimizations That Aren't (In a Multithreaded World)", *C/C++ Users Journal*, June 1999.

Weisfeld, M., "Synchronizing Processes Using Critical Sections", *C/C++ Users Journal*, September 1992.

Weisfeld, M., "A Synchronization Class Using Critical Sections", *C/C++ Users Journal*, November 1995.

Weisfeld, M., "Building Command Lines for Child Processes", *C/C++ Users Journal*, November 1996.

Texts concerning debugging in general:

Bugg, K., *Debugging Visual C++ Windows*, CMP Books, Gilroy, CA, 1998.

Ford, A. R., and Teorey, T. J., *Practical Debugging in C++*, Prentice-Hall, Englewood Cliffs, NJ, 2002.

Lencevius, R., *Advanced Debugging Methods*, Kluwer, Dordrecht, 2000.

Pappas, C. H., and Murray, W. H. III, *Debugging C++: Troubleshooting for Programmers*, McGraw-Hill, New York, 2000.

Robbins, J., *Debugging Applications*, Microsoft Press, Redmond, WA, 2000.

HANOI TOWERS PUZZLE

In Chapter 5 we discussed recursion and mentioned the Hanoi towers puzzle and its recursive solution. For completeness we include a simple C program to solve the problem. The puzzle consists of three pegs, with wooden disks stacked on one. The disks are of different sizes. The only rule of the game is that a bigger disk can never rest atop a smaller one. The task is to move all the disks from the leftmost peg to the rightmost peg – with the aid of the middle peg (see Figure A.1). We shall refer to the peg from which we are moving the disks as *origin*, the peg to which we must move the disks as *destination*, and the peg we can use in the interim as *help*.

origin **help** **destination**

Figure A.1   Hanoi towers puzzle

HANOI TOWERS PUZZLE

The recursive solution is based on the following observations. Moving two disks is easy (the top disk to help, the bottom disk to destination, the top disk to destination on top of the bottom disk). Moving three disks is also easy: pretend that the bottom disk is a part of the base; move the remaining two disks from origin to help using destination (easy to do, we did two disks just a few sentences back); now we have two disks nicely stacked on help; move the remaining third disk from origin to destination and pretend that it is a part of the base; now move two disks from help to destination using empty origin. And so on, ... More generally: To move n disks from origin to destination using help, we move the top $n - 1$ disks from origin to help using destination, then the remaining disk from origin to destination, then the remaining $n - 1$ from help (using origin) to destination.

The C program presented is rather simple (no graphics), but it does represent the pegs "graphically" on the screen in a schematic way. After each move, the program pauses and waits for the user to hit "enter" and so continue to the next move.

```
#include <stdio.h>
#include <string.h>
#include <stdlib.h>

#define HEIGHT 10

typedef int PEG[HEIGHT];

PEG A, B, C;

void set_pegs(int nofdisks);
void ht(int nofdisks,PEG origin,PEG help,PEG destination);
int remove_top(PEG peg);
void put_top(PEG peg,int disk);
void move(PEG from,PEG to);
void show_pegs(void);
char *make_disk(int disk);

/* function main ------------------------------------------------- */
int main(int argc,char** argv)
{
  if (argc != 2) {
    printf("usage - %s <nofdisks>\n",argv[0]);
    exit(1);
  }
```

```
if (sscanf(argv[1],"%d",&nofdisks) != 1) {
  printf("number of disks must be 2 - %d\n",HEIGHT);
  exit(0);
}

if (nofdisks < 2 || nofdisks > HEIGHT) {
  printf("number of disks must be 2 - %d\n",HEIGHT);
  exit(0);
}

set_pegs(nofdisks);
show_pegs();
ht(nofdisks,A,B,C);
printf("done\n");
return 0;

}/*end main*/

/* function set_pegs -------------------------------- */
void set_pegs(int nofdisks)
{
 int i;

 if (nofdisks > HEIGHT) {
   printf("too many disks (%d) for the height of the pegs (%d)\n",
          nofdisks,HEIGHT);
   exit(1);
 }

 for(i = 0;  i < HEIGHT;  i++)
    A[i] = B[i] = C[i] = -1;

 for(i = 0;  i < nofdisks;  i++)
    A[i] = nofdisks-1-i;

}/* end set_pegs */

/* function ht ------------------------------------------- */
void ht(int nofdisks,PEG origin,PEG help,PEG destination)
{
 if (nofdisks == 2) {   // base case
   move(origin,help);
   show_pegs();
   move(origin,destination);
```

```c
      show_pegs();
      move(help,destination);
      show_pegs();
      return;
   }

   // recursion
   ht(nofdisks-1,origin,destination,help);
   move(origin,destination);
   show_pegs();
   ht(nofdisks-1,help,origin,destination);

}/* end ht */

/* function remove_top ---------------------------------- */
int remove_top(PEG peg)
{
 int i, res;

 for(i = 0; i < HEIGHT; i++)
  if (peg[i] == -1) break;

 if (i == 0) {
   printf("peg is empty\n");
   exit(0);
 }

 i--;
 res = peg[i];
 peg[i] = -1;
 return res;

}/* end remove_top */

/* function put_top ------------------------------------ */
void put_top(PEG peg,int disk)
{
 int i;

 for(i = 0; i < HEIGHT; i++)
  if (peg[i] == -1) break;

 if (i == HEIGHT) {
   printf("peg is full\n");
```

```
   exit(1);
 }

 peg[i] = disk;

}/* end put_top */

/* function move ------------------------------------------ */
void move(PEG from,PEG to)
{
 int disk;

 disk = remove_top(from);
 put_top(to,disk);

}/* end move */

/* function show_pegs ----------------------------------- */
void show_pegs(void)
{
 int i;

 for(i = HEIGHT-1; i >= 0; i--) {
  printf("%s",make_disk(A[i]));
  printf("  %s",make_disk(B[i]));
  printf("  %s\n",make_disk(C[i]));
 }

 printf("%s",make_disk(-2));
 printf("  %s",make_disk(-2));
 printf("  %s\n",make_disk(-2));
 fflush(stdout);
 getchar();
 fflush(stdin);

}/* end show_pegs */

/* function make_disk ----------------------------------- */
char *make_disk(int disk)
{
 static char buf[26];
 int i, j;

 if (disk == -2)    /* make base */
   strcpy(buf,"HHHHHHHHHHHHHHHHHHHHHHHHH");
```

```
   else if (disk == -1)    /* make peg */
     strcpy(buf,"             |              ");
   else{
     for(j = 0; j < 1+HEIGHT-disk; buf[j++] = ' ');
      for(i = 0; i <= disk; buf[j++] = '=',i++);
       buf[j++] = '|';
       for(i = 0; i <= disk; buf[j++] = '=',i++);
       for(i = 0; i < 1+HEIGHT-disk; buf[j++] = ' ',i++);
       buf[j] = '\0';
   }

   return buf;
}/* end make_disk */
```

TRACING OBJECTS IN C++

In Chapter 10 we discussed some possible strategies for tracing memory leaks in C++ programs. In the following code we illustrate both localization tracing and object tracing. The program itself is the file count.cpp.

```cpp
extern "C" {
  #include <stdio.h>
  #include <string.h>
  #include <stdlib.h>
  #include "trace.hpp"
}

#ifdef _OBTRACE_ON
  #include "obtrace.hpp"
#endif

#ifdef _OBTRACE_ON
  class XClass : private OBTRACE<XClass>
#else
  class XClass
#endif
```

```cpp
{
public:
  XClass() { value=0; }
  XClass(int i) { value=i;}
  #ifdef _OBTRACE_ON
    // method ReportAll -------------------------------------
    static void ReportAll() {
      OBTRACE<XClass>::ReportAll(stdout,"XClass");
    }end ReportAll


    // method ReportCount -----------------------------------
    static void ReportCount() {
      OBTRACE<XClass>::ReportCount(stdout,"XClass");
    }end ReportCount
  #endif // _OBTRACE_ON

protected:
  int value;

};//end class XClass

#ifdef _OBTRACE_ON
  class YClass : private OBTRACE<YClass>
#else
  class YClass
#endif
{
public:
  YClass() { string[0]='\0'; }
  YClass(char* p) { strcpy(string,p); }

  #ifdef _OBTRACE_ON
    // method ReportAll -------------------------------------
    static void ReportAll() {
      OBTRACE<YClass>::ReportAll(stdout,"YClass");
    }//end ReportAll

    // method ReportCount -----------------------------------
    static void ReportCount() {
      OBTRACE<YClass>::ReportCount(stdout,"YClass");
    }//end ReportCount
  #endif // _OBTRACE_ON
```

```
protected:
  char string[10];

}//end class YClass

#ifdef _OBTRACE_ON
  char* OBTRACE<XClass>::init=NULL;
  char* OBTRACE<YClass>::init=NULL;
#endif

XClass ox1(2);
YClass oy1("hello");

// function doit1 -------------------------------------
int doit1()
{
 TRACE(doit1)

 XClass* ox2 = new XClass(12);
 //delete ox2;

 RETURN1(1)

}//end doit1

// function doit2 -------------------------------------
void doit2()
{
 TRACE(doit2)

  XClass ox3(3);
  XClass* ox4 = new XClass(0);

  doit1();

  //delete ox4;
  YClass* oy2 = new YClass("by");
  #ifdef _OBTRACE_ON
    YClass::ReportCount();
  #endif

  //delete oy2;

  RETURN
}//end doit2
```

```
#ifdef _OBTRACE_ON
   void Report()
   {
     XClass::ReportAll();
     YClass::ReportAll();
   }
#endif

// function main ---------------------------------------------
int main()
{
 TRACE(main)

 #ifdef _OBTRACE_ON
   atexit(Report);
 #endif

 doit2();

 RETURN1(0)

}//end main
```

Let us examine what is in the program. Two classes, XClass and YClass, are defined – just simple classes, for we are mainly interested in tracing them. Note that each entry to a function is marked with TRACE(name) and that each return from a function is RETURN whereas each return with a value of an expression is RETURN1(expression). Observe also that no ; is used after these "commands". We #included our own header file for tracing, trace.hpp:

```
#ifndef _TRACE_HPP
#define _TRACE_HPP

extern "C" {
 #include <stdio.h>
 #include <string.h>
 #include <stdlib.h>
}

#ifdef _TRACE_ON
  extern "C" {
```

```
      extern void POP_TRACE();
      extern void PUSH_TRACE(char*);
      extern char* REPORT_TRACE(int);
    }
    #define TRACE(a) PUSH_TRACE(#a);
    #define RETURN { POP_TRACE(); return; }
    #define RETURN1(a) { POP_TRACE(); return(a); }
    #define REPORT() REPORT_TRACE(3)
  #else
    char* TRACELOC="global";
    #define TRACE(a) TRACELOC=#a;
    #define RETURN return;
    #define RETURN1(a) return(a);
    #define REPORT() TRACELOC
  #endif

  #endif    // _TRACE_HPP
```

This means that if our program count.cpp is compiled without defining
_TRACE_ON, our tracing will consist simply of setting the global variable
TRACELOC to the function's name (thus a call from function A to function B
will reset the name to B and on the return to A it will still be B). RETURN and
RETURN1 are each defined as an ordinary return. On the other hand, if our
program count.cpp were compiled with a definition of _TRACE_ON, then
TRACE would translate to pushing the name onto the stack of function
names, RETURN would translate to popping the stack of function names
and then plain return, and RETURN1(exp) would translate to popping the
stack of function names and then plain return(exp). These functions are
defined in the source file trace.c, which must be compiled and linked
with our program.

```
#include <stdio.h>
#include <string.h>

// the function trace stack is a simple linked list of
// pointers to function identifiers
// the head of the list is the top of the stack
struct TRACE_NODE_STRUCT {
  char* floc;                         // ptr to function identifier
  struct TRACE_NODE_STRUCT* next;  // ptr to next frame
};
```

TRACING OBJECTS IN C++

```
typedef struct TRACE_NODE_STRUCT TRACE_NODE;
static TRACE_NODE* TRACETop = NULL; //ptr to top of the stack

/* function PUSH_TRACE -------------------------------------- */
void PUSH_TRACE(char* p)              // push p on the stack
{
  TRACE_NODE* tnode;
  static char glob[]="global";

  if (TRACETop==NULL) {
    // initialize the stack with "global" identifier

    TRACETop=(TRACE_NODE*) malloc(sizeof(TRACE_NODE));

    // no recovery needed if allocation failed, this is only
    // used in debugging, not in production
    if (TRACETop==NULL) {
      printf("PUSH_TRACE: memory allocation error\n");
      exit(1);
    }

    TRACETop->floc = glob;
    TRACETop->next=NULL;
  }
  // now create the node for p

  tnode = (TRACE_NODE*) malloc(sizeof(TRACE_NODE));

  // no recovery needed if allocation failed, this is only
  // used in debugging, not in production
  if (tnode==NULL) {
    printf("PUSH_TRACE: memory allocation error\n");
    exit(1);
  }

  tnode->floc=p;
  tnode->next = TRACETop;   // insert fnode as the 1st in the list
  TRACETop=tnode;           // point TRACETop to the first node

}/*end PUSH_TRACE*/

/* function POP_TRACE -------------------------------------- */
void POP_TRACE()    // remove the op of the stack
```

```
{
  TRACE_NODE* tnode;
  tnode = TRACETop;
  TRACETop = tnode->next;
  free(tnode);

}/*end POP_TRACE*/

/* report 'depth' top entries from the stack in the form
   fun1:fun2:fun3:....:funk  meaning fun1 called from fun2
   that was called from fun3 ... that was called from funk
   where k = depth
   The calling path may be up to 100 characters, if longer
   it is truncated  */

/* function REPORT_TRACE ----------------------------------- */
char* REPORT_TRACE(int depth)
{
  int i, length, j;
  TRACE_NODE* tnode;
  static char buf[100];

  if (TRACETop==NULL) {   // stack not initialized yet, so we
    strcpy(buf,"global"); // are still in the 'global' area
    return buf;
  }

  /* peek at the depth top entries on the stack, but do not
     go over 100 chars and do not go over the bottom of the
     stack */

  sprintf(buf,"%s",TRACETop->floc);
  length = strlen(buf);   // length of the string so far
  for(i=1, tnode=TRACETop->next;
                      tnode!=NULL && i<depth;
                                  i++,tnode=tnode->next) {
    j = strlen(tnode->floc);   // length of what we want to add
    if (length+j+1 < 100) {    // total length is ok
      sprintf(buf+length,":%s",tnode->floc);
      length += j+1;
    }else                      // it would be too long
      break;
  }
```

```
    return buf;
}/* end RPORT_TRACE */
```

The stack in trace.c is as simple as possible – a linked list, with the top of the stack as the head of the list. The location is reported in the form fun1:fun2:...:funK, meaning function fun1 called from fun2 that itself was called from fun3.... The depth K of this reporting is controlled in trace.hpp by the preprocessing directive

```
#define REPORT() REPORT_TRACE(3)
```

when _TRACE_ON is defined; in our example, K = 3.

The classes for object counting, tracing, and reporting are defined in the header file obtrace.hpp, which is #included for compilation if _OBTRACE_ON is defined and otherwise not. Note all the places in our program that are related to object tracing – they are all conditionally included based on the flag _OBTRACE_ON. Besides the #inclusion of obtrace.hpp we need a different class header for each class involved (in our example, for XClass and YClass), and each class must include the reporting functions ReportAll() and ReportCount() and, most importantly, the definition and initialization of the static part of each tracing class,

```
char* OBTRACE<XClass>::init=NULL;
```

and

```
char* OBTRACE<YClass>::init=NULL;
```

The method ReportCount() will report the total number of objects at the moment of its invocation; ReportAll() will report all undeallocated objects and where they were created.

We will be playing with several variations, so we include a simple Makefile (in this example we are using a public domain GNU C compiler gcc and a public domain GNU C++ compiler g++ under Solaris operating system). The Makefile:

```
CFLAGS=

count: count.o trace.o
        g++ -o count count.o trace.o $(CFLAGS)
count.o: count.cpp trace.hpp obtrace.hpp
        g++ -c -D_TRACE_ON -D_OBTRACE_ON count.cpp $(CFLAGS)

count1: count1.o
        g++ -o count1 count1.o $(CFLAGS)
count1.o: count.cpp trace.hpp obtrace.hpp
        g++ -c -D_OBTRACE_ON count.cpp $(CFLAGS)
        mv count.o count1.o

count2: count2.o trace.o
        g++ -o count2 count2.o trace.o $(CFLAGS)
count2.o: count.cpp trace.hpp obtrace.hpp
        g++ -c -D_TRACE_ON count.cpp $(CFLAGS)
        mv count.o count2.o

count3: count3.o
        g++ -o count3 count3.o  $(CFLAGS)
count3.o: count.cpp trace.hpp obtrace.hpp
        g++ -c count.cpp $(CFLAGS)
        mv count.o count3.o

trace.o: trace.c
        gcc -c trace.c $(CFLAGS)
```

Let us first make count – it is the form with both localization tracing and object tracing on. Executing the program yields the following output:

```
[doit2:main:global] number of objects of class YClass = 2
undeallocated object of class XClass created in doit1:doit2:main
undeallocated object of class XClass created in doit2:main:global
undeallocated object of class XClass created in global
undeallocated object of class YClass created in doit2:main:global
undeallocated object of class YClass created in global
```

The first line is produced by call to YClass::ReportCount() doit2() called from main() and the next three lines by XClass::ReportAll() invoked by the atexit registered function Report() when the program exits. The last two lines are produced by YClass::ReportAll() invoked by Report().

We tried to keep the reporting simple and so it is writing only to standard output (not every operating system keeps standard files open and accessible past exit(), so it may not be executable in this form on your particular machine). Let us check the output to see whether it is correct. When YClass::ReportCount() is invoked there are two YClass objects, oy1 and *oy2. The "undeallocated object of class XClass created in doit1:doit2:main" is *ox2 (note the commenting out of the delete). The "undeallocated object of class XClass created in doit2:main:global" is *ox4 (again its delete is blocked) – ox3 was deleted automatically when it went out of scope. The "undeallocated object of class XClass created in global" is the global object ox1. The "undeallocated object of class YClass created in doit2:main:global" is *oy2 (its delete is also commented out), and finally the "undeallocated object of class YClass created in global" is the global object oy1. Let us uncomment all the commented deletes, recompile, and execute again; correctly we obtain

```
[doit2:main:global] number of objects of class YClass = 2
undeallocated object of class XClass created in global
undeallocated object of class YClass created in global
```

Commenting the deletes again and recompiling our program as count1, which keeps the object tracing on but turns off the localization tracing, produces the output

```
[doit2] number of objects of class YClass = 2
undeallocated object of class XClass created in doit1
undeallocated object of class XClass created in doit2
undeallocated object of class XClass created in global
undeallocated object of class YClass created in doit1
undeallocated object of class YClass created in global
```

which we know is correct from our previous analysis – notice the "flat" localization reporting. Also notice in the Makefile that for count1 we did not link our program with trace.o. If we uncomment the deletes, we get the same correct response with "flat" localization. Now we compile our program as count2, which keeps the localization tracing on but turns the object tracing off (again we must link our program with trace.o as we did for count); this time we get no output because there is no reporting. The reader is encouraged to play with the localization tracing and reporting.

Compiling our program as count3 turns off both the localization tracing and the object tracing; this time our program is again not linked with trace.o and there is no output. There is practically no overhead, and the program behaves almost as if we never programmed it to do localization or object tracing.

TRACING OBJECTS AND MEMORY IN C++

Our aim here is to take count.cpp and change it to trace not only objects but also allocation and deallocation by global operators new and delete. Toward this end we work with just one class YClass and have its only data member value be dynamically allocated. We therefore added a destructor to deallocate value. Here is the file memtrace.cpp:

```
extern "C" {
  #include <stdio.h>
  #include <string.h>
  #include <stdlib.h>
  #include "trace.hpp"
}

#ifdef _OBTRACE_ON
  #include "obtrace.hpp"
#endif

#include "memtrace.hpp"
// now redefine new
```

```
#ifdef _TRACE_ON
  #define new new(__FILE__,__LINE__,REPORT_TRACE(3))
#else
  #define new new(__FILE__,__LINE__,TRACELOC)
#endif

#ifdef _OBTRACE_ON
  class XClass : private OBTRACE<XClass>
#else
  class XClass
#endif
{
public:
  XClass() { value=0; }
  XClass(int i) {
    value = new int;
    *value = i;
  }
  ~XClass() { if (value) delete value; }
  #ifdef _OBTRACE_ON
    // method ReportAll -----------------------------------
    static void ReportAll() {
      OBTRACE<XClass>::ReportAll(stdout,"XClass");
    }//end ReportAll

    // method ReportCount ---------------------------------
    static void ReportCount() {
      OBTRACE<XClass>::ReportCount(stdout,"XClass");
    }//end ReportCount
  #endif // _OBTRACE_ON

protected:
  int* value;

};//end class XClass

#ifdef _OBTRACE_ON
  char* OBTRACE<XClass>::init=NULL;
#endif

XClass ox1(1);

// function doit1 --------------------------------------
int doit1()
```

```cpp
{
 TRACE(doit1)

 XClass* ox2 = new XClass(2);
 //delete ox2;

 RETURN1(1)

}//end doit1

// function doit2 -------------------------------------------
void doit2()
{
 TRACE(doit2)

  XClass ox3(3);
  XClass* ox4 = new XClass(4);

  doit1();

  //delete ox4;
  #ifdef _OBTRACE_ON
    XClass::ReportCount();
  #endif

  RETURN
}//end doit2

void Report()
{
  #ifdef _OBTRACE_ON
    XClass::ReportAll();
  #endif
  new_report(stdout);
}

// function main -------------------------------------------
int main()
{
 TRACE(main)

 #ifdef _OBTRACE_ON
   atexit(Report);
 #endif
```

```
    doit2();

    RETURN1(0)

}//end main
```

The overloaded operators new and delete are in the file memtrace.hpp that is #included. That is where the reporting function new_report() is defined as well. Note that (a) we redefine new in two different ways, depending on whether or not we trace the functions, and (b) as discussed in Chapter 10, we do not redefine delete. Here is the file memtrace.hpp:

```
#ifndef _MEMTRACE_HPP
#define _MEMTRACE_HPP

extern "C" {
  #include <stdio.h>
  #include <string.h>
}

struct NEW_STRUCT
{
 void *addr;
 char* file;
 int line;
 char* local;
 size_t size;
 struct NEW_STRUCT* next;
};
typedef NEW_STRUCT NEW;
NEW* newlist = 0;

void* operator new(size_t size,const char* file,
                   int line,char* local) {
    void *p;
    NEW* newp;

    // every allocation should be checked and exception
    // thrown if error
    newp = (NEW*) malloc(sizeof(NEW));
    newp->addr = malloc(size);
    newp->file = strdup(file);
```

```
    newp->line = line;
    newp->local = strdup(local);
    newp->size = size;
    newp->next = newlist;
    newlist = newp;
    return newp->addr;
}

void operator delete(void* p) {
  NEW *newp, *newp1;

  if (newlist == 0) {
    // here we should throw, spurious deallocation
    return;
  }
  if (newlist->addr == p) {
    newp = newlist;
    newlist = newlist->next;
    free(newp->file);
    free(newp->local);
    free(newp);
    return;
  }
  for(newp1 = newlist, newp = newlist->next;
          newp != 0;
              newp1 = newp, newp = newp->next) {
    if (newp->addr == p) {
      newp1->next = newp->next;
      free(newp->file);
      free(newp->local);
      free(newp);
      return;
    }
  }
// here we should throw, spurious deallocation
}

void operator delete(void *p,const char* file,
                     int line,char* local)  {
  operator delete(p);
}

void new_report(FILE *fp) {
 NEW* newp;
```

```
if (newlist == 0) {
  fprintf(fp,"all deallocated :-)\n");
  fflush(fp);
  return;
}

for(newp = newlist; newp != 0; newp = newp->next) {
  fprintf(fp,"undealloc. segment at address %x from file=%s,\n",
          newp->addr,newp->file);
  fprintf(fp,"  line=%d, local=%s, size=%u\n",
          newp->line,newp->local,new->size);
}

fflush(fp);
}

#endif      // _MEMTRACE_HPP
```

Again, for keeping track of allocation and deallocation we chose a simple linked list, newlist. The files trace.hpp, trace.c, and obtrace.hpp are as before. The Makefile:

```
CFLAGS=

trace.o: trace.c
        gcc -c trace.c $(CFLAGS)

memtrace: memtrace.o trace.o
        g++ -o memtrace memtrace.o trace.o $(CFLAGS)
memtrace.o: memtrace.cpp memtrace.hpp trace.hpp obtrace.hpp
        g++ -c -D_TRACE_ON -D_OBTRACE_ON memtrace.cpp $(CFLAGS)
```

As in Appendix B, we first compile it as memtrace with both localization tracing and object tracing. We obtain the following output:

```
[doit2:main:global] number of objects of class XClass = 4
undeallocated object of class XClass created in doit1:doit2:main
undeallocated object of class XClass created in doit2:main:global
undeallocated object of class XClass created in global
undealloc. segment at address 22500 from file=memtrace.cpp,
   line=31, local=doit1:doit2:main, size=4
```

```
undealloc. segment at address 224f0 from file=memtrace.cpp,
   line=65, local=doit1:doit2:main, size=8
undealloc. segment at address 224d0 from file=memtrace.cpp,
   line=31, local=doit2:main:global, size=4
undealloc. segment at address 224c0 from file=memtrace.cpp,
   line=79, local=doit2:main:global, size=8
undealloc. segment at address 22460 from file=memtrace.cpp,
   line=31, local=global, size=4
```

The object count and undeallocated objects are clear (see the discussion in Appendix B). More interesting are the undeallocated segments. The one of size 4 at address 22500 is value of the global object ox1. The one of size 8 at address 224f0 is the dynamic object *ox2. The one of size 4 at address 224d0 is value of the object *ox2. The one of size 8 at address 224c0 is the dynamic object *ox4, while the one of size 4 at address 22460 is its value. There is no trace of the object ox3 and its value, for both were "destroyed" when it went out of scope. Now uncomment the deletes in memtrace.cpp and recompile. Running it again yields:

```
[doit2:main:global] number of objects of class XClass = 2
undeallocated object of class XClass created in global
undealloc. segment at address 224b8 from file=memtrace.cpp,
   line=31, local=global, size=4
```

There is only one undeallocated object, the global ox1, and only one undeallocated segment of size 4 at address 224b8, its value. Now, let us comment out the global object ox1, recompile, and run again:

```
all deallocated :-)
```

So there, a smiley!

THREAD-SAFE AND PROCESS-SAFE REPORTING AND LOGGING FUNCTIONS

Here we present the reporting and logging functions referred to in the text of the book on several occasions, especially in Chapter 11. This particular example is POSIX 1 compliant.

All functions comply with the same syntax and semantics for arguments as the printf() function (i.e., variable number of standard arguments). Functions named in all lowercase (sys_exit(), sys__exit(), msg(), msg_exit(), msg__exit(), and msg()) write their messages to the standard output (i.e., to the screen of the terminal under normal circumstances), whereas functions whose names begin with an uppercase letter (Sys_exit(), Sys__exit(), Sys(), Msg_exit(), Msg__exit(), and Msg()) write into a single log file.

The functions sys(), msg(), Sys(), and Msg() save on entry the current signal mask, block all signals, and than write the message – hence they cannot be "interrupted". On return, they reinstate the original signal mask.

The functions sys_exit(), sys__exit(), msg_exit(), msg__exit(), Sys_exit(), Sys__exit(), Msg_exit(), and Msg__exit() block all signals on entry. They do not save the original signal mask because they do not return; these functions exit using the system call exit(1) (functions sys_exit(), msg_exit(), Sys_exit(), and Msg_exit()) or _exit(1) (functions sys__exit(), msg__exit(), Sys__exit(), and Msg__exit()).

Functions msg_exit(), msg__exit(), msg(), Msg_exit(), Msg__exit(), and Msg() just write the requested message and either return (msg() and Msg()) or exit using exit(1) (msg_exit() and Msg_exit()) or _exit(1) (msg__exit() and Msg__exit()).

Functions sys_exit(), sys__exit(), sys(), Sys_exit(), Sys__exit(), and Sys() write a more elaborate system error message (together with the requested message) describing the error that happened based on errno. Thus they should be used only after a system call failed. These functions either return (sys() and Sys()) or exit using exit(1) (sys_exit() and Sys_exit()) or _exit(1) (sys__exit() and Sys__exit()).

Functions Sys_exit(), Sys__exit(), Sys(), Msg_exit(), Msg__exit(), and Msg() on entry lock the log file for writing (an exclusive lock); upon exit or return, they unlock the log file (using functions writelock() and fileunlock()). The file locking protects the integrity of the file if different processes try to write into it. If compiled with the _multithread flag, the POSIX mutexes (a mutual exclusion implementation for POSIX threads, a kind of a lock) are installed and used to protect the log.

All the functions use an integer pointer logi (declared in the log.h file), which must point to a location where the next sequential message number is stored. Each function uses that number for its message number and then increments its value by 1 so that the next function can use it. The location could be within the dataspace of the process (as we used it in several examples): first define and initialize the real index, int logindex=0, and then define logi and point it there – int* logi = &logindex. Or it could be a shared memory segment. If the logging functions are used for many processes for the same log then the message numbering will be out of sequence, for each process will keep track of the message numbering for itself only. If we want a correct numbering for all processes together then they must all use the same index, so we keep it in a shared memory segment. This would be a typical and intended use:

```
#include "log.h"
...
create_log("mylog");
int logindex=0;
int* logi=&logindex;
```

```
...
```
1. register atexit a cleanup function for a removal of a shared
   memory segment for logi, provided you are the parent process
2. create a shared memory segment, attach to it, its address is
   in logaddr
```
...
```
```
logi = loagddr;
```

3. fork all child processes
   they inherit both the shared memory segment and logaddr
   so the logging functions will be OK

Access to the shared memory segment need not be protected (since only the "owner" of the log will access it), so the mutual exclusion is enforced via file locking. For the multithreaded version:

```
#include "log.h"
...
create_log("mylog");
int logindex=0;
int* logi=&logindex;
...
```
1. create all threads
   they inherit logi
   so the logging functions will be OK

There is likewise no need to safeguard access to logindex since only the "owner" of the log will access it; here the mutual exclusion is enforced using the mutual exclusion of the log.

All reporting and logging functions return a char pointer that consists of a string with a possible error message. If a function executes without an error, a null pointer is returned (meaning no error message). If the pointer returned is not null then the string it points to contains an error message about what has happened. It is up to the programmer who is using these functions to decide what to do if an error has occurred.

The program using the logging functions must #include log.h and must define and initialize the mutex tloc as follows:

```
pthread_mutex_t tlock = PTHREAD_MUTEX_INITIALIZER
```

Here is log.h file:

```
#ifndef _log_h
#define _log_h

extern int *logi;
#ifdef _multithread
 extern pthread_mutex_t tlock;
#endif

#ifdef __cplusplus
    extern "C"
        #include <stdio.h>
        #include <string.h>
        #include <sys/types.h>
        #include <fcntl.h>
        #include <errno.h>
        #include <stdarg.h>
        #include <stdlib.h>
        #include <unistd.h>
        #include <time.h>
        #include <signal.h>
        #include <sys/stat.h>
        #include <pthread.h>

        char* sys_exit(char *fmt, ...);
        char* sys__exit(char *fmt, ...);
        char* sys(char *fmt, ...);
        char* msg_exit(char *fmt, ...);
        char* msg__exit(char *fmt, ...);
        char* msg(char *fmt, ...);
        char* Sys_exit(char *fmt, ...);
        char* Sys__exit(char *fmt, ...);
        char* Msg_exit(char *fmt, ...);
        char* Msg__exit(char *fmt, ...);
        char* Sys(char *fmt, ...);
        char* Msg(char *fmt, ...);
        char* create_log(char*);
 #else
   #include <stdio.h>
   #include <string.h>
   #include <sys/types.h>
   #include <fcntl.h>
   #include <errno.h>
   #include <stdarg.h>
   #include <stdlib.h>
```

```c
#include <unistd.h>
#include <time.h>
#include <signal.h>
#include <sys/stat.h>
#include <pthread.h>

extern char* sys_exit(char *fmt, ...);
extern char* sys__exit(char *fmt, ...);
extern char* sys(char *fmt, ...);
extern char* msg_exit(char *fmt, ...);
extern char* msg__exit(char *fmt, ...);
extern char* msg(char *fmt, ...);
extern char* Sys_exit(char *fmt, ...);
extern char* Sys__exit(char *fmt, ...);
extern char* Msg_exit(char *fmt, ...);
extern char* Msg__exit(char *fmt, ...);
extern char* Sys(char *fmt, ...);
extern char* Msg(char *fmt, ...);
extern char* create_log(char*);
#endif

#endif /* _log_h */
```

To view or download the complete code, please visit Prof. Franek's website: www.cas.mcmaster.ca/~franek.

GLOSSARY

_exit()   UNIX system call that terminates its process; similar to exit() but does not execute "atexit" functions.

absolute address   A synonym for *physical address*.

absolutization   The process that replaces relative addresses of the form (*segment, offset*) – or just plain *offset* for a single segment – by the actual addresses.

activation (of a function)   An execution of the function.

activation frame   A data structure to save all data relevant for running of a function (procedure), including the storage for all local objects and input parameters.

activation record   A synonym for *activation frame*.

address operator &   An operator for calculating the logical address of a variable in compile time.

address reference   Referring to an item by its address.

allocation from arena   Technique of allocating an arena first and then managing the allocation/deallocation within the arena by the program itself (rather then by the process memory manager); used for compaction and serialization of complex data structures and objects, or for managing memory in safety-critical and/or fault-tolerant systems.

GLOSSARY

ANSI-C standard Standardization of the programming language C by the American National Standards Institute.

argument (of a function) An input to the function; can be viewed as a named "slot" (sometimes referred to as *dummy variable*) that is filled with a value just prior to a call to the function, and during execution the function works with the argument as if it were a regular variable.

argument passing Parameter passing to functions.

array index range checking Checking whether an index used to access an array item is within the correct range.

assignment method A synonym for operator=.

auto (C/C++ keyword) Storage class *automatic*.

auto_ptr<X> The template-based C++ Standard Library definition of smart pointers.

backtracking algorithm A class of algorithms that systematically generate or traverse a space of solutions. The name alludes to their main feature: when they are stuck, they "backtrack" to the previous position from which they can once again start generating or traversing.

base class If a class A is an extension of a class B, then B is called the base class of A; a synonym for *superclass.*

big endian byte order A byte order for numbers of at least 2 bytes in which the more significant byte is placed to the left of a less significant byte; most UNIX boxes use big endian byte order.

binary code A sequence of bits (customarily depicted as 0s and 1s) representing a particular value. In C/C++ there are three fundamental binary codes employed – coding for characters, coding for integers, and coding for real numbers. Some might recognize only two since the coding for characters and integers is the same, but we ought to make a conceptual distinction between them.

binary heap A labeled binary tree in which every node has a label that is strictly bigger than the labels of all its descendants.

binary search tree A binary tree with nodes storing values; the tree is organized so that a parent node has a value strictly larger (resp., smaller) than the left (resp., right) child node. This arrangement allows access to nodes in no worse than $O(n)$ time with average $O(\log n)$ access time.

binary tree Linked data structure consisting of nodes; each node (parent) is at most linked to two other nodes (its children), and no node is linked to its predecessor node. (In the terminology of graph theory, this is an acyclic graph.)

blanked memory Memory in which each of its bits is cleared (set to 0).

blocking/nonblocking system call A system call dealing with some I/O devices; for instance, read on a pipe may either wait until some data arrives (so-called blocking call) or, if there is no data waiting to be had, it returns (so-called nonblocking call).

buffer A common term referring to a contiguous segment of memory used for storing binary data.

byte code A special code to which Java programs are "compiled" in order to speed their interpretation by the Java virtual machine.

C++ standard Current standard for Programming Language C++, JTC1.22.32, ISO/IEC 14882, published 1 September 1998.

C++ Standard Library A set of common classes and interfaces that greatly extend the core C++ language.

C99 The current standard for Programming Language C, ISO/IEC 9899:1999, published 1 December 1999.

cache A fast and expensive (and hence small) memory used to store prefetched data in order to speed up execution; access to the cache is much faster than access to the main memory.

caching The process of pre-fetching data anticipated to be needed by the running program into the cache and attendant memory mapping, so that the running program has no "knowledge" of the fact that it is working with data in the cache rather than with data in the main memory; caching is used to speed up the execution.

call (to a function) A C/C++ language construct indicating that the function should be executed at the point where the construct is located.

call-by-address A synonym for call-by-reference.

call-by-location A synonym for call-by-reference.

call-by-name A particular way of implementing a function call, in which the variables passed to the function replace the names of arguments; used for macro-expansion and inlining.

call-by-reference A particular way of implementing a function call, in which the arguments are passed by their references.

call-by-value A particular way of implementing a function call, in which the arguments are passed by their value (i.e., their copies).

callee The function being called.

caller The function doing the calling.

calling convention The type of calling sequence used; thus we speak of the C calling convention, the Java calling convention, the Pascal calling convention, and so on.

calling sequence   A sequence of steps performed prior to the execution of the called function. Some of the steps are performed by the caller, some by the callee.

calloc()   A standard C/C++ function that provides a platform-independent interface to the process memory manager; used to allocated and clear the memory.

child process   After a fork() in UNIX, one of the copies of the (parent) process being forked continues with a new process ID, customarily called the child process; the term is also used in the context of other operating systems for a process created by another process.

class   A collection of definitions of data items and operations intended to model some important commonality among many objects.

class member   A data item or a method.

class method   A function that belongs to the class definition; intended to be used by all objects of the class and mainly on the object's own data.

cleared memory   A synonym for *blanked memory.*

command line   The prompt line offered by many operating systems to type in a command.

command-line argument   If program execution is initiated by a command typed on the command line, additional words after the command are passed to the program being invoked; these are referred to as command-line arguments.

command-line argument structure   The data structure created by the operating system using the command-line arguments passed to the program being invoked.

compaction   A process that stores a linked data structure in a single contiguous segment of memory.

compile-time array index range checking   Checking during compilation whether the indicated operation violates the known range of the array (e.g., during initialization).

constructor   One of a set of specialized methods that is invoked during an object's creation; can be viewed as a "blueprint" for object creation.

copy constructor   A constructor used by the compiler for passing objects by value (i.e., copying them); the signature of the copy constructor for a class C is C(const C&).

copy-restore   A call method in which arguments are passed to the callee by value; upon termination of the callee, the newly computed values are copied to the activation frame of the caller.

dangling pointer   A pointer pointing to a previously meaningful location that is no longer meaningful; usually a result of a pointer pointing to an object that is deallocated without resetting the value of the pointer.

dangling reference   A reference to an object that no longer exists.

data abstraction   A principle by which implementation details of an abstract data type are hidden so that the user manipulates only the well-defined abstract properties of abstract data types.

data hiding   A synonym for *information hiding*.

data structure   A collection of simpler data items linked through explicit links (see *linked data structure*) or through implicit links.

declaration (of an object)   A C/C++ construct informing the compiler that a particular symbol represents an object of a given type; no creation is involved.

default constructor   An explicit constructor with no arguments, or an implicit constructor provided by the compiler.

definition (of an object)   A C/C++ construct that causes the compiler to create an object out of "raw" memory.

delete   A C++ operator to delete a memory segment previously dynamically allocated by the operator new; unlike the C allocators, delete can be overloaded to provide a custom-made or debugging version, and errors can be handled through exceptions.

delete[]   A C++ operator to delete a memory segment previously dynamically allocated by the operator new[]; unlike the C allocators, delete[] can be overloaded to provide a custom-made or debugging version, and errors can be handled through exceptions.

dereference operator *   A synonym for *indirection operator*.

derived class   A class extending another class; a synonym for *subclass*.

destructor   A special method of each class that is automatically used when an object of the class is being destroyed (either implicitly when a function in which it is local is terminating, or explicitly when an object is being deallocated using the operator delete).

distributed computing   Setup of a computing environment in which data and/or code used by a program may physically reside on other machines of the network yet be accessible for the program as if they resided on the same machine; in particular, this enables many programs running on different machines to cooperate toward the same goal.

dynamic data   Data stored in dynamically allocated memory; also, a section in the program address space for dynamically allocated memory.

dynamic memory allocation   The process of requesting and obtaining additional memory segments during the execution of a program.

dynamic memory deallocation   The process of "returning" previously allocated dynamic memory to the process memory manager.

dynamic multi-dimensional array A dynamically created data structure that allows access through multiple indexes with the same syntax as that used for static multi-dimensional arrays.

dynamic one-dimensional array An array whose segment to hold the array items has been allocated dynamically.

elementary data type Data types that a programming language recognizes and can deal with automatically; in C/C++ these include char, int, float, and pointers to these and pointers to pointers (recursively).

encapsulation A principle according to which both the data and the operation with it are enclosed within a module and not generally available to other modules.

environment Usually, a set of environment variables for a process.

environment variable A set of variables that are set prior to a program's execution and to which the program has access.

exception An event that occurs during program execution that disrupts the normal flow of instructions.

exception-safe code Code that preserves certain invariants (usually the use and ownership of resources) after an exception occurs – usually by restoring the state of the process to the one that obtained before the exception.

exception-unsafe code Code that is not exception-safe.

exec() A family of UNIX system calls to execute a program within the process in which it is used.

executable file A synonym for *load module.*

executable module A synonym for *load module.*

extendibility A characteristic of software whose functionality may be extended if necessary.

fault-tolerant software A software system so designed that it continues to work even if fatal errors in execution are encountered.

FIFO A named pipe; an acronym standing for "first in, first out".

flat-table approach A program structure resembling cards spread on a flat table, where a function (procedure) is likened to a card; the main implication is that functions cannot be defined within functions.

flow of control Sequence indicating which of the functions has "control" (i.e., is being executed).

foreign key An item in a table A of a relational database whose value comes from another table B. Only in table B can the value be modified; in table A, the value is used as a "link" – in essence linking A to B. Foreign keys are used to capture relationships among tables.

fork() A UNIX system call to create a new process.

fragmentation During dynamic memory allocation, the process manager may need to carve out a segment to allocate from a bigger one. The left-over segment may be too small to be of any use; this unpleasant aspect of allocation is often called fragmentation.

free() A standard C/C++ function providing a platform-independent inter-face to the process memory manager; used to deallocate memory.

free store A synonym for *system heap*.

function A subprogram module in C/C++ with a precisely defined interface; in general the term *function* refers to a module that returns a value. In C/C++, modules are presumed to return a value (even if they do not), so the term is used for all subprogram modules.

function argument A synonym for *argument* (of a function).

function call A synonym for *call* (to a function).

function header A construct in C/C++ syntax that describes the function's interface.

garbage collection If only implicit dynamic allocation is allowed then deallo-cation must also be done by implicit means, which is often called garbage collection.

garbage collector Software that provides implicit memory deallocation by deallocating objects that are no longer referenced by some other object.

getenv() A UNIX system call to obtain the value of a particular environment variable.

GetEnvironmentVariable A Windows system call to obtain the value of a par-ticular environment variable.

global item An item that can be referenced (accessed) in all functions (with some restrictions) of the program.

Hanoi towers puzzle The Hanoi towers puzzle was invented by the French mathematician Edouard Lucas in 1883. Three pegs are given, one of which contains a certain number of wooden disks of different sizes. The disks must always be organized so that only a smaller disk can sit on top of a bigger one. The monks are supposed to move the disks from one peg to an-other. This is a complex problem that nevertheless can easily be "solved" using recursion (see Appendix A).

hidden allocation A problem that arises when a service or object is requested from a module without realizing that the module has allocated some mem-ory to serve that request.

incorrect assignment An assignment that does not properly destroy the dynamic parts of an object before assigning them new values; usually in the form of a missing explicit assignment.

index-out-of-range run-time error An attempt to access an array item with an index that is outside of the range.

indirection operator * An operator referencing the "virtual object" at the address a pointer is pointing to; used for fetching and storing of values.

information hiding A principle akin to the military term "need to know basis" whereby only the module that "guards" the data should have direct access to it while all other modules should gain access only through the "guard"; this enables much safer programming, for it prevents accidental data corruption.

inheritance A mechanism by which objects of a derived class automatically have the same properties as objects of the base class without those properties being explicitly restated.

inlining A method by which a compiler, in order to reduce the function overhead, places a direct code instead of a function call while maintaining the syntax convention and convenience of function calls.

innate data type A synonym for *elementary data type*.

instance A synonym for *object*.

instantiation A synonym for *object construction*.

insufficient destructor A destructor that does not properly deallocate all the dynamic parts of an object; usually in the form of a missing explicit destructor.

interpreted program A program that is read in its source form by an *interpreter* that then does whatever the statements of the program indicate should be done.

interpreter A program that reads (interprets) programs in their source form and executes whatever the statements of the program being interpreted indicate should be done.

invocation (of a function) A synonym for *function call*.

ipcrm A UNIX command for removal of a shared memory segment or a semaphore (provided the user has the required permissions to do so).

ipcs A UNIX command for generating statistics on all shared memory segments and semaphores within the system.

Java virtual machine An interpreter for Java byte code.

lightweight process A UNIX term denoting a thread that is implemented by the operating system.

linked data structure A data structure consisting of components connected by links, usually pointers.

linking Term used to denote either the whole process of forging a set of object modules into a single load module or the second phase of that process, when address references from one object module to another (so-called external references) are resolved with respect to the beginning of the load module being created.

list　A linked data structure consisting of nodes to hold data and links to the next element in the list (so-called singly linked list) or, in addition, links to the previous element in the list (doubly linked list).

little endian byte order　A byte order for numbers of at least 2 bytes in which the less significant byte is placed to the left of a more significant byte; Intel processors use little endian byte order.

load file　A synonym for *load module*.

load module　A file containing a binary code of a program with all address references resolved and ready to be loaded to the memory and executed.

loading　The process of copying the contents of a load module to memory while modifying logical addresses to physical.

local item　An item defined within a function (or block) with default storage class *auto*.

logical address　An address in the form of an offset from either the beginning of the load module or an activation frame.

macro-expansion　A method by which a macro defined through the #define preprocessor directive is replaced by the code.

maintainability　A property of software allowing reasonably easy modifications as requirements change during the software's lifetime.

malloc()　A C/C++ standard function that provides an interface to the process memory manager; used for requesting additional dynamic memory.

malloc.h　A slightly obsolete standard C header file for dealing with allocation and deallocation of memory.

memory alignment　Usually refers to the fact that the address of an item starts at a machine-word boundary in memory (to enable a more efficient memory access in terms of machine words).

memory allocation　A synonym for *dynamic memory allocation*.

memory deallocation　A synonym for *dynamic memory deallocation*.

memory leak　A commonly used term indicating that a program is dynamically allocating memory but not properly deallocating it, which results in a gradual accumulation of unused memory by the program to the detriment of other programs, the operating system, and itself.

memory manager　A synonym for *process memory manager*.

memory-mapped I/O operation　An operating system approach to "sending" data to various I/O devices; for instance, "storing data" at a special address X is interpreted by the operating system as a request to send the data to a disk.

memory mapping The process of assigning physical addresses to logical addresses.

memory segment A contiguous section of memory; referred to in other contexts as a *buffer*.

messaging A system of sending and receiving messages by processes.

modularization Breakup of a program into smaller and more manageable modules with precisely defined mutual interaction, usually through precise interfaces.

multithreading Running several threads in a process simultaneously.

mutex A binary semaphore implementing mutual exclusion for threads.

named pipe A pipe between unrelated processes; a synonym for *FIFO*.

network byte order A standard byte order for numbers of at least 2 bytes to be transferred across a network; the big endian byte order is used as the network byte order.

new or **new[]** A C++ operator providing an interface to the process memory manager, in some ways similar to `malloc()` but in many other ways quite different; used to allocate dynamic arrays. In particular, it can be overloaded to provide a custom-made or debugging version, and errors can be handled through exceptions.

NULL A special C constant, defined in `stdio.h` as `'\0'` (or 0, or `(void*)`), that can be used as the null value for pointers.

null pointer A pointer with value 0 or an address of 0 that is interpreted as "no address".

object A complex data structure together with methods (functions) that can manipulate the data contained in the object.

object code The contents of an object file; in essence, a program translated to machine instructions including the binary code for data.

object file A synonym for *object module*.

object module A binary file containing essentially the binary code for machine instructions and the data of a program.

one-dimensional array A synonym for *static one-dimensional array*.

operating system memory manager The top-level memory manager that allocates large blocks of memory to individual process memory managers (it also serves other purposes for the operating system).

operator[] An indexing operator that can be overloaded (redefined) for any class defined in C++.

operator= Predefined C++ operator known as *assignment*; by default, it uses *memberwise copy*.

GLOSSARY

orphaned allocation A problem that arises when the address of an allocated segment is not preserved for later deallocation.

overflow Generally, when a binary code to be stored at some location is longer than the memory space reserved for it; in a narrower interpretation, a result of an arithmetic operation that is too big for the size of the result's data type.

overloading Using the same name for operations on different data types.

padding "Junk" space attached to some items in a structure in order to facilitate easy memory access based on machine-word boundaries.

parameter (of a function) A synonym for *function argument*.

parent process A process that creates another process – it is the parent of the newly created process.

passing by address A synonym for *passing by reference*.

passing by location A synonym for *passing by reference*.

passing by reference A method in which – instead of values of the arguments – their references (in C/C++, a pointer) are passed.

passing by value A method in which the values (copies) of arguments are passed to the function.

physical address The address of a byte in the physical memory.

pipe A memory-implemented special file for data exchange between related processes.

placement syntax A special syntax for memory operators that enables the use of additional arguments.

placement-delete A user-defined "counterpart" to placement-new; used for overloading of delete or delete[].

placement-new An overload of new or new[]; most often used to build objects in memory obtained by other means (and hence without allocation).

pointer A value or a variable with two attributes: (i) an address and (ii) a data type of what should be found at that address.

pointer arithmetic A way of moving pointers left or right in discrete "jumps" according to their data types.

pointer dereferencing Referencing the "virtual object" to which a pointer points (see *indirection operator*).

polymorphism A synonym for *overloading*.

pop An operation on *stack*: the item on the top is removed.

preprocessing directives A command in C or C++ that is not a part of the program to be compiled; destined for the preprocessor of the compiler, its goal is to modify the source code before it is actually compiled. Most preprocessing directives start with #.

preprocessor Part of the compiler that scans the source file prior to compilation and modifies it according to preprocessing directives embedded in the program; in essence, it works as a sophisticated text replacement facility.

private A designation of class members that are not generally accessible and whose properties are noninheritable.

procedure A term reserved for a module that does not return a value; in C/C++, it is assumed that every module returns a value (even if it does not) and thus the term *function* is always used.

process A program in execution.

process image Image of the address space of the program running as the process.

process memory manager A program that: keeps track of dynamically allocated and deallocated memory in terms of the process with which it is associated; serves the allocation and deallocation requests of this process; and (if it runs out of memory to allocate) requests a large block of free memory from the operating system memory manager.

process system stack A dynamic stack, unique to the running process, that is used for saving the context of a function (procedure) when calling another function (procedure) and for returning a value by the called function.

program memory manager A synonym for *process memory manager.*

program system stack A synonym for *process system stack.*

protected A designation of class members that are not generally accessible but whose properties are inheritable.

pthread_create() A POSIX system call to initiate a new thread.

pthread_exit() A POSIX system call to terminate the running thread.

pthread_join() A POSIX system call to wait for a thread.

pthread_self() A POSIX system call to obtain the thread ID.

public A designation of class members that are generally accessible.

push An operation on *stack*: a new item is placed on the top.

putenv() A UNIX system call to define a new environment variable or to change its value.

readability Characteristic of a source program that can be read and comprehended easily by those who did not design or write the program.

realloc() A C/C++ standard function providing an interface to the process memory manager; used for requesting additional dynamic memory or extending/reducing an already dynamically allocated segment with the preservation of data in it.

real-time system A software system that guarantees a response within fixed time limits regardless of the data being processed; the limits usually require a fast response.

recursion A programming language feature in which a function can call itself; it is the construction counterpart to mathematical induction.

recursive descent parser A parser for a grammar that is written using the "recursive descent" technique, in which nonterminal symbols of the grammar are represented and the execution of these functions reflect the grammar rules; not all context-free grammars can be parsed in such a manner.

relative address A synonym for *logical address*.

relativization A process in which actual addresses in a data structure stored within one or more contiguous segments of memory are replaced by offsets from the beginning of the segment in which they are located.

relocation The first phase of the process of forging a set of object modules into a single load module when the address references within an object module (so-called internal references) are resolved.

resource owner The module using the resource and responsible for "releasing" it when no longer needed.

return sequence A sequence of steps undertaken at the termination of a function; some of the steps are performed by the callee, some by the caller.

row-major formula A formula that translates multiple indexes into a single index, thus allowing proper access to a one-dimensional array in which a multi-dimensional array is stored.

row-major storage format A format used to store multi-dimensional arrays in one dimension.

run-time array index range checking A check performed during program execution before any access to the array; used to see whether the index is within proper range.

safety-critical software A software system that cannot fail because its working is critical for safety (e.g., nuclear power plant control system, aircraft flight control system, etc.).

scanner A "lexical analyzer" – usually an input module for a parser that turns the input from a stream of characters to a stream of tokens according to lexical analysis of the language.

semaphore A data structure – a synchronization primitive – to implement mutual exclusion for various processes sharing the same resource.

serialization A process in which a linked data structure is stored within several contiguous segments of memory with all addresses relativized.

SetEnvironmentVariable A Windows system call to set a value of an environment variable.

shared memory   Memory that is shared by several processes.

shared memory segments   The implementation, in UNIX System V, of shared memory.

signal handler   A function that is executed when the particular signal for which it is intended is delivered to a process and caught by the process.

signals   One-bit messages signifying that some event has happened; sometimes referred to as software interrupts.

simple data type   A synonym for *elementary data type*.

size_t   An ANSI-C defined data type to facilitate tight type checking; defined as unsigned long.

sizeof operator   A C/C++ operator calculating (in compile time) the size of memory required by a particular data type or by the resulting data type of an expression.

sleep()   A UNIX system call to put a process in suspension for a specified amount of time.

smart (or **safe**) **pointer**   A C++ object, which behaves and is used like a pointer, that deallocates the object being referenced when it goes out of scope.

source code   A program written in *source language*.

source file   A synonym for *source module*.

source language   A high-level language (like C or C++) in which a program is written.

source module   An ASCII text file containing a program or a part of a program written in a high-level language like C or C++.

spawning a process   Creating a new process and running a new program within it; in UNIX this usually refers to fork() followed by an exec().

stack   A data structure resembling a deck of cards; a new item can only be put on top of the deck (the *push* operation) or removed from the top of the deck (the *pop* operation).

standard function   A function whose behavior is guaranteed irrespective of platform and that comes with most compilers. In other contexts such functions are usually called *built-in* or *innate*, but for C/C++ they are provided as an addition for the programmer's convenience.

static (C/C++ keyword)   Changes the storage class of a local variable from *auto* to *static*; restricts the lexical scope of a global variable to the source file where the definition is located.

static data   The data whose memory layout is prepared by the compiler and stored within an area of the program address space that does not change its layout throughout the whole execution of the program; also, a section in the object module, the load module, and the program address space holding static data that in C/C++ programs correspond to global objects and local objects of storage class *static*.

static memory allocation   Memory layout for static data prepared by the compiler.

static multi-dimensional array   An array created by the compiler at compile time and accessible through multiple indexes; C/C++ uses the row-major storage format to store this as (essentially) a one-dimensional array.

static one-dimensional array   An array allocated by the compiler during compilation; the programmer does not have to allocate or deallocate the store, since these operations are performed automatically.

stdlib.h   A more up-to-date (than malloc.h) standard C header file for dealing with allocation and deallocation of memory.

strcat()   A standard function for string concatenation.

strcpy()   A standard function for copying a string from one location to another.

string   In essence, a character array terminated by NULL.

strlen()   A standard function for computing the length of a string (the terminator NULL is not counted).

structure   A data structure created by application of the C/C++ constructor struct.

subclass   A synonym for *derived class*.

superclass   A synonym for a *base class*.

symbolic reference   A reference to an item by its name.

system call   A call to an operating system function providing some service; the usual interface with the operating system is through a set of system calls.

system heap   A set of free memory blocks maintained in the form of a binary heap by the operating system memory manager.

system stack   A synonym for *process system stack*.

system stack unwinding   If an exception is thrown then the system stack is unwound – deallocating all local variables on the stack along the way – to the point where the last catch statement is located.

System V   A special variant of the UNIX operating system.

template class   A type-parameterized C++ class; for a particular definition, the actual type must be specified. The compiler "creates" the proper definition for the given type from the template.

testability   Property of software that lends itself to testing and debugging in a reasonable and systematic way.

testing and debugging   A phase in the software cycle when a freshly designed or modified software component is tested for correctness of its execution and the discovered errors (commonly called bugs) are rectified.

thread   A software object that can be dispatched to – and executes in – an address space.

traversal   A systematic process in which every component of a linked data structure is visited.

tree   A linked data structure consisting of nodes to store data and links to so-called child nodes.

undetermined ownership   A memory problem that results when we obtain an object from another module without realizing that we are now responsible for deallocation of the object.

uninitialized variable   A variable that is evaluated prior to storing any reasonable value there.

user space   The memory in which the process image is loaded.

user thread   A thread that is implemented by the user program and not by the operating system.

validation   Process of establishing that software is performing as intended.

value   A binary code for the appropriate data type.

variable   As a concept, an "entity" that can attain certain values; in programming, we can imagine that it is a "data container".

virtual memory system   A software system that provides a sophisticated mapping of logical addresses to physical addresses in a way that allows execution of programs with address spaces larger than the physical memory; usually relies on paging, where only some parts (pages) of the program address space are present in the physical memory at a time.

INDEX

absolutization, 139, 148, 149, 154, 156, 157, 239
access link, 61
activation, 10, 61, 62, 76, 77, 136, 168, 239
  frame, 4, 16–18, 39, 59, 61–4, 67, 68, 76–8, 108, 112, 113, 122, 123, 239, 242
  record, 16, 61, 239
  tree, 62, 76
address, 4, 13, 14, 16, 21, 31, 32, 38, 41, 239, 246, 247, 249
  absolute, 239
  base, 92
  logical, 13, 14, 16, 18, 239, 247, 248, 251, 254
  operator, 31, 239
  physical, 14, 18, 239, 247–9, 254
  reference, 8, 9, 12, 13, 18, 239, 246, 247, 251
  relative, 13, 18, 138, 251
  space, 4, 7, 13–19, 207, 243, 252, 254
  of variable, 22

allocation from arena, 48, 52, 147, 239
ANSI-C Standard, 240
argument, 59–61, 63, 64, 67, 76, 77, 79, 114, 115, 118–20, 123, 126, 240–3, 245, 249
argument passing, 31, 59, 61, 63, 67, 76, 77, 79, 81, 84–7, 92, 100, 104, 161, 240–2, 249
array, 8, 10, 81–3
  base, 83, 85–7
  dynamic, 81, 87, 88, 93, 95, 103–5, 248
  dynamic multi-dimensional, 97, 103, 104, 244
  dynamic one-dimensional, 87, 93, 103, 244
  dynamic two-dimensional, 102, 103, 105, 189, 205
  indexing, 81
  multi-dimensional, 4, 97
  one-dimensional, 4, 81, 82, 248
  representation, 83, 92, 97
  static, 81, 83, 88

array *(cont.)*
    static multi-dimensional, 97, 253
    static one-dimensional, 248, 253
    static two-dimensional, 97, 99
array passing, 81, 84–7, 92, 100, 104
assignment, 123, 124, 126, 127, 240, 248
auto
    object, 59, 77
    storage class, 10, 77, 240, 247, 252
    variable, 135, 204
auto_ptr, 181, 183, 185, 240
automatic
    object, 108, 109, 113, 118, 162
    storage class, 10, 240
    variable, 17

backtracking algorithm, 240
base address, 83
base class, 107, 240
binary
    code, 21–3, 25, 32, 33, 41, 43, 240, 249, 254
    heap, 47, 240, 253
    search tree, 133, 138, 240
    tree, 50, 51, 133, 156, 240
blocking system call, 241
buffer, 28, 95, 161, 189, 195, 196, 206, 241, 248
byte code, 241, 246
byte order, 33, 240, 247

C++ allocator, 4
C++ standard, 241
C++ Standard Library, 181, 183, 240, 241
C99, 109, 110, 241
cache, 241
caching, 14, 241
call, 59, 60–2, 76, 241, 245, 246
call-by-address, 63, 241
call-by-location, 241
call-by-name, 63, 76, 241
call-by-reference, 63, 77, 241
call-by-value, 63, 76, 77, 241

callee, 60, 63, 64, 76, 241, 242, 251
caller, 60–64, 76, 241, 242, 251
calling convention, 77, 79, 241
calling sequence, 61, 63, 64, 77, 242
calloc(), 4, 38, 45, 48–50, 52, 54, 55, 57, 116, 121, 165, 166, 242
child process, 191, 193, 194, 205, 207, 236, 242
class, 107, 242
    member, 242
    method, 242
command-line arguments, 189, 190, 205, 242
compaction, 132, 137, 138, 148, 149, 154–7, 242
compilation, 4, 5, 7–9, 15, 18, 26, 28, 31, 39, 40, 42, 43, 45, 56, 57, 62, 83, 84, 88, 95, 100, 108, 129, 166, 168, 176, 220, 223, 225, 232, 233, 235, 242, 249, 250, 253
compile time, 15, 39, 62, 115, 239, 252
compile-time checking, 84, 92, 242
compiler, 1, 2, 7, 8, 15, 17, 19, 22–5, 27–9, 31, 37, 39, 41–3, 48, 54, 55, 57, 61, 62, 64, 76, 81–4, 86, 88, 89, 92, 93, 95, 100, 101, 104, 108–10, 114, 118, 121, 122, 126, 128, 163, 166, 169, 170, 173, 178, 179, 223, 242, 243, 246, 249, 250, 252, 253
constructor, 106, 109–12, 114–16, 118–20, 122–8, 242, 243
control link, 61
copy constructor, 122–4, 126, 127, 242
copy-restore, 63, 242

dangling pointer, 39, 242
dangling reference, 243
data container, 4, 21, 24, 26, 31, 32, 36, 41, 106, 254
data hiding, 106, 243
data structure, 8, 26, 243, 253
debug_free(), 166, 167, 169, 170
debug_malloc(), 166, 167, 169, 170, 176
debugging, 53, 159, 254

INDEX

declaration, 81, 86, 243
default constructor, 106, 114, 115, 120, 124, 126, 128, 243
default destructor, 106, 114, 126
definition, 81, 86, 243
dereference operator, 32, 243
dereferencing, 32, 40, 249
derived class, 107, 115
destructor, 106, 113–16, 120, 122, 126, 127, 243
distributed computing, 155, 156, 243
doubly linked list, 247
dynamic
  allocation, 7, 16, 17, 38–41, 45, 51, 52, 54, 55, 57, 62, 63, 76, 87, 88, 92–4, 108–10, 112, 113, 162, 167, 196, 205, 227, 243–5, 247, 250
  construction, 108
  creation, 62, 119
  data, 16, 18, 108, 243
  data section, 16, 18, 19, 43
  data structure, 53, 244
  deallocation, 45, 243
  extension, 138
  function call, 64
  list, 47
  memory, 4, 52, 55, 92, 109, 111, 137, 155, 247, 250
  object, 38, 92, 118, 120, 126, 138, 161, 162, 179, 180, 182, 205, 208, 233
  pseudo-array, two-dimensional, 105
  smart pointer, 181
  stack, 250
  string, 91, 112, 124
  structure, 205

elementary data type, 244, 246, 252
encapsulation, 106, 107, 247
endian
  big, 33, 35, 240, 248
  little, 33, 36, 247
environment, 187, 188, 205, 244
environment variable, 188–90, 205, 244, 245, 250, 251

exception, 22, 52, 117, 119–22, 162–4, 173, 179, 181, 182, 184–6, 243, 244, 248, 253
exception-safe, 163, 181, 184–6, 244
exception-unsafe code problem, 162, 165, 182, 244
exec(), 193, 206, 244, 252
executable, 225
  file, 7, 8, 244
  module, 7, 8, 244
  statement, 109, 110
execution environment, 60
external component problem, 164, 165, 182
extendibility, 59, 244

fault-tolerant software, 52, 53
FIFO, 196, 206, 244, 248
flat-table approach, 9, 244
flow of control, 60, 80, 244
foreign key, 133, 244
fork(), 5, 184, 191–4, 205, 207, 208, 242, 244, 252
fragmentation, 46, 47, 245
free(), 4, 45, 48, 50, 52–4, 56, 57, 94, 108, 113, 116, 121, 127, 160, 166, 167, 169–71, 202, 245
free store, 47, 245
function, 7, 8, 59, 76, 245
  argument, 59
  call, 59, 76, 241, 245
  parameter, 60
function header, 245

garbage collection, 3, 40, 245
garbage collector, 40, 41, 245
getenv(), 188, 189, 245
GetEnvironmentVariable, 189, 245
global
  data, 10
  definition, 203
  item, 245
  object, 9, 10, 18, 110, 225, 233, 253
  operator, 116, 126, 127, 138, 171, 173, 174, 176, 183, 227

global *(cont.)*
  stack, 183
  variable, 18, 77–9, 95, 168–70, 174,
    188, 203–5, 220, 252

Hanoi towers puzzle, 5, 76, 78,
  210–15, 245
hidden allocation problem, 160, 164,
  182, 245

inconsistent conceptual levels, 28, 29
incorrect assignment problem, 162,
  165, 182, 184, 245
index range checking, 3, 81, 91, 240,
  242, 246, 251
indirection operator, 32, 81, 99, 102,
  243, 246, 249
information hiding, 246
inheritance, 107, 246
initialized data, 10
initialized data section, 11
inlining, 246
innate data type, 246
instance, 109, 246
instantiation, 109, 246
insufficient destructor problem, 161,
  165, 182, 184
interpretation, 39, 41
interpreted program, 246
interpreter, 39, 246
interprocess communication, 4, 14,
  184, 194, 206, 208
invocation, 61, 63, 77, 189, 223, 246
invoke, 62, 111, 115, 116, 126, 139, 189,
  224, 225, 242
ipcrm, 199, 246
ipcs, 199, 246

Java, 3, 39, 41, 246
Java virtual machine, 40, 246

lightweight process, 191, 246
linked
  data structure, 4, 5, 38, 92, 132, 133,
    135–7, 147, 149, 155–7, 208, 242,
    243, 246, 247, 251, 254

  list, 133, 157, 180, 220, 223, 232, 247
  tree, 139, 157
linker, 13, 89
linking, 4, 5, 7–9, 12, 18, 19, 45, 89, 95,
  166, 167, 169, 176, 220, 225, 226,
  246
LINUX, 47, 160
load
  file, 8, 247
  module, 7, 9, 13, 15, 18, 19, 21, 246,
    247, 251, 252
  time, 11
loader, 13, 15
loading, 4, 5, 7, 9, 15, 18, 45, 247
local
  data, 10, 59, 61, 64
  item, 247
  object, 10, 18, 39, 59, 61, 77, 239, 253
  variable, 10, 17, 67, 77, 135, 181, 203,
    204, 252, 253
localization
  reporting, 225
  tracing, 5, 184, 216, 224–6, 232

machine
  16-bit, 22
  32-bit, 22, 26, 30
  64-bit, 22
  code, 8
  instruction, 8, 11, 18, 19, 248
  status, 61, 64
  word, 26, 27, 247, 249
macro-expansion, 63, 76, 241, 247
maintainability, 59, 247
malloc(), 4, 16, 28–30, 38, 43, 45,
  48–50, 52, 54–7, 87, 88, 90, 94,
  103, 109, 113, 116, 117, 121, 133,
  156, 160, 165, 166, 169–71, 174,
  202, 221, 230, 247, 248
malloc.h, 48, 247
memory
  access, 3, 4, 25–7, 38–41, 49, 53,
    123, 190, 204, 247, 249
  alignment, 139, 149, 156, 157, 247
  allocated by the compiler, 15

allocation, 4–5, 15–17, 38, 40–3, 45–9, 51–5, 57, 91, 111, 115, 119, 136, 158, 165, 167, 178, 184, 196, 204, 243, 245, 247, 250, 253
allocation from arena, 132, 138, 139, 148, 155–8
allocator, 51, 116, 120, 126, 165
blanked, 49, 240, 242
cleared, 49, 242
deallocation, 4, 40, 45, 46, 52, 53, 120, 126, 136, 138, 158, 167, 178, 184, 204, 243, 245, 247, 253
deallocator, 120
dynamic allocation, 7
leak, 3–5, 40, 41, 47, 49, 53, 55, 91, 108, 109, 111, 112, 114–16, 121, 124–6, 128, 159–71, 174, 176–9, 183, 184, 185, 195, 196, 201, 203, 204, 207, 208, 216, 247
management, 19, 20, 46, 54–5
manager, 16, 52, 56, 247
mapping, 14, 15, 38, 40, 247, 248
operator, 114, 116, 126, 249
static allocation, 7, 15, 53, 54, 253
memory-mapped file, 14, 195
memory-mapped page file, 195
message, 4
messaging, 194, 195, 206, 248
method, 8, 30, 106, 107
modularization, 59, 76, 248
Msg(), 201, 202
msg(), 197, 198, 234, 235
msg_exit(), 234, 235
msg_exit(), 234, 235
multithreading, 184, 201, 204, 207, 208, 248
mutex, 201, 207, 235–7, 248

naked pointer, 179
network byte order, 33, 248
new_handler, 117
nonblocking system call, 241
nonexecutable statement, 109, 110
NULL, 39, 248

object, 106, 107, 248
  code, 8, 248
  construction, 4, 109, 110, 114, 116–18, 120–4, 129, 136, 138, 160, 161, 173, 176, 179, 184, 242, 246
  counting, 176, 177, 179, 180, 183, 223, 225, 233
  destruction, 4, 5, 113, 114, 116, 120, 123, 124, 136, 161, 177, 184
  file, 8, 11, 12, 248
  module, 8–13, 18, 19, 246, 248, 251, 252
  orientation, 106
  passing, 122, 123, 242
  tracing, 5, 208, 216, 223–7, 232, 233
  undeallocated, 223, 225, 233
  virtual, 41, 246, 249
operating system memory manager, 46, 47, 54, 248, 250, 253
operator delete, 4, 48, 106, 115, 116, 120–2, 125–7, 129–31, 138, 149, 156, 183, 243, 249
  overloaded, 138, 149, 156, 159
operator new, 4, 16, 38, 48, 51, 91, 106, 110, 115–22, 125–31, 137–41, 143, 149, 150, 156, 162–4, 171–4, 176, 183, 186, 218, 227–30, 243, 248, 249
  overloaded, 138, 149, 156, 159
operator[], 108, 248
orphaned allocation problem, 159, 164, 182, 184, 249
overflow, 22–4, 28, 49, 249
ownership, 180
  transfer, 180

padding, 26–30, 148, 149, 156, 249
parent process, 191, 193, 194, 205, 206, 249
passing
  by address, 63, 249
  by location, 249
  by reference, 31, 38, 63, 84, 86, 92, 100, 104, 123, 134, 135, 249
  by value, 63, 84–6, 92, 100, 123, 249

physical memory, 4, 14–16, 27, 249, 254

pipe, 4, 195, 196, 206, 241, 244, 248, 249

placement syntax, 118–21, 126, 173, 249

placement-delete, 121, 122, 129, 249

placement-new, 119, 121, 122, 126, 129, 137, 249

pointer, 3, 4, 31, 32, 36–41, 50, 54–5, 77, 81–3, 85–7, 89, 92, 93, 95, 99, 109, 114, 117–19, 121, 122, 126, 134, 137, 139, 147, 149, 154–6, 246, 248, 249

pointer arithmetic, 36, 37, 249

pointer indexing, 82

polymorphism, 108

pop, 16, 62, 64, 169, 175, 176, 220, 249, 252

preprocessing directive, 166, 183, 223, 247, 249, 250

preprocessor, 166, 174, 175, 183, 249, 250

private (class member), 250

procedure, 250

process, 187, 188, 191–6, 198–200, 205–8, 242, 244, 248–52
  ID, 191–4, 206, 242
  image, 191, 193–5, 199, 205–7, 250, 254

process memory management, 17

process memory manager, 45–8, 50, 52, 54, 121, 156, 239, 242, 243, 245, 247, 248, 250

process system stack, 17, 250, 253

process-safe, 5, 234

program address space, 13, 15, 18, 243

program counter, 61, 64, 200

program memory manager, 16, 250

program system stack, 7, 16

protected (class member), 250

pthread_create(), 201, 250

pthread_exit(), 202, 250

pthread_join(), 202, 250

pthread_self(), 202, 250

public (class member), 250

push, 16, 62, 175, 176, 220, 250, 252

putenv(), 250

readability, 59, 250

real-time systems, 251

realloc(), 4, 38, 45, 48–57, 88, 94, 95, 116, 121, 165, 166, 184, 207, 250

record, 26

recursion, 3, 4, 16, 62–4, 67, 76, 77, 80, 136, 139, 210, 245, 251

recursive
  descent parser, 66, 135, 251
  format, 101
  function, 133
  implementation, 136
  language, 16
  manner, 133
  pointers, 244
  solution, 210, 211
  use of struct, 26

relational database, 244

relativization, 137–9, 147–9, 154–7, 251

relocation, 8, 12, 18, 19, 251

return sequence, 61, 63, 64, 251

rfree(), 169

rmalloc(), 169

row-major access formula, 97, 99–101, 104, 251

row-major format, 97, 99–101, 104, 105, 251, 253

safety-critical software, 52, 53, 251

scanner, 251

semantics, 1, 2, 7, 18, 36, 37, 49, 50, 169, 234

semaphor, 251

serialization, 132, 135, 138–9, 149, 155–7, 251

SetEnvironmentVariable(), 251

shared memory segment, 4, 14, 195–9, 206, 207, 235, 236, 246, 252

INDEX

shmat(), 198
shmctl(), 198
shmget(), 197
SIGABRT, 195
SIGCONT, 198
SIGFPE, 195
SIGILL, 195
SIGINT, 195
SIGKILL, 198
signal handler, 198, 252
signals, 194, 195, 198, 206, 234, 252
SIGSEGV, 195
SIGSTOP, 198
SIGTERM, 195
simple data type, 252
sizeof, 26, 28–30, 36, 37, 87, 103, 117,
    118, 133, 152, 153, 165, 166, 221,
    230, 252
smart (safe) pointer, 159, 165, 179,
    180, 181, 204, 208, 252
source
    code, 8, 11, 22, 199, 249, 252
    file, 7–10, 15, 59, 95, 166, 168, 178,
        220, 250, 252
    language, 8, 252
    module, 8, 18, 252
    program, 7, 10, 15, 18, 41, 250
    statement, 39
spawning a process, 252
stack, 16, 17, 62, 76, 78, 175, 176,
    183, 184, 220, 223, 249, 250,
    252
standard
    argument, 234
    file, 225
    function, 8, 53
    output, 225, 234
static
    allocation, 99
    data, 252
    memory, 4, 15, 109, 111, 112
    object, 10, 109, 204, 205
    storage class, 9, 18, 252
stdlib.h, 48, 253
strcat(), 56, 89, 90, 253

strcpy(), 43, 55–7, 88–90, 94, 109,
    115, 120–2, 125, 127, 128, 214, 215,
    217, 222, 253
strdup(), 91, 129, 130, 160, 230, 231
string, 4, 81, 88, 253
strlen(), 43, 90, 109, 113, 115, 120–2,
    125, 127, 128, 160, 222, 253
struct, 7, 26, 30, 220, 230, 253
symbol section, 31
symbolic language, 7, 8
symbolic reference, 8, 10, 12, 18, 21,
    31, 253
syntax, 1–3, 8, 118–21, 126, 173, 234,
    244, 249
Sys(), 234, 235
sys(), 198, 234, 235
Sys__exit(), 234, 235
sys__exit(), 234, 235
Sys_exit(), 234, 235
sys_exit(), 192, 197, 198, 234, 235
system
    call, 48, 253
    heap, 47, 55, 62, 76, 77, 108, 118, 129,
        135, 155, 160, 161, 182, 245, 253
    stack, 4, 17, 19, 62–4, 66, 67, 76–8,
        80, 108, 129, 135, 136, 155, 162,
        168, 178, 180, 181, 204, 253

template class, 253
testability, 59, 253
thread, 4, 5, 187, 191, 199–201, 204–8,
    246, 248, 250, 254
thread-safe, 5, 234
traversal, 133, 254
tree, 133–5, 138, 139, 147–9, 154–7,
    240, 254

undetermined ownership problem,
    159, 161, 164, 165, 179, 182–4, 204,
    205, 254
uninitialized
    data, 10, 15
    data section, 11, 13
    pointer, 38, 88, 93
    variable, 254

INDEX

UNIX, 5, 14, 25, 35, 45, 160, 167, 187–91, 194–6, 198, 199, 205–8, 239, 240, 242, 244–6, 250, 252, 253
user space, 188, 190, 191, 194, 195, 206, 254
user thread, 191, 207, 254

validation, 59, 254
value, as binary code, 254

variable, 4, 7, 21, 22, 24, 26, 31, 41, 254
virtual
   data container, 32, 36, 37, 82
   memory, 14, 53, 254
   object, 249

Windows, 14, 20, 160, 185, 189–91, 194–6, 205–9, 245, 251